FERTILIZERS AND MANURES

FERTILIZERS AND MANURES

By

Dr. Renuka Sharma

DPH

DISCOVERY PUBLISHING HOUSE PVT. LTD.
NEW DELHI-110 002

Published by:
Tilak Wasan
DISCOVERY PUBLISHING HOUSE PVT. LTD.
4383/4B, Ansari Road, Darya Ganj
New Delhi-110 002 (India)
Phone : +91-11-23279245, 43596064-65
Fax : +91-11-23253475
E-mail : discoverypublishinghouse@gmail.com
sales@discoverypublishinggroup.com
parul.wasan@gmail.com
web : www.discoverypublishinggroup.com

First Edition: **2014**

ISBN: 978-93-5056-390-8

Fertilizers and Manures

Printed at:
Dynamic Printers
Delhi

Preface

Plant requires food/nutrients/elements for its growth and development which are absorbed through soil. The nutrient supplying sources are manures and fertilizers. Application of manures and fertilizers to the soil is one of the important factors which help in increasing the crop yield and to maintain the soil fertility. N, P and K are the 3 major elements required for the crop growth. Organic fertilizers include substances such as dried blood and seaweed derivatives, which are of animal and plant origins respectively. Inorganic fertilizers are usually wholly manufactured, as in the case of sulphate of ammonia; or they may be processed from a mined or quarried mineral, as in the case of ground limestone.

—Author

Contents

1

Introduction

DEFINITION

Organic or inorganic plant foods, which may be either liquid or granular, used to amend the soil in order to improve the quality or quantity of plant growth. Fertilizers or fertilizers are compounds given to plants with the intention of promoting growth; they are usually applied either via the soil, for uptake by plant roots, or by foliar spraying, for uptake through leaves. Fertilizers can be organic (composed of organic matter, *i.e.*, carbon based), or inorganic (containing simple, inorganic chemicals).

They can be naturally-occurring compounds such as peat or mineral deposits, or manufactured through natural processes (such as composting) or chemical processes (such as the Haber process).

Fertilizers typically provide, in varying proportions, the three major plant nutrients (nitrogen, phosphorus, and potassium), the secondary plant nutrients (calcium, sulphur, magnesium), and sometimes trace elements (or micronutrients) with a role in plant nutrition: boron, manganese, iron, zinc, copper and molybdenum.

INORGANIC FERTILIZERS

- Examples of naturally-occurring inorganic fertilizers include diatomaceous earth and limestone.
- Examples of manufactured or chemically-synthesized

inorganic fertilizers include ammonium nitrate, potassium sulphate, and superphosphate, or triple superphosphate.

Synthesised materials are also called artificial fertilizers, and may be described as straight, where the product predominantly contains the three primary ingredients of nitrogen (N), phosphorus (P) and potassium/potash (K), often described as NPK fertilizers. They are named or labelled according to the content of these three elements, thus a 5-10-5 fertilizer would have 10 per cent phosphate in its ingredients. If nitrogen is the main element, they are often described as nitrogen fertilizers.

Alternatively they may be described as compound where there is a mix of nutrients. Chemist Justus von Liebig (in the 19th century) contributed greatly to understanding the role of inorganic compounds in plant nutrition and devised the concept of Liebig's barrel to illustrate the significance of inadequate concentrations of essential nutrients. At the same time he deemphasised the role of humus. This theory was influential in the great expansion in use of artificial fertilizers in the 20th century.

Nitrogen fertilizer is often synthesised using the Haber-Bosch process, which produces ammonia. This ammonia is applied directly to the soil or used to produce other compounds, notably ammonium nitrate, a dry, concentrated product. It can also be used in the Odda Process to produce compound fertilizers such as 15-15-15.

Inorganic fertilizers sometimes do not replace trace mineral elements in the soil which become gradually depleted by crops grown there. This has been linked to studies which have shown a marked fall (up to 75 per cent) in the quantities of such minerals present in fruit and vegetables.

One exception to this is in Western Australia where deficiencies of zinc, copper, manganese, iron and molybdenum were identifed as limiting the growth of crops and pastures in the 1940's and 1950's. Soils in Western Australia are very old, highly weathered and deficient in many of the major nutrients and trace elements. Since, this time these trace elements are routinely added to inorganic fertilizers used in Agriculture in this state. In many countries there is the public perception that inorganic fertilizers 'poison the soil' and result in "low quality" produce.

However, there is very little (if any) scientific evidence to support these views. When used appropriately, inorganic fertilizers enhance plant growth, the accumulation of organic matter and the biological activity of the soil, while reducing the risk of water run-off, overgrasing and soil erosion. The nutritional value of plants for human and animal consumption is typically improved when inorganic fertilizers are used appropriately.

ORGANIC FERTILIZERS

- Examples of naturally occurring organic fertilizers include manure and slurry, urine, peat, seaweed and guano. Green manure crops are also grown to add nutrients to the soil. Naturally occurring minerals such as mine rock phosphate, sulphate of potash and limestone are also considered Organic Fertilizers.
- Examples of manufactured organic fertilizers include compost, dried blood, bone meal and seaweed extracts. Other examples are natural enzyme digested proteins, fish meal, and feather meal. A listing of products may be found at Organic Materials Review Institute and California Organic Fertilizers Inc..

The decomposing crop residue from prior years is another source of fertility. Though not strictly considered "fertilizer", the distinction seems more a matter of words than reality.

Some ambiguity in the usage of the term 'organic' exists because some of synthetic fertilizers, such as urea and urea formaldehyde, are fully organic in the sense of organic chemistry. In fact, it would be difficult to chemically distinguish between urea of biological origin and that produced synthetically. On the other hand, some fertilizer materials commonly approved for organic agriculture, such as powdered limestone, diatomaceous earth, and Chilean saltpeter, are inorganic in the use of the term by chemistry.

Although the density of nutrients in organic material is comparatively modest, they have some advantages. For one thing organic growers typically produce some or all of their fertilizer on-site, thus lowering operating costs considerably.

Then there is the matter of how effective they are at promoting plant growth, chemical soil test results aside. The answers are encouraging. Since, the majority of nitrogen supplying organic fertilizers contain insoluble nitrogen and are slow release fertilizers their effectiveness can be greater than conventional nitrogen fertilzers.

Implicit in modern theories of organic agriculture is the idea that the pendulum has swung the other way to some extent in thinking about plant nutrition. While admitting the obvious success of Leibig's theory, they stress that there are serious limitations to the current methods of implementing it via chemical fertilization.

They re-emphasise the role of humus and other organic components of soil, which are believed to play several important roles:

- Mobilising existing soil nutrients, so that good growth is achieved with lower nutrient densities while wasting less.
- Releasing nutrients at a slower, more consistent rate, helping to avoid a boom-and-bust pattern.
- Helping to retain soil moisture, reducing the stress due to temporary moisture stress.
- Improving the soil structure.

Organics also have the advantage of avoiding certain long-term problems associated with the regular heavy use of artificial fertilizers;

- The possibility of 'burning' plants with the concentrated chemicals (*i.e.*, an over supply of some nutrients).
- The progressive decrease of real or perceived "soil health", apparent in loss of structure, reduced ability to absorb precipitation, lightening of soil colour, etc.
- The necessity of reapplying artificial fertilizers regularly (and perhaps in increasing quantities) to maintain fertility.

- The cost (substantial and rising in recent years) and resulting lack of independence.

Organic fertilizers also have their disadvantages. As acknowledged above, they are typically a dilute source of nutrients compared to inorganic fertilizers, and where significant amounts of nutrients are required for profitable yields, very large amounts of organic fertilizers must be applied. This results in prohibitive transportation and application costs, especially where the agriculture is practiced a long distance from the source of the organic fertilizer.

The composition of organic fertilizers tends to be highly variable, so that accurate application of nutrients to match plant production is difficult. Hence, large-scale agriculture tends to rely on inorganic fertilizers while organic fertilizers are cost-effective on small-scale horticultural or domestic gardens. Finally, some organic fertilizers such as manures can contain bacteria or heavy metals harmful to human health.

In practice a compromise between the use of artificial and organic fertilizers is common, typically by using inorganic fertilizers supplemented with the application of organics that are readily available such as the return of crop residues or the application of manure.

It is important to differentiate between what we mean by organic fertilizers and fertilizers approved for use in organic farming and organic gardening by organisations and authorities who provide organic certification services. Some approved fertilizers may be inorganic, naturally occurring chemical compounds, *e.g.*, minerals.

FARMWAY

Farmway are one of the largest suppliers and distributors of fertilizers in the North of England. We have a main distributorship for GrowHow UK Ltd and distribute a wide range of Farmway Own Brand fertilizers, plus imported fertilizers, *i.e.*, imported nitrogen, prilled and granular urea and compounds. We also supply straights.

We can offer advice and full recommendations using our FACTS qualified personnel:-

Contact	Location	Telephone
Tony Simpson	Piercebridge Business Support Unit	01325 504600
John Close	Stokesley Country Store	01642 717600
Colin Jewell	Stokesley Country Store	01642 717600
Eddie Coulson	Hexham Country Store	01434 613930
Rob Harrison	Thirsk Country Store	07584 706396
Rose Riby	Driffield Country Store	01377 249700
Andrew Grayshon	Ripley Country Store	01423 774400
Richard Martin	Piercebridge Business Support Unit	07710 087306

GROWHOW NITROGEN

GrowHow manufacture the most well recognised fertilizer brands in the UK in a distinct blue bag, manufacturing high quality product. GrowHow's brand will help you achieve both yield and specification aspirations and meet your expectation in every respect. GrowHow has developed a range of services aimed at giving UK farmers the tools needed to maximise the full potential from your fertilizer purchase.

PRODUCTS

Nitram 34.5 Per Cent

A concentrated form of ammonium nitrate fertilizer, high quality, free flowing, and the UK's best known brand of straight nitrogen.

DoubleTop 27N + 30SO3

The sulphur rich top dressing has the right balance of Nitrogen to Sulphur for first top dressing. DoubleTop is the perfect choice for the cereal and oilseed rape grower at the forefront of husbandry, with high yields and quality cereals to the farmer in a sulphur deficient area.

SingleTop 27N + 12SO3

The flexible sulphur top dressing product for arable and grass crops, contains sulphate which is the most effective source of sulphur for maximum grass growth and yields.

CropMaster 27:4:4 + 6SO3

The simple, one-product solution for sulphur-responsive areas, balances the nutrients recycled by grasing animals. Also a very flexible, spring-applied top dressing, containing Sulphur and added P and K, contains sulphate the most effective source of sulphur for maximum crop growth and yield.

Swardsman 25:5:5

The all-season grasing fertilizer has proved reliable in all situations for more than 25 years. Swardsman is used as a flexible grasing product for medium or low intensity grassland farms.

Twenty Ten Ten 20:10:10

The quality NPK fertilizer for less intensive grassland situations on low fertility soils. Hos lower N levels to suit less intensive situations such as hay production and extensive grasing.

Twenty Ten Ten is a general purpose fertilizer which can be used for many applications on the farm.

Cut and Graze 21:5:9

The all purpose fertilizer which gives more tonnes for less money in extensive systems. Just one product to stock, freeing up storage space.

Kayenne 26:0:15 Kayenne Sulphur 25:0:13 + 7SO3

For high yielding second and third cut silage. High nitrogen content can mean less product to store and apply.

Early Bite 25:10:0

The first choice for early spring grasing. A potash-free product and therefore less risk of grass staggers. Early Bite has a high proportion of nitrogen in ammonium form, which is protected from leaching and all the phosphate is applied in early spring when it gives better yields than a little and often approach.

MultiCut 25:4:13 MultiCut Sulphur 23:4:13 + 7SO3

The all-season silage fertilizers, balances slurry so that costs can be reduced by making maximum use of the farm's own slurry and FYM resources.

Number Four 15:15:20

Providing NPK in a single application. A cost effective single, first NPK dressing, balanced with straight nitrogen, ideal for spring or winter cereals, grass ley resseds, maincrop potatoes and grass cutting systems on low phosphate and potash soils.

Number Seven 17:17:17

General purpose NPK fertilizer. A leach resistant and so more environmentally friendly NPK fertilizer for oilseed rape, potatoes, spring crops, grass ley reseeds, and grass cutting systems on low phosphate and potash soils.

P AND K OFF-TAKES AND USEFUL CONVERSIONS

P and K Off-Takes

The chart below will help you decide which GrowHow products are the best choice under a spring-applied arable system where Phosphate and Potash are used in the sping.

Crop	Units/Tonne of Yield P_2O_5	Units/ Tonne of Yield K_2O
Cereals		
Grain only	15	11
Grain and Straw		
- Winter wheat/barley	17	23
- Spring wheat/barley	17	27
Winter/spring oats	17	34

(Contd...)

Oilseed Rape		
Seed only	27	22
Seed and Straw	30	34
Peas (dried)	17	20
Potatoes	2	11.4
Hay	12	35
Silage		
25 per cent DM	3.4	11.8
30 per cent DM	4.1	14.1
Average fresh weight silage yields		
1st cut 10 Tonnes/acre		
2nd cut 7 Tonnes/acre		
3rd cut 4 Tonnes/acre		
1 Cubic metre of silage weighs		
20 per cent DM = 0.725 Tonnes		
25 per cent DM = 0.660 Tonnes		

Conversions

Imperial	units/acre × 1.25 = kg/ha
	50kgs bags/acre × 123.5 = kgs/ha
Metric	kg/ha × 0.8 = units/acre
	kgs/ha × 0.00809 = 50kgs bags/acre

Fertilizer Analysis

Imperial

1 unit = 1 per cent of a cwt

So a fertilizer with the analysis 15:15:20 contains:

15 units N

15 units P_2O_5

20 units K_2O

Metric

Under the metric system the unit of measurement is kg

Recommendations are given in kg/ha

A fertilizer with the analysis 15:15:20 contains:

15 per cent N 15 per cent P_2O_5 20 per cent K_2O

So in a 50kg bag:-

15 per cent of the 50kg is N, *i.e.*, 7.5kg N

15 per cent of the 50kg is P_2O_5 *i.e.*, 7.5kg P_2O_5

20 per cent of the 50kg is K_2O, *i.e.*, 10kg K_2O

15:15:20 on the bag means:

15 units N or 7.5kg N

15 units P_2O_5 or 7.5kg P_2O_5

20 units K_2O or 10kg K_2O

Sulphur Conversions

From	To	Multiply By
S	SO_4	2.996
SO_4	S	0.333
S	SO_3	2.5
SO_3	S	0.4

FARMWAY BRANDED QUALITY FERTILIZERS

Farmway branded quality fertilizers are manufactured and bagged locally using the highest quality raw materials. We supply a full range and these can be ordered from our Customer Services Department, any of our Country Stores, or your local sales representative. Farmway branded fertilizer keep up with the modern farmer, are up-to-date with developments as they occur, excellent quality, great choice, overhead costs kept to a minimum, making the products more competitive. This, backed with the Farmway excellent service gives farmers quality and profitability.

FARMWAY FERTILIZERS GENERAL RECOMMENDATIONS

Crops	Fertilizer	Kg Per Ha	50Kg Per Acre
Autumn Grown Cereals	0:24:24	250kg to 375kg	2 to 3
	5:24:24		
	0:18:36		
	0:20:30		
	5:24:24		
Spring Grown Cereals	20:10:10	500kg to 600kg	4 to 5
	20:8:14	20:5:15	20:8:12

APPLY FARMWAY NITROGEN AND SULPHUR PRODUCTS AS REQUIRED

Crops	Fertilizer	Kg Per Ha	50Kg Per Acre
Oilseed Rape	0:24:24	250kg to 375kg	2 to 3
Winter Sown	0:20:30		
	5:24:24		
	5:20:30		
	16:16:16		
Oilseed Rape	20:10:10	375kg to 500kg	3 to 4
Spring Sown	20:8:14		
Peas and Beans	0:24:24	250kg	2
	5:24:24		
Kale	20:10:10	500kg to 600kg	4 to 5
	20:14:14		
	20:8:14		
Cabbage	13:13:20	500kg to 600kg	4 to 5
	15:15:21		
	16:16:16		
Sugar Beet	13:13:20	375kg to 750kg	3 to 6
Fodder Beet	0:20:30		
Mangels	20:10:10		
	20:8:14		
	17:6:24		

APPLY SALT SYLVINITE AND FARMWAY NITROGEN AND SULPHUR AS REQUIRED

Crops	Fertilizer	Kg Per Ha	50Kg Per Acre
Swedes	9:15:15	750kg to 1000kg	6 to 8
Turnips	10:20:10		
Grassland	12:15:20	375kg to 500kg	3 to 4
Silage	25:5:5		
March	20:10:10		
Application			
	20:8:14		
	20:5:15		
May	25:0:16	500kg	4

(*Contd...*)

Appliction			
(After First			
Cut)			
July	25:0:16	375kg to 500kg	3 to 4
Application			
(After	20:10:10		
Second Cut)	20:8:14		
	20:5:15		
Grasing		250kg	2
March	26:13:0	250kg	2
Application			
June	25:0:16		
Application			
OR		250kg to 375kg	2 to 3
April	25:5:5		
Application	25:5:5		
May			
Application			
June	25:5:5		
Application			
OR	20:8:14	375kg to 500kg	3 to 4
June	20:5:15		
Application	20:10:10		
Hay		375kg to 500kg	3 to 4
April/May	20:8:14		
Application	20:5:15		
	20:10:10		

APPLY FARMWAY NITROGEN AND SULPHUR PRODUCTS AS REQUIRED

Crops	Fertilizer	Kg Per Ha	50 Kg Per Acre
Potatoes First Earlies And Canning	16:16:16	1000kg to 1225kg	8 to 10
Second Earlies and Maincrop	13:13:20 15:15:21 16:16:16	1350kg to 1750kg	11 to 14
Seed	12:15:20	1250kg	10

APPLY FARMWAY NITROGEN AS REQUIRED

The general recommendations shown will vary and must be adjusted dependant on the crop rotation, growing conditions and the levels of Nitrogen, Phosphate and Potash available in the soil..

Poland covers an area of 312 600 km^2, or about 31 million ha, of which 60 per cent is farmland and 29 per cent woodland (*Table 1.1*). Almost the whole territory is located in the Baltic Sea Basin, with a very small area of the southeastern part of the country in the Black Sea Basin. The rivers Oder and Vistula flow across the whole Polish territory and a number of small rivers discharge directly into the Baltic Sea. More than half of the coastal inhabitants of the Baltic Sea Basin live in Poland, using 40 per cent of the arable land situated there; hence, the high impact of the country on the pollution of this sea.

The productive farmland of about 18 million ha supports a population of 38.8 million people, *i.e.*, about 0.46 ha per person. Private farmers are the major landholders, occupying 76 per cent of the farmland, the remainder belonging to the Agency of State Treasury Fund for Land Ownership and the few cooperatives. About 28 per cent of the total labour force is currently employed in agriculture and each farmer produces sufficient food to support about six non-farming persons.

Table 1.1 Land Utilisation in Poland, Averages For 1999-2001

Area	Million ha	Per cent
Agricultural area	18.41	58.9
Arable land	14.08	76.5
Grassland	4.06	22.0
Permanent plantations	0.27	1.5
Forests	9.04	28.9
Open waters	0.82	2.6
Urban and industrial area	3.00	9.6
Total	**31.27**	**100**

Natural farming conditions are poor, due to the prevalence of light, sand-derived soils and the unfavourable climate. The length of the growing period averages 210 days and is comparable to that in Scandinavian countries. During May to

September, evapotranspiration in Poland exceeds rainfall, resulting in a continuous water deficit, especially on light soils with low water holding capacity. Generally the quality-rating index for the climate in Poland is about 75 to 80 points and for the soils also about 75 to 80 points, as compared with the average of 100 points for western Europe. As a result of combined soil and climate ratings, the average value of the agricultural production area is about 57 to 64 points (Table 1.2).

Table 1.2 Comparison of Natural Conditions of Agriculture in Poland and Western Europe.

Characteristics	Unit	Western Europe	Poland
Climate	Valuation	100	75 to 80*
Soils	Valuation	100	75 to 80**
Climate and soils	Valuation	100	57 to 64
Agricultural land per person	ha	0.14 to 0.85	0.27 to 0.31
Agricultural Production	Cereal units/ha	48.2 to 54.2	30.9

Note: * Calculated by Górski T. based on the duration of growing season.

** Calculated by Witek T. based on soil maps of Europe. The above-synthesised index has been used to calculate that, for each inhabitant of Poland, there are about 0.27 to 0.31 ha (instead of 0.45 ha) of farmland, a value comparable to that of western Europe. Thus, the inputs (particularly of fertilizers) necessary to obtain a yield of 3.1 tonnes of cereals per hectare in Poland (present capacity) would produce yields of 4.8 to 5.4 tonnes cereal grains in France, Belgium, The Netherlands and Germany.

SOILS

The agricultural landscape originates from the period of glaciations. The Scandinavian glacier covered the present day Polish territory three times, shaping the oldest soils in the southern part of the country (Mindel glaciations) and the youngest in the northern part of the country (Wurm glaciations). Due to the high diversity of the parent rocks (Table) and to different geological and pedological processes, a substantial number of soil types and sub-types have developed in Poland. According to the Polish soil classification system, there are 35 different soil types and 78 sub-types. The most common soil types are brown soils, acid brown soils, grey brown podsolic soils, rusty soils and podsolic soils. A much smaller area is covered by chernozem soils, rendzina soils, black soils and alluvial soils.

Table 1.3 Parent Rocks of the Polish Soils

Parent Rocks	% of the Total Area	% of the area Agric. Land	% of the Area Arable Soils
Gravels	0.9	0.5	0.6
Loose/slightly loamy sands	34.6	24.8	27.8
Loamy sands	10.2	12.4	16.2
Light loams	15.8	18.8	16.7
Medium and heavy loams	9.6	13.2	12.8
Clays	0.8	1.0	0.6
Loess	3.5	4.8	9.1
Silts of water origin	4.2	4.6	4.8
Alluvial soils	4.7	5.8	5.2
Rendzinas	1.1	1.6	1.6
Peats, mucks	8.5	9.6	0.7
Massive rocks different origin	6.1	3.9	3.9

Grasslands are located mainly on alluvial muck soils, muck soils and peat soils. Most of the soils have developed from loose, post-glacial rocks and only a small area is covered by soils derived from massive rock. The soils classified as very suitable or suitable for agriculture account for only 23 per cent of arable land. Those classified as of moderate suitability cover about 47 per cent. Marginal and unsuitable soils account for 30 per cent of the land. Parts of the unsuitable Polish soils are still under cultivation but the area of set-aside land is increasing steadily.

The soils in Poland are commonly acid and low in plant nutrients (Table 1.3). Unfertile and acid soils account for 50 per cent to 65 per cent of arable land and only 34 per cent to 50 per cent of soils can be rated as highly fertile.

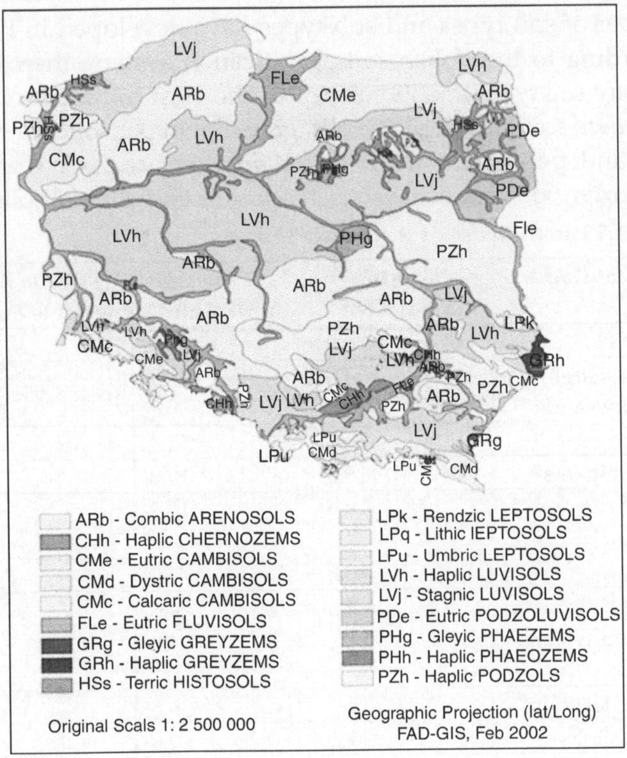

Fig 1.1 Dominant Soil Map of Poland

Table 1.4 Fertility Status of Polish Soils

Soil pH and Nutrient	pH %	P_2O_5 %	K_2O %	Mg %
Very acid and very low nutrient	22	10	18	10
Acid, low nutrient	30	27	30	27
Slightly acid, medium nutrient	28	27	29	27
Neutral, high nutrient	15	17	11	17
Alkaline, very high nutrient	5	19	12	19
Total	**100**	**100**	**100**	**100**
Soil fertility index*	34	49.5	37.5	42.6

Note: *Alkaline, very high + neutral, high + 1/2 slightly acid,medium.

Unpublished data

Soil acidity is correlated with the low content of available magnesium and is one of the most limiting factors for soil productivity in Poland. The next most limiting factor is the low potassium status of soils. This has deteriorated during the past five years due to a very low consumption of potassium fertilizers.

AGRICULTURAL STRUCTURE

The course of the history of Poland in the last 200 years has contributed substantially to the present day status of agriculture. From the end of 18th century until the First World War Poland was conquered and divided between Austria, Prussia and Russia. The serfs were enfranchised in 1811, 1848 and 1863 in the Prussian, Austrian and Russian-annexed parts of Poland respectively. In the partition period, agriculture developed most quickly in the Prussian and very slowly in the Russian annexed parts of the country. After the Second World War, Poland lost a substantial part of territory in the East and recovered the old, historical, part of the territory in the West.

On the recovered territory, the agricultural land was partly managed by the big state-owned farms and partly attributed to the peasants who had moved from the lost territory. In 1990/91 the formerly state-owned farms were taken over by the Agency of State Treasury Fund for Land Ownership and are being restructured. The main forms of this process are the leasing and selling of farms to individuals or joint venture companies.

For all these reasons, the structure of agriculture in Poland with respect to ownership rights, size and economic conditions of farm holdings is extremely varied. According to the last inventory, made in 1996, the total number of farm holdings in Poland is 3 066 535, mostly in the private sector and only 2 016 farms in the public sector.

Of the number of private farm holdings, 66.6 per cent, *i.e.*, roughly 2 million, have an area over one ha and are classified as individual farms. The remaining 33.4 per cent, with an area below one ha each, are classified as agricultural plots. As regards the numbers, most of the individual farms fall in the 1 to 7 ha category (68.2 per cent) and only 8.5 per cent of the farms in the category of more than 15 ha (Figure). In terms of area, the small farms (1 to 7 ha) occupy 30.8 per cent of the agricultural land and the large ones (over 15 ha) 35.5 per cent of the agricultural land. The average size of an individual farm in Poland is about seven ha. The average size of a farm in the public sector is about 600 ha.

REGIONS IN POLAND

The natural, economic and socio-technical conditions of agriculture are very different across Poland. Consequently, a number of systems have been developed for dividing the country's territory into regions or zones. On 1 January 1999 a new administrative division of Poland into 16 provinces (Table 1.5) came in force.

Table 1.5 Codes Used for the Different Provinces or Regions*

Code	Region/Province
Dls	Dolnoslaskie
Kuj	Kuj. pomorski
Lub	Lubelskie
Lus	Lubuskie
Lod	Lódzkie
Mal	Malopolski
Maz	Mazowie
Opl	Opolskie
Pdk	Podkarpackie
Pod	Podlaskie
Pom	Pomorskie
Sls	Slaskie
Swi	Swietokrzyskie
Wrm	Warm. Mazurskie
Wlp	Wielkopols
Zpm	Zach.-pomorski
Poland	Poland

Note: * These codes are used in the tables that follow.

Some of the factors taken into consideration in delimiting the new provinces were the natural, economic and socio-technical conditions for agriculture. Therefore the new provinces, with some approximation, can be treated as the regions for analyses concerning agriculture, including this report on fertilizer use by crops.

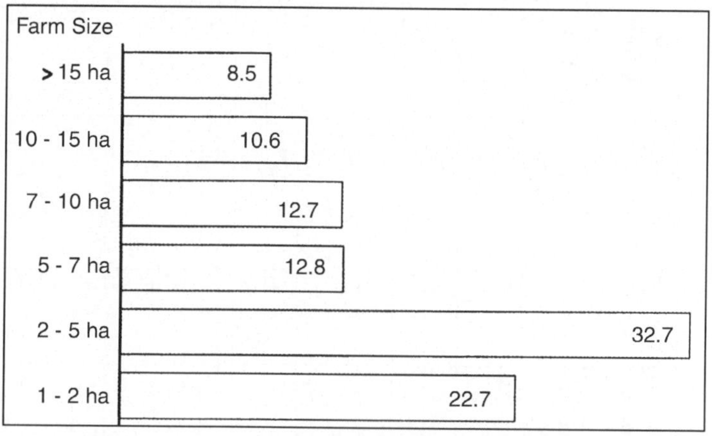

Fig 1.2 Structure of Individual Farms According to Number in Percentage of Farms Number

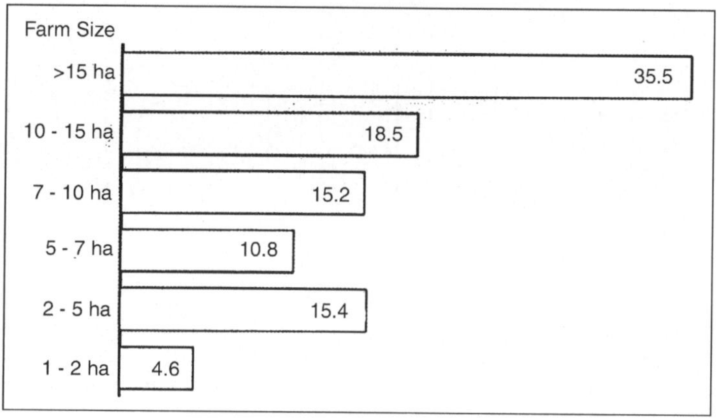

Fig 1.3 Structure of Individual Farms According to Area in Percentage of Farms Area

Table 1.6 General Characteristics of the Regions/Provinces in P oland

Regional code	Land Valorization Index*	Soil Index*	Organic Content	Average Farm Size	Fertilizers	Actual Cereal Production	Potential Production***
			Percent	ha	kg NPK/ha	t/ha	t/ha
Dls	74.9	46.9	3.04	8.7	76.0	3.78	5.0
Kuj	71.0	58.3	1.85	10.4	115.7	3.03	4.5
Lub	74.1	39.1	2.02	5.5	80.0	2.66	4.8
Lus	62.3	42.9	2.11	9.9	87.1	2.82	4.1
Lod	61.9	32.1	2.12	6.1	72.4	2.37	4.0
Mal	69.3	34.6	2.25	3.0	71.4	2.82	4.7
Maz	59.9	38.1	1.94	6.7	75.2	2.34	3.9
Opl	81.4	49.6	2.33	7.1	119.9	4.16	5.2
Pdk	70.4	31.4	2.39	3.3	62.9	2.69	4.7
Pod	55.0	29.3	2.06	10.3	75.8	2.14	3.8
Pom	66.2	47.9	2.65	11.5	113.8	2.87	4.3
Sls	64.2	39.9	2.59	3.7	63.3	3.08	4.4
Swi	69.3	33.1	1.83	4.4	65.5	2.42	4.5
Wrm	66.0	42.8	2.22	15.7	74.7	2.74	4.5
Wlp	64.8	49.9	1.99	9.1	109.1	3.23	4.1
Zpm	67.5	38.8	2.29	14.5	106.4	3.08	4.3
Poland	66.6	42.6	2.20	6.6	85.8	2.85	4.3

Note: * A composite factor of the agricultural land usability, including soil quality, agro climate, relief and soil amelioration (higher value = better conditions).

** A composite factor of the soil pH and the content of available phosphorus, potassium and magnesium (higher value = better the soil fertility status).

*** Based on soil bonitation, share of individual crops in the crop structure and crop yield in the field experiments (non-limiting treatments).

The general characteristics of these regions are presented in Table 1.6. According to the results of multivariate statistical analysis, the 16 regions can be grouped into three clusters (*Figure 1.4*).

There are eight regions in the first cluster: Dls, Kuj, Lus, Opl, Pom, Sls, Wlp and Zpm. They are characterised by a highly efficient crop production that approaches most closely the potential level. This can be explained by a higher consumption of fertilizers than the average for Poland and a generally good soil fertility status. It is interesting that natural conditions for crop production in some regions of this cluster are not particularly good (*e.g.*, Lus, Sls and Pom).

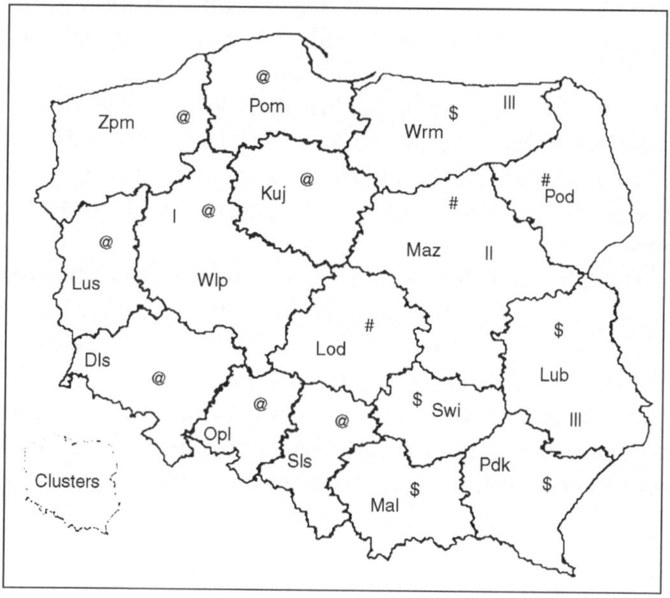

Fig 1.4 Regions and Clusters of Regions in Poland

However, in these regions a quite substantial area of agricultural land is excluded from agricultural production and left as set-aside land. This concerns, most probably, the worst soils, originating from gravel and sand as the parent rocks.

Wlp region deserves particular attention. In spite of poor natural conditions the level of agricultural production is very high. This can be explained by historical reasons. With the exception of region Sls, the size of farms in other regions of this cluster exceeds the average farm size for Poland as a whole. Generally speaking, agriculture in most regions in this cluster is fully developed and is up to western Europe standards. The consumption of mineral fertilizers is fairly high, the soil fertility status is rather good and the farm size is higher than the average for Poland.

A substantial area of the land belongs to the public sector, which makes possible the enlargement of individual farms. The third cluster includes three regions located in Central Poland: Lod, Maz and Pod. These are characterised by extensive farm management practices reflected in a low consumption of mineral fertilizers, light soils of low fertility and medium-sized farms. The public sector is practically absent from agriculture and few farms have an area over 50 ha. Nevertheless the size of farms is slightly higher than the average for Poland, which gives some hope for further development of its agriculture. Another positive feature is the high stocking level and consequent production of manure.

In an intermediate position, cluster two comprises five regions in the eastern part of the country: Lub, Mal, Pdk, Swi and Wrm. These regions, with exception of Wrm, have a prevalence of very small farms and a subsistence type of agriculture. In spite of better soils, but of low fertility, crop production is much lower compared with cluster one. This can be explained partly by a very low consumption of fertilizers, not compensated by manure production.

CROPS

Most arable land in Poland is under cereals (Table). Cereals cover about 70 per cent of arable land in five regions Kuj, Lub, Opl, Pod and Wlp. In the three first-mentioned regions this is explained by the good soils and prevalence of farms oriented towards crop production. In the Pod region, cereals (mainly rye, oats and mixtures) are used for cattle production and in Wlp region for pig production.

Only in southeastern Poland (Mal, Pdk and Sls) is the share of cereals as low as 50 per cent. Winter and spring wheat prevail, followed by rye, mixed cereals and winter and spring barley. Triticale and oats are grown on smaller areas.

In recent years, for the first time in the history of Polish agriculture, the share of wheat has been higher than the share of rye. This trend is particularly noticeable in regions Dls, Lub and Opl, which are characterised by good quality, fertile soils. A particular feature of cereal production in Poland is the high share of cereal mixtures (mainly oats + barley) covering over 10 per cent of the arable land. On light, acid soils cereal mixtures give a higher yield than each of its components. In the western part of Poland (regions Dls, Opl and Wlp), maize, grown for both grain and silage, is gaining in importance.

Table 1.7 Land Utilisation in Regions of Poland (Thousand ha)

Regional code	Agric. area	Grassland	Cereals	Potatoes	Other crops
Dls	1163	256	563	53	146
Kuj	1163	138	689	50	220
Lub	1714	337	904	134	186
Lus	554	139	225	16	46
Lod	1252	215	636	155	141
Mal	882	244	285	91	158
Maz	2391	560	1120	224	240
Opl	581	82	343	25	104
Pdk	943	290	299	89	186
Pod	1201	402	560	77	179
Pom	909	181	456	42	146
Sls	618	151	229	42	100
Swi	732	148	314	74	153
Wrm	1305	394	524	35	181
Wlp	1892	300	1108	101	329
Zpm	1114	229	518	32	159
Poland	18414	4 065	8778	1238	3211

The share of potatoes and fodder crops is decreasing. Potatoes are grown on an area accounting for 13 to 15 per cent of arable land in only five regions. In all these regions very small, self-subsistence farms account for most of the agricultural land.

In northern and western Poland (regions Kuj, Lus, Wrm, Zpm) the share of potatoes is already close to 4 per cent to 5 per cent of arable land.

Sugar beet and rapeseed maintain their position, with the highest concentration in Dls, Kuj, Opl, Pom, Wlp and Zpm regions, characterised by bigger, more intensive farms. In recent years, winters have been rather unsuitable for rapeseed production but it is most likely that this crop will recover a leading position in Poland. Fodder crops including maize for silage, fodder beet, annual and perennial crops, cover on average about 8 per cent of the arable land. A very serious drop in cattle and sheep numbers explains the low and still falling share of these crops. During the past decade, a new phenomenon for Polish agriculture is a quite substantial proportion of set aside and fallow land. This occurred after transformation from a centrally planned to a market oriented economy. In Lus, Pdk, Sls, Wrm and Zpm regions, the proportion of the abandoned area amounts to 20 to 30 per cent of the arable land. In the regions where most land belongs to individual farmers the problem of abandoned land is less serious.

The lowest share of set-aside land is registered in Opl and Wlp regions, which are characterised by intensive agriculture (Table). The share of set-aside land must be taken into consideration when analysing the consumption of mineral fertilizers in terms of kg NPK ($N + P_2O5 + K_2O$) per ha of agricultural land (including the set-aside area). The set-aside area is evidently left without fertilization.

The yield of cereals in Poland is low by western standards and the three-year average is only 2.85 t/ha. The highest yielding cereal crop, excepting maize for grain, is wheat (mainly winter wheat), followed by triticale and barley (mainly spring barley). The yields of rye and oats are almost one third lower but on very light and light soils these are the prevailing cereal crops. The coefficient of cereal yield variation is fairly high, which reflects large differences in the yield level between several regions and between vegetative periods in Poland (*Figure 1.5*).

The lowest yields are recorded in the central and eastern parts of Poland (regions Lod, Maz, Pod and Swi) and the highest in western and southern parts of the country (regions Dls, Opl, Sls, Wlp and Zpm). These differences can be explained partly by the combined effects of climatic conditions and the prevailing cereal species and partly by the different agro-technical measures, *i.e.*, fertilization, plant protection and others.

The yield of potatoes is hardly half that of sugar beet but the coefficient of yield variation of both crops, between the regions, is rather small. The reasons for similar, low variation coefficients are, however, quite different for the two crops. On most farms potatoes are grown on the poorest soils, and with a low level of production inputs. On the other hand, sugar beet, a highly profitable crop, is concentrated on the best soils and is cultivated properly and well fertilized.

Table 1.8 Set-aside Areas and Yields of Certain Crops in Regions of Poland

Regional Code	Set Aside Area 103 ha	Yields Cereals t/ha	Potatoes t/ha	Sugar Beet t/ha
Dls	114	3.78	19.90	38.77
Kuj	59	3.03	17.90	36.60
Lub	86	2.66	16.87	37.43
Lus	116	2.82	18.93	30.17
Lod	84	2.37	15.50	30.90
Mal	75	2.82	15.13	35.60
Maz	172	2.34	16.53	30.03
Opl	22	4.16	19.03	42.40
Pdk	137	2.69	17.07	31.73
Pod	58	2.14	17.73	34.73
Pom	103	2.87	18.27	33.23
Sls	121	3.08	17.20	42.87
Swi	76	2.42	15.33	33.80
Wrm	168	2.74	18.10	33.93
Wlp	73	3.23	19.23	38.37
Zpm	168	3.08	19.97	36.57
Poland	1 631	2.85	17.10	36.33

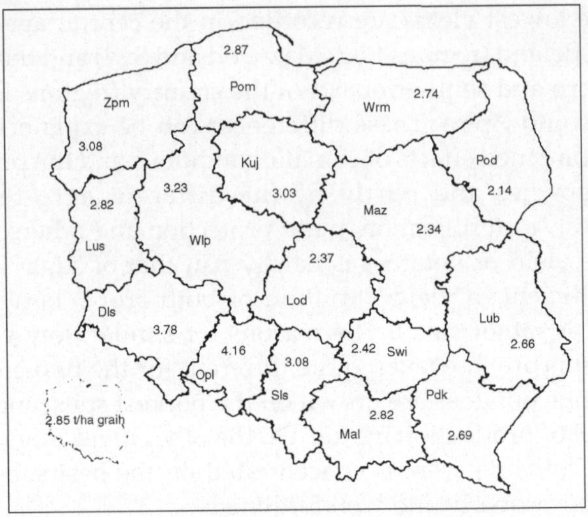

Fig 1.5 Yields of Cereals in Poland (t/ha)

Rapeseed is still a low-yielding crop and the average yield for Poland approximately exceeds two tonnes of seeds. The most important factor determining the yield of rapeseed, at a regional level, seems to be the quality of the soil, which is rather disappointing in view of the high input of fertilizers and pesticides commonly applied on this crop.

The average yield of pulses, *i.e.*, bean, peas and lupin, is very low and the cultivation of these crops is at the limit of profitability, which explains the continually decreasing share of pulses, in Poland.

2

The Fertilizer Sector

MINERAL FERTILIZER PRODUCTION

The history of the Polish fertilizer industry can be traced back to the second half of the 19th century. In the period between the first and second World Wars, two nitrogen fertilizer plants, four phosphorus fertilizer plants and three potassium salt mines were operating in the country. Some of these old plants, after considerable reconstruction, are still in operation but after the Second World War the fertilizer industry was practically rebuilt from scratch. In the second half of the 1980s it reached a peak production capacity of 1 640 thousand tonnes of N and 945 thousand tonnes of P_2O_5 annually. Potassium fertilizers, some 1350 thousand tonnes of K_2O, were imported from the former USSR and former East Germany.

The fertilizer industry was a very important part of the central planned economy and its production capacity matched the demand for fertilizers by Polish agriculture. There were almost no fertilizer exports. Fertilizer production and distribution were subsidised by the State and the demand for low-cost products exceeded production substantially. Mineral fertilizers were much more easily available for the state farms, which were supported for political reasons, than to the individual ones.

State farms, covering about 17 per cent of the agricultural land, consumed more than 30 per cent of the total fertilizers sold in the country. In 1991, the first year of transformation to a market oriented economy, the subsidy on fertilizers was removed and the demand from an impoverished agriculture dropped dramatically. The fertilizer factories reacted by reducing production and starting to export fertilizers. Few plants were closed. At present five large nitrogen plants and six phosphorus and compound fertilizer plants are operating in Poland. The production capacity of these factories, particularly the phosphorus plants, is not yet fully realised and a substantial part of the production is exported to European countries and overseas.

Table 2.1 The Large Polish Fertilizer Plants (Capacities in Thousand Tonnes Product Per Annum)

Plant	Fertilizers produced	Capacities
Zaklady Azotowe Pulawy	Urea	730
	Ammonium nitrate	1 220
	UAN (solution)	900
Zaklady Chemiczne Police	Urea	400
	NP. fertilizers	460
	NPK fertilizers	960
Zaklady Azotowe Kedzierzyn	Urea	175
	Calcium amm. nitrate	1120
	UAN (solution)	150
Zaklady AzotoweTarnow	Calcium amm. nitrate	450
	Ammonium sulphate	410
Zaklady Azotowe Wloclawek	Ammonium nitrate	790
Zaklady Nawozów Gdansk	Triple superphosphate	150
	NPK, PK fertilizers	310
Kopalnie Zaklady Tarnobrzeg	Single superphosphate	550
	NP, NPK & PK	200
Superfosfat Zaklady Szczecin	Single superphosphate	480
	NPK & PK fertilizers	
Zaklady Chemiczne Lubon	Single superphosphate	250
	NPK, NP, PK	320
Fabryka Nawozów Ubocz	Single superphosphate	250
	NPK fertilizers	160
Zaklady Przemyslu Wroclaw	Single superphosphate & NPK fertilizers	300
Zaklady Chemiczne Zlotniki	NMg, Mg fertilizers	

MINERAL FERTILIZER CONSUMPTION

Domestic fertilizer consumption reached its lowest level in 1992 (1135 thousand tonnes total NPK and 62 kg NPK/ha of agricultural land) and has been slowly recovering ever since. In 2001 consumption reached 1615 thousand tonnes, of which 55 per cent was accounted for by N, 20 per cent by P_2O_5 and 25 per cent by K_2O. The share of nitrogen in the total NPK is much higher than before 1990 and nitrogen consumption is increasing at a faster rate compared with phosphorus and potassium.

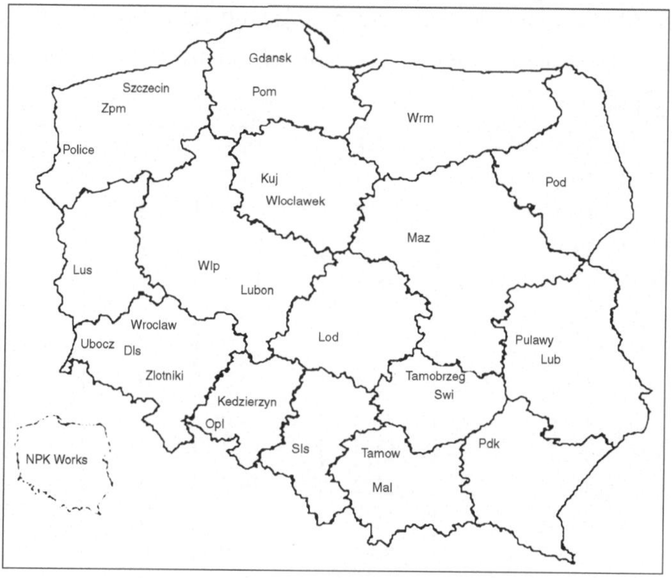

Fig 2.1 Location of Fertilizer Plants in Poland

Table 2.2 Production, Consumption and Trade of Mineral Fertilizers

Fertilizers	Item	Thousand Tonnes Nutrient		
		1998	1999	2000
Nitrogen N	Production	1 406	1 272	1 576
	Consumption	832	862	861
	Import	127	245	126
	Export	637	438	686
	Unaccounted*	64	217	155
Phosphorus P_2O_5	Production	593	535	639
	Consumption	317	308	297
	Import	29	36	38
	Export	194	173	135
	Unaccounted*	111	90	245
Potassium K_2O**	Consumption	380	387	368

Note: * Unfortunately the data concerning exports and imports are not fully available and reliable. The data concerning production and consumption in agriculture are reliable.

** There is no production of potassium in Poland. The consumption is that of imported material.

The consumption of nutrients varies greatly between the different regions of Poland. The average figures are shown in Table.

Table 2.3 Consumption of Mineral Fertilizers (kg/ha of Agricultural Land)

Region or Province	N	P_2O_5	K_2O	NPK
Dls	37.4	16.9	20.1	74.4
Kuj	76.9	16.8	22.5	116.2
Lub	39.7	17.8	20.8	78.2
Lus	51.0	16.5	17.8	85.2
Lod	48.3	11.2	13.0	72.5
Mal	33.2	18.2	19.3	70.7
Maz	35.6	17.9	21.8	75.3
Opl	68.4	22.6	36.7	127.7
Pdk	23.6	12.6	13.8	50.0
Pod	41.9	16.6	17.8	76.4
Pom	58.2	29.0	37.3	124.5
Sls	36.3	11.2	16.1	63.6
Swi	36.2	14.9	13.6	64.7
Wrm	44.5	12.3	16.3	73.1
Wlp	67.4	17.4	23.9	108.7
Zpm	62.1	15.8	26.2	104.2
Poland	47.4	16.7	20.9	85.1

The consumption of mineral fertilizers in Poland increased by about 10 per cent in 2001 compared with the figure. It concerned all nutrients almost proportionally and therefore the $N:P_2O_5:K_2O$ ratio remained practically unchanged (1:0.35:0.44). The highest rates of mineral fertilizers, exceeding 110 kg NPK/ha, are applied in five regions in western and northern Poland (Figure 2.2). In the eastern and southern parts of the country, the consumption of mineral fertilizers is below 75 kg NPK/ha of agricultural land. These figures are to some extent misleading because of the different proportions of set-aside land, practically unfertilised, in the various regions of Poland.

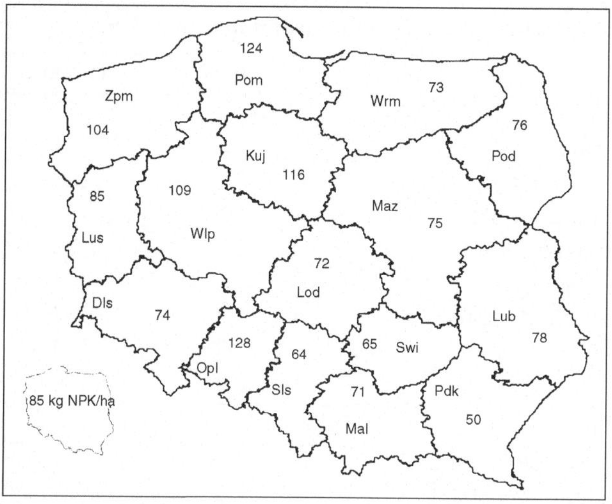

Fig 2.2 Consumption of Fertilizers by Region (kg Nutrient/ha)

The products sold in Poland in 1998 are shown in Table 2.4 and the relative importance of the different products is shown in Figure 2.3 for nitrogen and Figure 2.4 for phosphorus.

Until 1994 practically the whole amount of fertilizers was distributed in solid form. A new product, urea ammonium nitrate solution (UAN), launched by the Zaklady Azotowe, Pulawy S.A. plant, challenged the established distribution system for fertilizers.

At the beginning of 1990s UAN was sold exclusively on foreign markets. The export of this product in 1993 and 1994 reached the level of about 600 000 tonnes. Since, 1994, with the logistical and financial support of ZA Pulawy plant, a network of liquid fertilizer storage and distribution stations has been built, mainly in the Northern and Western regions of Poland. The storage stations are usually provided with two tanks each of 20 m^3 capacity, located on a pad to secure against the accidental leakage of UAN. Due to the lower production and transport costs, the price per nitrogen unit in UAN is a few to several per cent lower in comparison to solid nitrogen fertilizers. The consumption of UAN, starting from 25 000 tonnes in 1994, has been increasing steadily to the estimated amount of over 100 000 tonnes recently.

Table 2.4 Structure of Fertilizer Consumption in Poland

	2000	Percent
Nitrogen		
Ammonium sulphate	14	1
Urea	223	25
Ammonium nitrate	400	45
Calcium amm. nitrate	148	16
Nitrogen solutions	41	4
Ammonium phosphate N	10	1
NPK N	60	8
Total N	896	100
Phosphate		
Single superphosphate	18	7
Triple superphosphate	20	8
Other straight P_2O_5	-	-
Amm. phosphate P_2O_5	26	9
PK P_2O_5	25	9
NPK P	181	67
Total	270	100
Potash		
Potassium chloride	160	43
PK K_2O	30	8
NPK K_2O	180	49
Total K_2O	370	100
Total N + P_2O_5 + K_2O	1536	

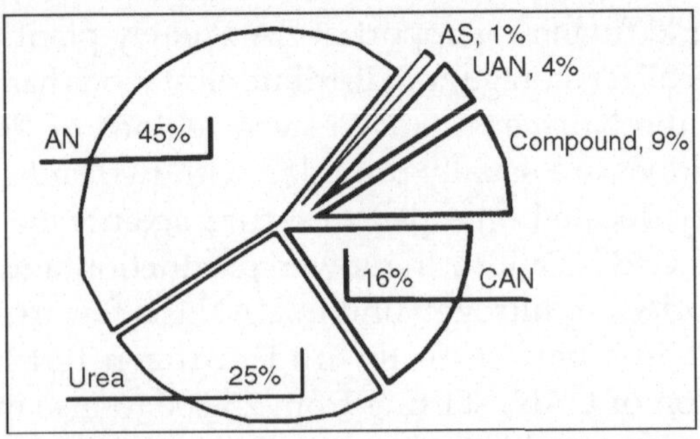

Fig 2.3 Structure of Nitrogen Fertilizer Consumption

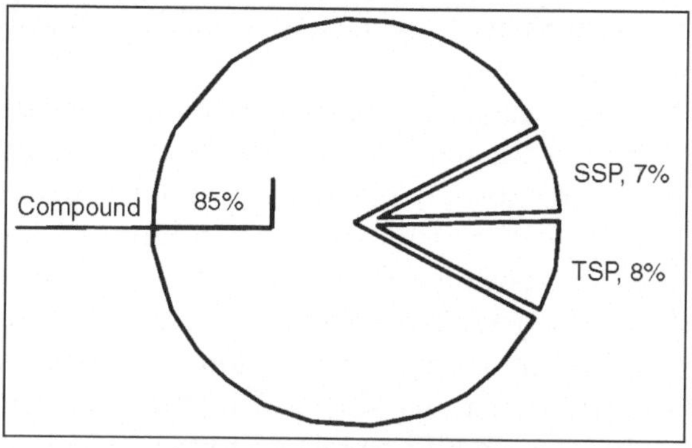

Fig 2.4 Structure of Phosphorus Fertilizer Consumption

ORGANIC MANURES

Table 2.5 Consumption of Nutrients in Manure and as Proportion of Total Nutrients in Mineral Fertilizers and Manure (kg/ha of Agricultural Land)

Region or Province	N	P_2O_5	K_2O	NPK	Per centage of Total NPK in Manure*
Dls	14.1	6.6	18.0	38.7	34
Kuj	36.4	18.5	48.0	102.9	47
Lub	24.8	10.8	34.8	70.4	47
Lus	13.3	6.3	17.3	36.9	30
Lod	32.5	14.7	45.9	93.0	56
Mal	34.3	13.9	49.4	97.6	58
Maz	31.6	13.5	45.7	90.8	55
Opl	27.3	13.9	34.9	76.0	37
Pdk	26.4	10.3	37.9	74.6	60
Pod	39.1	16.4	58.9	114.4	60
Pom	25.0	12.3	33.5	70.7	36
Sls	24.0	10.6	32.4	67.0	51
Swi	27.7	11.4	40.0	79.0	55
Wrm	22.2	9.7	31.3	63.2	46
Wlp	45.4	24.0	59.5	129.0	54
Zpm	13.9	6.8	18.5	39.2	27
Poland	28.7	12.9	39.6	81.1	49

The consumption of nutrients in organic materials, mainly manure, also decreased due to a reduction in the number of animals. Nevertheless, as a consequence of an even larger fall in the consumption of mineral fertilizers, the share of nutrients in manure increased substantially to reach about 50 per cent of the total amount of NPK consumed. The consumption of nutrients in manure varies considerably, by a factor 3, from below 40 kg NPK ($N+P_2O_5+K_2O$) in Dls, Lus and Zpm regions to over 120 kg NPK/ha in Wlp region. This consumption is naturally correlated with the density of animal stock. In fact the consumption of nutrients in manure should be related to the area of arable land and not to the total agricultural land, because in Poland manure is applied almost exclusively on arable land. This would increase the share of nutrients in manure in the total amount of NPK per ha of arable land far above 50 per cent.

FERTILIZER CONSUMPTION BY CROP

Statistical data concerning the consumption of fertilizers by crops are unavailable and for the sake of this report an indirect approach had to be used. This approach is based on so-called 'coefficients of preference'. This coefficient represents the ratio of the actual fertilizer rate for a given crop to the average rate applied to one ha of agricultural land. Coefficients of preference were calculated from the survey conducted during the past five years on the representative set of farms in Poland.

Unfortunately the coefficients of preference concern the total amount of NPK and do not separate out the individual nutrients. Consequently some crops seem to be under-estimated and others over-estimated with respect to calculated rates of nitrogen, phosphorus and/or potassium fertilizers.

The previous method under-estimated the rates on potatoes, rapeseed and vegetables, and over-estimated those on maize, grassland and perennial fodder crops. The main drawback of both methods is the assumption that the whole area of a given crop is fertilized, while some farmers do not apply fertilizers at all or use fertilizers only on a few, high profitable crops.

NITROGEN

The actual (or most probable) rates of nitrogen for crops grown in regions of Poland are presented in Table 2.6 The rates of nitrogen are the highest for sugar and fodder beets (in spite of manure application), maize, rapeseed and wheat. High rates of nitrogen are also applied on vegetables and triticale. The lowest rates are applied on rye, oats, pulses and fodder crops. The low rate for grassland is to a certain extent misleading because there are no separate coefficients of preference for meadows and pastures. Part of the area of pastures is, moreover, not fertilized. However, due to the alternative utilisation of most grassland in Poland (for both hay and grasing) it seems practical to calculate the average rate of nitrogen for the total grassland area.

Table 2.6 Actual Rates of Nitrogen Applied to Crops in the Regions of Poland

Region or Province	Grass Land	Wheat	Grain Maize	Pota- toes	Sugar Beet
Dls	29	49	62	36	91
Kuj	59	98	124	75	182
Lub	34	56	71	41	105
Lus	53	88	112	65	164
Lod	46	77	98	57	145
Mal	30	51	64	37	95
Maz	35	58	74	43	108
Opl	46	77	97	56	143
Pdk	18	31	39	22	57
Pod	39	66	83	48	123
Pom	50	83	105	61	155
Sls	32	53	68	39	100
Swi	28	46	59	34	87
Wrm	43	71	90	52	133
Wlp	56	93	118	68	173
Zpm	54	89	113	66	167
Poland	39	65	82	47	121

PHOSPHORUS

Present phosphorus rates are presented in Table. These rates are the highest for sugar and fodder beet, maize and rapeseed. Rates of phosphorus per hectare of agricultural land are higher in Opl and Pom regions than the average for Poland, however in Pom region the share of set-aside (unfertilized) land is three times higher in comparison to Opl region. Therefore the rates of phosphorus for the individual crops in Pom region far exceed those in Opl region.

Table 2.7 Actual Rates of Phosphorus Applied to Crops in the Regions of Poland

Region or province	Rapeseed	Wheat	Grain maize	Potatoes	Sugar beet
Dls	32	22	28	16	41
Kuj	31	21	27	16	40
Lub	37	25	32	18	47
Lus	42	28	36	21	53
Lod	26	18	223	13	34
Mal	41	28	35	20	52
Maz	43	29	37	21	55
Opl	37	25	32	19	47
Pdk	24	16	21	12	31
Pod	38	26	33	19	49
Pom	61	41	52	30	77
Sls	24	16	21	12	31
Swi	28	19	24	14	36
Wrm	29	20	25	14	37
Wlp	35	24	30	18	45
Zpm	33	23	29	17	43
Poland	33	23	29	17	43

POTASSIUM

The rates of potassium application are presented in Table. They are highest for sugar beet, maize and rapeseed and lowest for rye, pulses and fodder crops. Care is taken with potassium fertilization in western and northern Poland but it is neglected in the middle and eastern parts of the country.

Table 2.8 Present Rates of Potash Applied to Crops in the Regions of Poland

Region or Province	Rapeseed	Wheat	Grain Maize	Potatoes	Sugar Beet
Dls	38	26	33	19	49
Kuj	42	29	36	21	53
Lub	43	29	37	21	55
Lus	45	31	39	22	57
Lod	31	21	26	15	39
Mal	43	29	37	222	55
Maz	52	36	45	26	66
Opl	60	41	52	30	77
Pdk	26	18	23	13	33
Pod	41	28	35	20	52
Pom	78	53	67	39	99
Sls	35	24	30	17	44
Swi	25	17	22	13	32
Wrm	38	26	33	19	49
Wlp	48	33	42	24	62
Zpm	55	38	48	28	71
Poland	42	29	36	21	53

NUTRIENT BALANCES

The balances are calculated as soil surface nutrient balances according to the method prepared in Poland in the context of the MAINTAINE research project supported by EC. This method is in general agreement with the official OECD methodology. The original method or model called MACROBIL was aimed at balancing nutrients at the farm level.

It has been adapted slightly for the purposes of this report where regions and the whole of Poland are regarded as the equivalents of the big farms. The model was fed with the following data: area and yield of the crops, number of animals of different kinds and ages (calves, cattle, sows, fattening pigs and so on), consumption of mineral fertilizers and balance coefficients for phosphorus and potassium. In the nitrogen balance, on the input side the nutrients in fertilizers, manure, and crop by-products incorporated into the soil, biological N fixation and N atmospheric deposit are identified. The same items, apart from biological fixation and atmospheric deposition, are given for phosphorus and potassium.

The right side of the balance consists of the nutrients removed with the total yield of the crop. For the sake of interpretation of the final balance, the input of nitrogen is expressed in units of so-called acting N as well as total N. Acting nitrogen is the amount of N from the given source (*e.g.*, manure, crop residues, biological fixation) showing the same effect as the corresponding amount of nitrogen in mineral fertilizers. The amount of acting nitrogen is calculated according to the formula:

*Acting Nitrogen = total Nitrogen * nitrogen equivalent*

The nitrogen equivalents are derived from the result of field experiments and relate the efficiency of N from a given source to the efficiency of N in mineral fertilizers taken for 1. Nitrogen equivalents are less than one for some sources, such as cereal and rape straw, and may even be negative (nitrogen immobilisation). Nitrogen equivalent for fertilizers equals one (by definition).

The amounts of removed phosphorus and potassium also are corrected by balance equivalents. The balance equivalent is the ratio between the phosphorus and potassium uptake at the actual (or planned) yield and the optimal rate of these elements. These equivalents were calculated on the basis of long term field experiments with increasing rates of phosphorus and potassium fertilizers. For calculations at the regional level these equivalents were modified and correspond to the soil fertility status.

The input of total nitrogen in the whole of Poland and in all individual regions is higher than nitrogen removal, giving a positive nitrogen balance or N surplus. Nevertheless only in a few regions, are the surpluses of nitrogen slightly in excess of 40 kg N per ha of agricultural land, which is considered to be acceptable in most countries of the European Union. The balance of acting nitrogen is in the whole country still positive but in several regions deficiencies of this element are recorded.

The input of phosphorus in Poland and in most regions except Dln and Sls is higher than the P removed by the crop and there is an apparent P surplus. Nevertheless the output of phosphorus should be slightly higher (the balance coefficient for Poland is 1.12) than removal and hence, the phosphorus input and output are practically in balance. In six regions (Dln, Lod, Pdk, Sls, Wrm and Zpm) the phosphorus balance, taking account of the soil fertility, is negative.

Table 2.9 Nitrogen Balance, kg N/ha of Agricultural Land Region or Province

Region or Province	Input		Removal*	Balance	
	N Total	N Acting	N Total	N Total	N Acting
Dls	73.3	53.8	71.7	2.0	-18.0
Kuj	139.0	112.3	74.0	65.1	38.3
Lub	86.2	67.1	62.2	24.0	4.9
Lus	81.8	67.8	45.0	36.8	22.9
Lod	100.7	79.3	56.6	44.2	22.7
Mal	92.8	69.5	69.7	23.1	-0.2
Maz	86.6	65.2	55.6	31.0	9.6
Opl	123.2	93.1	94.6	28.5	-1.5
Pdk	72.8	52.6	59.5	13.3	-6.9
Pod	100.1	75.9	62.1	39.0	13.9
Pom	103.9	84.5	60.7	43.2	23.8
Sls	82.1	62.9	60.0	22.1	2.9
Swi	85.3	65.9	53.5	31.7	12.4
Wrm	86.7	69.7	59.3	27.4	10.4
Wlp	135.9	105.2	77.1	58.8	28.1
Zpm	95.0	79.8	55.0	40.0	24.9
Poland	97.6	75.7	63.5	34.2	12.2

Note: * The amounts of nutrients removed with the crop products.

Potassium input in the country as a whole and in practically all regions except Dln exceeds removal but due to the poor potassium status of most soils, the output of this element should in any case be higher than the mere removal (the balance coefficient for Poland is 1.30). In consequence the potassium balance calculated as the difference of input and output for the country as a whole is negative and in some regions potassium deficiencies exceed 10 kg K_2O per ha of agricultural land.

Table 2.10 Phosphorus Balance, kg P_2O_5/ha of Agricultural Land

Region or Province	Input	Removal*	Output**	Balance
Dls	26.0	29.1	30.2	-4.2
Kuj	37.5	30.2	30.2	7.4
Lub	29.9	24.4	29.0	0.9
Lus	23.9	18.4	18.8	5.2
Lod	26.6	22.1	27.1	-0.6
Mal	32.9	24.5	30.8	2.1
Maz	32.1	21.3	24.0	8.1
Opl	40.3	39.3	37.4	2.9
Pdk	23.9	21.3	26.5	-2.6
Pod	33.5	23.0	30.1	3.3
Pom	42.5	24.2	24.7	17.9
Sls	22.8	22.8	26.9	-4.1
Swi	27.1	20.2	26.6	0.5
Wrm	22.7	22.1	25.4	-2.7
Wlp	43.3	31.6	31.0	12.3
Zpm	24.1	22.8	27.1	-3.0
Poland	30.9	24.8	27.8	3.2

Note: * The amounts of nutrients removed with the crop products.
** Output = removal multiplied by the balance equivalent.

It may be surprising that, with the low consumption of nutrients in fertilizers and manure, the nutrient balances show surpluses or comparatively low deficiencies. This can be explained by the low or even very low crop yields recorded in the country and consequently the low nutrient removal with the harvested crop products.

The productivity of agriculture differs considerably among the regions in Poland. In this context, it is interesting that the nutrients removed per unit of yield are practically the same in all regions, which proves that there is a very close relation between the crop yields and the amount of nutrients at the disposal of the crop. Reversing this relationship, one can conclude that further growth of crop production depends considerably on the increased consumption of fertilizers and manure. The crop yields converted into cereal units and the uptake of nutrients per cereal unit are presented in Tables 2.11, 2.12 and 2.13.

Table 2.11 Potash Balance, kg K_2O/ha of Agricultural Land

Region or Province	Input	Removal*	Output**	Balance
Dls	53.6	60.5	65.3	-11.7
Kuj	85.3	66.8	75.5	9.8
Lub	64.5	51.2	65.6	-1.0
Lus	41.8	36.6	53.1	-11.3
Lod	63.5	51.4	77.0	-13.6
Mal	74.2	57.2	65.8	8.4
Maz	71.8	47.3	72.3	-0.5
Opl	94.4	80.9	94.6	-0.2
Pdk	57.4	60.5	63.7	-6.2
Pod	79.5	50.1	73.7	5.8
Pom	79.0	51.5	63.9	15.1
Sls	54.8	49.5	58.9	-4.1
Swi	59.1	44.2	58.3	0.8
Wrm	52.0	48.8	58.6	-6.5
Wlp	95.0	68.5	97.2	-2.2
Zpm	54.1	45.8	60.9	-6.8
Poland	68.7	54.1	70.3	-1.6

Note: * The amounts of nutrients removed with the crop products.
** Output = removal multiplied by the balance equivalent.

Table 2.12 Crop Yields and Nutrients Uptake Per Yield Unit in Regions of Poland.

Region	Crop yields converted into cereal units/ha*		Nutrients uptake per cereal unit kg per unit		
	Agricultural land	Arable land	N	P_2O_5	K_2O
Dln	30.4	34.8	2.36	0.96	1.99
Kuj	32.2	33.8	2.30	0.94	2.07
Lub	27.6	29.7	2.25	0.89	1.86
Lus	19.7	22.7	2.28	0.93	1.86
Lod	25.0	25.4	2.27	0.88	2.06
Mal	26.6	28.2	2.62	0.92	2.15
Maz	24.4	24.8	2.28	0.87	1.94
Opl	39.9	43.3	2.37	0.98	2.03
Pdk	23.3	24.9	2.56	0.92	2.17
Pod	23.0	11.1	2.70	1.00	2.18
Pom	25.1	27.2	2.42	0.96	2.05
Sls	24.3	25.7	2.47	0.94	2.04
Swi	23.3	24.5	2.30	0.87	1.90
Wrm	22.2	23.3	2.67	1.00	2.20
Wlp	33.0	35,3	2.34	0.96	2.08
Zpm	23.4	26.5	2.35	0.97	1.96
Poland	26.5	28.5	2.40	0.94	2.04

Note: *Cereal units as given in table below

Table 2.13 Equivalents of Crop Yields in Cereal Units

Crop, Product and Yield in kg	Cereal Units
Cereals, grain, 100 kg	1.0
Pulses, grain, 100 kg	1.20
Rape, seeds, 100 kg	2.00
Potato, sugar beets, tubers or roots 100 kg	0.25
Fodder beets, roots, 100 kg	0.12
Fodder crops, green matter 100 kg	0.10 to 0.14
Meadows and grasses, hay, 100 kg	0.40 to 0.50
Vegetables, fresh matter 100 kg	0.20

3

Prices and Profitability of Fertilizers

PRICES OF MINERAL FERTILIZERS

Until 1990 the sale or rather the distribution of fertilizers was organized uniformly and the retail prices were lower than the production costs (the ratio of prices to production costs was 0.51, 0.17 and 0.43 for nitrogen, phosphorus and potassium fertilizers respectively). In a transformed economy, the market determines the prices of fertilizers. In the years 1989 to 1993 the prices of nitrogen fertilizers (N) increased 30 times, phosphorus (P_2O_5) 36 times and potassium (K_2O) 44 times.

In the years the prices of fertilizers increased at the rate comparable to the rate of inflation. In the years the price trend flattened out (Table 3.1) and the price increases were below the inflation rate. This means that mineral fertilizers have become relatively cheaper. This can be explained by the surplus of fertilizers from domestic production and the strong competition for the market between the fertilizer plants. Another reason is the substantial, although only partly controlled, import of cheap fertilizers from eastern European countries. The prices of fertilizers are almost the same in all regions as a consequence of the policy of the fertilizer producers.

During the same period, the prices of agricultural products also increased but until 1994 at a slower pace than the prices of fertilizers.

Table 3.1 Prices of Basic Fertilizers in the Years 1998-2001

Fertilizer & % nutrients	Prices PLN*/kg nutrient (N, P_2O_5, K_2O)			
	1998	1999	2000	2001
Calcium amm. nitrate 28%	1.51	1.50	1.66	1.96
Ammonium nitrate 34%	1.28	1.21	1.39	1.61
Urea 46%	1.16	1.16	1.30	1.51
Single superphosphate 18%	1.72	1.97	1.98	2.19
Triple superphosphate 46%	1.81	1.85	1.96	2.08
NP fertilizer 18-46	1.50	1.59	1.62	1.65
NPK fertilizer 8-24-24	1.37	1.48	1.61	1.70
Potassium chloride 57%	0.80	0.93	1.02	1.04
Yearly rate of increase**	8.0%	5.0%	8.0%	9.0%
Yearly rate of inflation**	8.5%	9.8%	8.6%	3.6%

Note: * 100 PLN = 24.6 euros in June 2002

** In relation to the previous year.

In the years 1994 to 1997, the rate of increase of the prices of wheat was slightly higher than the rate of increase of the fertilizer price. In consequence, the fertilizer/grain price ratio widened at the beginning of the 1990s and narrowed slowly in the second half of this decade. During the years the index of the grain and fertilizer price relationship opened again and the farmer had to sell about 3 kg of wheat grain to buy 1 kg N, about 4 kg of wheat grain to buy 1 kg P_2O_5 and almost 2 kg of grain to buy 1 kg K_2O (Table 3.2).

Table 3.2 Price of 1 kg Nutrient Expressed in kg of Winter Wheat Grain

Fertilizer & % Nutrients	Price Ratio			
	1998	1999	2000	2001
Calcium amm. nitrate 28 %	3.2	3.6	2.8	3.6
Ammonium nitrate 34 %	2.7	3.0	2.5	3.0
Urea 46 %	2.5	2.7	2.3	2.8
Single superphosphate 18%	3.3	4.2	3.6	3.9
Triple superphosphate 46 %	3.7	4.3	3.6	3.9
NP fertilizer 18-46	3.1	3.6	3.0	3.1
NPK fertilizer 8-24-24	2.9	3.3	2.9	3.2
Potassium chloride 57 %	1.6	2.0	1.8	2.0

In view of the fact that the profitability of nitrogen fertilizers is 3 to 4 times higher than that of phosphorus and potassium, it is obvious why the consumption of phosphorus and potassium dropped more dramatically compared with the consumption of nitrogen fertilizers.

The only fertilizer product still subsidised by the State is lime, but the share of the subsidy in the total cost of production and distribution of limestone and dolomitic limestone shows a decreasing trend (Table).

Table 3.3 Subsidisation of Calcium and Magnesium Amendments

Item	Subsidies			
	1997	1999	2001	
Total subsidy in PLN*106	192	64	64	
Subsidy change, %	10.8	–35	–1.1	
Yearly rate of inflation, %	13	9.8	3.6	
Subsidy as % of the cost	44	25	25	

At the end of the central planning period, the subsidy accounted for more than 70 per cent of the total cost of liming and in 1993 it still amounted to 66 per cent. In 1997 this share was cut down to 44 per cent and in 1999/2001 to a mere 25 per cent of the total cost of liming. This is a crucial problem for Polish agriculture since, high acidity is one of the most limiting factors of soil fertility and crop yields in the country.

PROFITABILITY OF FERTILIZER USE

The data from the former 49 provinces were used to create models for relating yield and fertilizer consumption. Two models, one simplified and the other a full model were developed. The following crop prices were used to estimate profitability (*Table 3.4*). The prices of plant products given in this table are averages for the whole country. They show large fluctuations between years and regions. With the exception of a few products, *i.e.*, sugar beet, rapeseed grain, high quality wheat grain and some special products (tobacco, hemp), demand is too low in comparison with production. In 1998 the prices of most crops decreased dramatically (by 10 to 20 per cent) and farmers could hardly cover their costs.

Table 3.4 Prices of Plant Products in the Years

Product	Price, PLN, Per Tonne				
	1998	1999	2000	2001	Average
Wheat, grain	478	430	497	511	479
Rye, grain	332	294	380	364	342
Sugar beet	89	98	101	112	100
Rapeseed, seeds	895	644	806	830	793

The average price of 1 kg NPK ($N+P_2O_5+K_2O$) for the years was 1.41 PLN, and the average price of 1 kg of wheat grain (taken to be equivalent to the value of 1 kg of grain unit) was 0.48 PLN. The profitability of mineral fertilization of grain in Poland is therefore fairly high and can be roughly estimated at 3.1 PLN yield value per 1 PLN spent on fertilizers. The more complete model gave a somewhat lower response than the simplified model but it was still substantial at 2.4 PLN yield value per 1 PLN spent on fertilizers.

Similar calculations have been performed for certain other crops. The simplified model gave an average mineral fertilizer efficiency of 30 tonnes potatoes and 50 tonnes of sugar beet per kg NPK (Table).

Table 3.5 Profitability of Mineral Fertilization for Selected Crops

Crop	Yield increase per 1 kg NPK	Value of yield increase PLN	Cost of fertilizers PLN/kg NPK	Cost/value ratio
Wheat	9.84	4.71	1.41	3.3
Barley	7.77	4.19	1.41	3.0
Triticale	7.27	3.42	1.41	2.4
Rapeseed	6.61	5.24	1.41	3.7
Potato	30.32	3.64	1.41	2.6
Sugar beet	50.27	5.03	1.41	3.6

Until 1989, the fertilizer industry and the fertilizer distribution system were elements of the centrally planned economy, with the sales monopolised by the 'Agrochem Company'. Most of the domestically produced and imported (potassium salts) fertilizers were distributed centrally among the provinces and channelled by Agrochem either directly to the state farms or to the marketing cooperatives, which had outlets in each commune (the smallest administrative unit covering a few to several villages). This system collapsed within a few months after introduction of the market-oriented system in 1989/1990.

Most of the marketing cooperatives went bankrupt and the Agrochem Company was partly dissolved and partly privatised. The fertilizer market was in total confusion with few entrepreneurs seeking an easy profit and a crowd of farmers queuing for fertilizers at the factory gates. The prices rocketed to the rate 5 to 7 kg of wheat grain for 1 kg of nutrient and fertilizers were practically inaccessible for most farmers. Large fertilizer plants were fighting for survival. They began to export fertilizers and to rebuild the distribution channels in a market driven way.

In 1991/92 the wholesale centres and dealer networks were implemented and each big producer established uniform factory prices for the whole country. The discussion of trading policies are not revealed but it is believed that most of the large factories are selling almost equal amounts of fertilizers through their own dealers network and through wholesale centres. In the case of one factory only, almost the total production is sold through its own dealer network. Today more than 3 000 retailers, connected with the main producers, are active on the fertilizer market, which intensifies the competition for the clients.

For farmers, the prices of fertilizers are the same at the factory gate and at the local retailer level due to the discounts given by the producers to the distributors. The usual margin of profit offered to retailers is 5 to 10 per cent of the fertilizer value. The payment system for delivered fertilizers is very flexible. In the case of the wholesaler the immediate remittance system is commonly used but in the case of dealers the payment is executed when the dealer acquires the dues from the farmer.

During the past four years the State has intervened slightly on the fertilizer market through preferential credit offered to farmers. The credit for purchasing the fixed amount of fertilizers at a low interest rate (half of the normal rate) is available for the period from planting to harvest. The amount of money secured for this kind of credit by the banks is, however, limited and only partly satisfies the farmers demand. The overall productivity of agricultural land in Poland amounts to about 3 tonnes of cereal grain per ha or about 650 kg grain per inhabitant. This, relatively low productivity can be explained by the poor, prevalently sandy soils showing high acidity and low content of available nutrients. This productivity, after correction for the soil and climatic conditions, corresponds to the productivity of 4 820 to 5 420 kg grain units in continental western Europe.

To ensure food self-sufficiency for the country, crop production should be increased by at least 10 per cent. The easiest way to achieve this goal would be to increase mineral fertilizer consumption. The fertilizer market collapsed after the introduction of the economic reforms in 1990 and has been recovering slowly in recent years at a yearly rate of a few per cent. Taking into consideration that the efficiency of mineral fertilizers is in the range of 7 to 9 kg of grain units per 1 kg NPK, for ensuring the country's food self-sufficiency the consumption of fertilizers should grow by about 45 kg NPK per ha of land under cultivation, *i.e.*, to the level of at least 130 kg NPK per ha.

A higher share than at present should be accounted for by phosphorus and potassium, at the expense of nitrogen. This can be justified by the fact that the soil surface balance of nitrogen shows a surplus, while phosphorus is practically balanced and the balance of potassium is negative.

The agricultural policy in Poland should vary between the regions. In the central and western regions of the country, agriculture is generally well developed, matches the western Europe standards and can more or less cope with the financial problems. In the northern part of the country, agriculture is going through a very difficult time due to transformation processes connected with the former land structure (the prevalence of state farms). In eastern Poland, with some exceptions, agriculture will face a permanent crisis due to the land fragmentation among the huge number of very small farms, unless some firm political and economic measures are taken.

4

Biophysical Carbon Sequestration

INTRODUCTION

As discussed, the process of CS, or flux of C into soils forms part of the global carbon cycle. Movement of C between the soil and the atmosphere is bidirectional. Consequently, carbon storage in soils reflects the balance between the opposing processes of accumulation and loss. This reservoir of soil C is truly dynamic. Not only is C continually entering and leaving the soil, the soil C itself is partitioned between several pools, the residence times of which span several orders of magnitude. Nor is soil C an inert reservoir, the organic matter with which it is associated is vital for maintaining soil fertility and it plays a part in such varied phenomena as nutrient cycling and gaseous emissions. A detailed description and analysis of soil C and organic matter can be found elsewhere. Taking into account specific biophysical characteristics of dry areas, different biophysical aspects of CS in dryland soils.

HALOPHYTES

A special feature of many dryland soils is salinity, either through natural occurrence or increasingly as a result of irrigation. Saline soils affect large parts of the drylands. Such lands are often abandoned, but halophytic plants are especially adapted to these conditions and offer potential for sequestering

C in this inhospitable environment. It has been estimated that 130 million ha are suitable for growing halophytes, which can be used for forage, feed and oilseed. Glenn *et al.* estimate that 0.6-1.2 gigatonnes of C per year could be assimilated annually by halophytes. Evidence from decomposition experiments suggests that 30-50 per cent of this C might enter long-term storage in soil. Although irrigation would be required to achieve these figures, a complete carbon budget still suggests a carbon actual rate of 22-30 per cent.

GRASSLANDS

Grasslands are the natural biome in many drylands, partly because rainfall is insufficient to support trees, and partly because of prevailing livestock management. However, grassland productivity and CS have been controversial. The productivity of tropical grasslands is now known to be much higher than was previously thought, and consequently they sequester much more C. Estimates for C stored under grassland are about 70 tonnes/ha, which is comparable with values for forest soils. Although many of the grassland areas in drylands are poorly managed and degraded, they offer potential for CS as a consequence.

The average annual input of organic matter into grassland is about double the 1-2 tonnes/ha that is contributed to cropped soils. This fact is borne out by the results of studies from various locations. The data have shown that grassland, even where subject to controlled grasing, generally has higher soil C levels than cropland. Chan and Bowman found that 50 years of cropping soils in semiarid New South Wales, Australia, had on average reduced soil C by 32 per cent relative to pasture. The reduction was linearly related to the number of years of cropping. Similarly, soils of tall-grass pasture under controlled grasing had greater soil C than adjacent cropland subject to conservation tillage.

The key factor responsible for enhanced carbon storage in grassland sites is the high carbon input derived from plant roots. It is this high root production that provides the potential to increase SOM in pastures and vegetated fallows compared with cropped systems. Root debris tends to be less decomposable than shoot material because of its higher lignin content. Consequently, the key to maintaining and increasing CS in grassland systems is to maximize grass productivity and root inputs. Grasses have also been shown to sequester more C than leguminous cover crops. Grasses also have the potential to sequester C on previously degraded land. Garten and Wullschleger used a modelling approach that estimated a 12-per cent increase in soil C could be obtained under switchgrass (*Panicum virgatum* L.) on degraded land in ten years.

Grasing is a feature of many grasslands, natural or managed. This might be expected to decrease the availability of residues that can be used to sequester C, especially as the quantity of C returned in manure is less than that consumed. However, provided there is careful grasing management, many investigations have found a positive effect of grasing on the stock of soil C. This was found to be the case for a composite pasture (alfalfa and perennial grasses) in the semi-arid pampas. Even under harsher conditions in the Syrian Arab Republic, grasing was found to have no detrimental impact on soil C. Schuman, Janzen and Herrick, have calculated that with proper grasing management, rangelands in the United States of America can increase soil carbon storage by 0.1-0.3 tonnes/ha/ year. For new grasslands, this can rise to 0.6 tonnes/ha/year.

The positive effect of grasing appears to result from the effect that it has on species composition and litter accumulation. Willms *et al.* found that when prairie was protected from grasing there was little effect on production but there was an increase in the quantity litter. Reeder and Schuman also found that there was an accumulation of litter in an ungrazed semi-arid system and that soil carbon levels were higher in the grazed lands. The litter acted as a store of immobilised C. The ungrazed grassland also experienced an increase in species that lacked the fibrous rooting system that is conducive to SOM formation and accumulation.

Therefore, grasslands can play a vital role in sequestering C. However, careful grasing management is essential. The historical record shows how susceptible semiarid grasslands are to overgrasing, soil degradation and carbon loss.

BURNING

Fires form part of the natural cycle in many biomes and are especially prevalent in grassland ecosystems. However, humans have also used fire to clear areas for agriculture and to clear crop residues.

The action of fire would seem to be counter to CS as it returns C fixed by vegetation directly to the atmosphere, thereby preventing its incorporation into the soil. The effect of fire is difficult to generalise because it depends upon the intensity and speed of the fire.

These factors are influenced by: the state of the vegetation, *i.e.,* its maturity and woody component; the accumulation of litter; and climate factors such as moisture level. They C in all the aboveground material that is fully combusted will be lost from the system. However, in grassland ecosystems, C lost to fires can be replaced quickly by increased photosynthesis and vegetative growth.

Even in savannah systems that contain woody species, it has been shown that C lost through combustion can be replaced during the following growing season. Regarding the soil, the intensity and speed of the fire will govern the depth to which it is affected. In one study where burning was used to clear forests, 4 tonnes C/ha was lost in the top 3 cm of soil, but this was replaced within one year under a pasture system.

Not all plant material is fully combusted by fire, and a variable amount of charcoal will be produced. Charcoal is extremely resistant to decomposition; it is not cycled like most organic matter, and has a mean residence time of 10 000 years. Consequently, in severely degraded soils that have been affected by several fires, charcoal and charred material can form a substantial proportion of the remaining organic C. However, it is not known whether charcoal and other charred material have any protective effect on the native organic matter.

Thus, although fires release CO_2 back into the atmosphere, the simultaneous production of charcoal can be regarded as a sequestration process that results in a substantial amount of C being accumulated within the soil for a long period.

AFFORESTATION

Forestry is recognised as major sink for C. However, as well as accumulating C aboveground, it can also make significant contributions to soil C even in drylands. A number of suitable species are available that enable viable afforestation in dryland environments. In particular, N-fixing trees generally lead to increased accumulation of soil C. For example, *Prosopis* and *Acacia* are adapted to subtropical semi-arid lands and are reported to increase the level of soil C by 2 tonnes/ha.

Some tree varieties are particularly suitable for growing on degraded lands, their deep rooting systems tapping resources unavailable to shallow-rooted crops. *Prosopis juliflora* has been grown on salt-affected soils in northwest India and increased the SOC pool from 10 tonnes/ha to 45 tonnes/ha in an eight-year period. Even where large-scale forestry is not appropriate, there is often scope for introducing trees around farmers' fields. Such is the case in semi-arid India where *Prosopis cineraria* has improved soil fertility as well as sequestering extra C. However, natural systems are complex and trees do not guarantee improved CS. Jackson *et al.* found that soil C decreased when woody vegetation invaded grasslands. Although there was an increase in aboveground and belowground biomass, these gains were offset by losses in soil C.

RESIDUES

Plant residues provide a renewable resource for incorporation into the SOM. Production of plant residues in an ecosystem at steady-state will be balanced by the return of dead plant material to the soil. In a native prairie, about 40 per cent of plant production is accumulated in the SOM. However, in agricultural systems, because plants are harvested, only about 20 per cent of production will on average be accumulated into the soil organic fraction.

Furthermore, in some farming systems, all aboveground production may be harvested, leaving only the root biomass. Of the plant residue returned to the soil, about 15 per cent will be converted to passive SOC. Schlesinger is more pessimistic, suggesting that only 1 per cent of plant production will contribute to CS in soil. The actual quantities of residue returned to the soil will depend on the crop, the growing conditions and the agricultural practices. For example, for a soybean—wheat system in subtropical central India, the annual contribution of C from aboveground biomass was about 22 per cent for soybean and 32 per cent for wheat. This resulted in 18 per cent of the annual gross carbon input being incorporated into the SOM. In semi-arid Canada, the conversion of residue C to SOC was reported to be 9 per cent in frequently fallowed systems, increasing to 29 per cent for continuously cropped systems.

Unless a root crop is being harvested, all belowground production is available for incorporation into the SOM. Roots are believed to be the major constituent of particulate organic matter although tillage reduces the net accumulation of C from roots substantially. In cool climates, belowground carbon inputs from roots alone can generally maintain soil carbon levels. However, this is not the case in warmer or semi-arid regions where residues are decomposed much more readily, providing sufficient moisture is available.

Consequently, when continuous cropping is practised in drylands, failure to return aboveground plant residue will lead invariably to a reduction in soil C. Many African soils demonstrate this phenomenon. Continuous cropping over a number of years without the recommended inputs has often halved their carbon content.

Both the quality and quantity of plant residues are important factors for determining the amount of C stored in soil. The quantity is highly dependent on the environmental conditions and agricultural practices. Differences between crops can be marked. A crop of maize will return nearly twice as much residue to the soil compared with soybean and, consequently, will result in a higher rate of SOM increase.

The advantage that cereals have over legumes for achieving maximum CS rates has also been demonstrated by Curtin *et al.* They have shown that while black lentil fallow in semi-arid Canada added between 1.4 and 1.8 tonnes C/ha, a wheat crop would add 2-3 times this amount of C annually. Similarly, in

Argentina, soybean, which produced 1.2 tonnes/ha of residue, resulted in a net loss of soil C, while maize, with 3.0 tonnes/ ha of residue, lessened the loss of soil C from the system significantly.

Even within one crop group, large differences in organic matter production occur. Abdurahman *et al.* compared dry leaf production from pigeon pea and cowpea. While the former yielded 3 tonnes/ha, cowpea produced 0.14 tonnes/ha. These examples illustrate how the choice of crop can have a major influence on how much C an agricultural system can sequester.

The importance of roots relative to shoots for providing soil C is another factor illustrated in an experiment to compare the fate of shoot-and root-derived C. In this study with leguminous green manure (hairy vetch), nearly half of the root-derived C was still present in the soil after one growing season whereas only 13 per cent of shoot-derived C remained. This implies that shoot residues are broken down rapidly on account of their higher N content and may serve as a nitrogen source for the following crop.

The chemical composition of plant residues affects their rate of decomposition. On average, crop residues contain about 40-50 per cent of C but N is a much more variable component. A high concentration of lignin and other structural carbohydrates together with a high C:N ratio will decrease the rate of decomposition. For example, measurement of CO_2 evolution from tree leaves of African browse species and goat manure showed a significant correlation with initial nitrogen content and a negative correlation with lignin content. Legume residues such as soybean are generally of high quality and so decompose rapidly. Although the chemical composition of the plant residue affects its rate of decomposition, there is little effect on the resulting SOM.

Where residues accumulate on the soil surface, their physical presence affects the soil. Mulches reduce water loss and soil temperature, both important factors for drylands, especially where the soil temperature is above the optimum for plant growth. The ability of soil to assimilate organic matter is not clear-cut. A linear relationship between application and accumulation of SOM is often quoted. However, measurement of CO_2 flux in central Ohio, the United States of America, showed this flux to increase with added application of wheat straw (0, 8 and 16 tonnes/ha). However, the SOC was 19.6, 25.6 and 26.5 tonnes/ha after four years, suggesting that CS was reaching saturation.

Care must be taken when applying residues, as large losses of C can still occur under certain conditions. For example, in western Kenya, 70-90 per cent of the added C was lost within 40 d when green manure from agroforestry trees was applied during the rainy season. In Niger, the addition of millet residue and fertilizer for five years had no significant effect on the carbon level in the sandy soils. Termite activity may have contributed to the low levels of soil C here because entire surface mulches can be consumed within one year.

The potential amount of residues available for applying to soils can be large. Gaur estimated that in India about 235 million tonnes of straw/stover are produced annually from five major cereals (not only from drylands). Even if half of this were used for feeding livestock, there would be more than 1 million tonnes available for adding to the soil. However, availability of sufficient plant residues is often a problem, especially where they are required for livestock feed.

This conflict of requirement occurs frequently in many dryland farming systems. In West Africa, crop residues are either removed or burnt. Consequently, the amount of soil C has declined steadily. Continuous cultivation and manure application can raise soil carbon levels by 40 per cent but this frequently involves mining C from neighbouring areas to support the livestock. Where plant and animal residues are in short supply, possibilities may exist for alternative organic inputs to the soil. For example, in India, waste products from a plant processing coir dust have been incorporated successfully into soil, and other experiments with industrial glue waste have increased soil carbon levels successfully.

With regard to the complete carbon budget, where plant residues accumulate *in situ*, there is no extra carbon cost involved. Consequently, the C fixed by plants in photosynthesis is available as a net gain to the soil. The situation becomes more complex where machinery is required to separate the residue from the harvestable components. Where plant residues are transported between fields the energy cost would need to be included.

Perhaps the major issue regarding residue application and carbon accounting is the question of whether C is simply being transferred from one place to another rather than being truly sequestered. If organic material from industrial processes or other sources were to be used for incorporation into the soil, then any C used in transport would have to be accounted for. However, where the material is truly a waste product, there should be no need to consider the C used in its production. In this case, the C available for sequestration should be viewed no differently from the CO_2 emitted from a fossil fuel source that is subsequently fixed by plants in photosynthesis and returned to the soil via crop residues.

APPLIED MANURES

The application of FYM has long been treated as a valuable source of organic matter to enhance soil fertility. One of the key characteristics of manure application is that it promotes the formation and stabilisation of soil macroaggregates and particulate organic matter. Manure is more resistant to microbial decomposition than plant residues are. Consequently, for the same carbon input, carbon storage is higher with manure application than with plant residues.

Following five years of application, soil receiving manure had 1.18 tonnes/ha more C present than soil receiving plant residues. Even after 15 years, there was a still a difference of 0.37 tonnes C/ha as calculated by the RothC soil carbon model. In the field, Gregorich *et al.* found that manured soils had large quantities of soluble C with a slower turnover rate than in control or fertilized plots.

The composition and, therefore, decomposition of manure varies between the species from which it originates and also within species according to their diet. Many field trials have found that manure is the best means for incorporating organic matter into soils and promoting carbon storage. For example, Li *et al.* found that manure yielded the largest amount of C sequestered over a range of soils and climate conditions, although soil texture was important, and the greatest rate of sequestration occurred where there was a high clay content. However, many traditional agrosystems add manure in combination with fertilizers.

Depending on the system, the application of even relatively high amounts of FYM does not guarantee an increase in soil C. A long-term study in Kenya has shown that SOM declined even when manure was applied and maize residue returned. It has been estimated that in order to maintain soil C in this system, 35 tonnes/ha of manure or 17 tonnes/ha manure with 16 tonnes/ha of stover would be required annually. Consequently, there is a carbon shortfall in this case, but it is difficult to see how the present system could remedy it.

In addition, high application rates of manure can sometimes cause problems in the soil through the accumulation of K^+, Na^+ and NH_4^+ and the production of water-repellent substances by decomposer fungi. An additional problem in drylands that restricts the quantity of manure that can be applied is 'burning' of the crop when insufficient moisture is available at the time of application. Consequently, farmers often wait until the rains have come before making an application, especially as precipitation is often erratic in arid regions. is often erratic in arid regions.

The production of sufficient manure for application to fields is a real problem for many smallholder farming systems. In Nigeria, direct manure input onto land from dry-season grasing is about 111 kg/ha of dry matter. This quantity will have little effect on the soil. More useful is the practice of night-parking cattle as manure production is usually greatest at dawn and dusk.

When 50 cattle were penned in an area of 0.04 ha for five nights, they produced the equivalent of 6.875 tonnes/ha of manure. Normally, cattle will be penned in fields for 2-3 nights in northern Nigeria and this can supply manure at a rate of 5.5 tonnes/ha. Alternatively, in densely populated parts such as the Kano closed-settlement zone, cattle and crop production are fully integrated. Cattle are kept permanently in pens and fed using feed grown on neighbouring fields. Their manure is collected and spread onto the croplands. Although an efficient system, some C will be lost as a consequence of the respiratory and growth requirements of the cattle. An additional problem associated with cattle rearing is that ruminants produce significant quantities of CH_4, which is a potent GHG.

There has been some debate as to the usefulness of animal manure in CS. Schlesinger has calculated that providing 13.4 tonnes/ha would require 3 ha of cropland in order to produce sufficient cattle feed. This means that manure production requires mining of C from neighbouring lands. Although this is a generalisation, it is argued that the 3:1 differential makes it unlikely that manure production *per se* could be used as a means of providing a net carbon sink in soils.

However, in many dryland smallholder cropping systems, manure application rates are much lower, and fodder production is also less efficient. Smith and Powlson have made the case that keeping cattle is part of many agricultural systems and, hence, that manure should be considered as a byproduct that can be added to arable land without necessarily including the carbon cost of its production.

Part of the disagreement with Schlesinger on the usefulness of manure depends on where the system boundary for carbon accounting is drawn. However, when conducting such a carbon audit, it is essential to remember that the purpose of agriculture is to feed people; offsetting GHGs can only be evaluated as a secondary activity.

INORGANIC FERTILIZERS AND IRRIGATION

Fertilization and irrigation are primary means for increasing plant production and crop yield. Any increase in biomass also offers increased scope for CS. Consequently, irrigation and fertilization have been recommended as, and proved to be, successful methods of increasing CS. Rasmussen and Rohde have shown a direct linear relationship between long-term nitrogen addition and accumulation of organic C in some semi-arid soils in Oregon, the United States of America. However, these technologies provide no additional organic matter themselves but do carry a carbon cost. Schlesinger has pointed out that pumping water requires energy and that the process of fertilizer manufacture, storage and transport is energy intensive. Consequently, Schlesinger has estimated that the gains in C stored using either fertilization or irrigation are offset by losses elsewhere in the system. Irrigation can also lead to the release of inorganic C from the soil.

Izaurralde, McGill and Rosenberg have argued that the calculations used by Schlesinger are based on very high rates of fertilizer application. For many dryland agriculture systems in the developing world, farmers do not have sufficient funds to apply large quantities of fertilizer even if they were available. With regard to the energy costs incurred in pumping water, solar-powered systems are being developed and dryland environments with frequently clear skies would be able to make the best use of solar radiation.

These examples serve to illustrate how important it is to consider the whole system when CS is being considered to offset CO_2 emissions. The exact carbon cost of irrigation and fertilization would require calculation for each system, but the carbon deficits associated with both technologies make their incorporation into net CS systems difficult to achieve. Water conservation, the growing of legumes and careful nutrient cycling are more likely to yield a positive carbon balance.

TILLAGE

Pretty *et al.* consider tillage to be one of the major factors responsible for decreasing carbon stocks in agricultural soils. Research and experimentation with reduced tillage practices are most prevalent in the Americas. The mould-board plough and disc harrow are believed to be the causes of the loss of soil C through the destruction of soil aggregates and the acceleration of decomposition by the mixing of plant residues, oxygen and microbial biomass. Soil aggregates are vital for CS, a process that is maximal at intermediate aggregate turnover. Of the organic matter fraction, the particulate organic matter is the most tillage sensitive.

It is difficult to quantify the effects of tillage on soil C because the effect are very site dependent, *e.g.*, coarse-textured soils are likely to be more affected by cultivation than are fine ones. However, reducing tillage should be most effective in hot, dry environments.

Reicosky conducted an experiment that used measurements of CO_2 efflux to investigate tillage-induced carbon loss from soil. The flux of CO_2 was monitored for 19 d following different forms of tillage practice. The mould-board plough buried most of the crop residue and produced the maximum CO_2 flux. The C released by the different treatments as a per centage of C in the crop residue was: 134 per cent with mould-board plough; 70 per cent with mould-board plough and disc harrow; 58 per cent with disc harrow; 54 per cent with chisel plough; and 27 per cent with no-tillage.

This demonstrates the correlation between CO_2 loss and tillage intensity, and demonstrates why farming systems that use mould-board ploughing inevitably lose soil C. Very large amounts of organic matter would be required to replace the loss incurred by such heavy tillage. Reicosky *et al.* estimate that 15-25 tonnes/ha manure plus crop residue would be needed annually in North America to offset these losses.

The flux of CO_2 from soil generated directly by the tillage process may not always reflect the overall release of CO_2 and hence, carbon storage of the system. This is illustrated by a comparison of conventional disc tillage and no-tillage in central Texas, the United States of America, by Franzluebbers, Hons and Zuberer.

Here, seasonal evolution of CO_2 was up to 12 per cent greater in the no-tillage system after 10 years. This was despite the fact that more C was sequestered by the no-tillage system. The authors suggest that a change in the dynamics of CS and mineralisation have occurred under the no-tillage system. Similarly, Costantini, Cosentino and Segat found that more CO_2 was released from no-tillage or reduced-tillage compared with conventional tillage despite there being increased levels of soil C. They ascribe this difference to an increase in the microbial biomass.

Rates of carbon loss through tillage depend considerably on the site and cropping system. Ellert and Janzen measured the flux of CO_2 following the passage of a heavy cultivator on a semi-arid Chernozem soil in the Canadian prairies. They found that although tillage increased rates of CO_2 loss by two to four times, values returned to normal after 24 hours.

They calculated that even with ten passes of the cultivator, only 5 per cent of crop residue production would be released from this cropping system. In another situation, ploughing of a wheat-fallow cropping system near Sydney, Australia, reduced soil C by 32 per cent after 12 years. Elimination of ploughing and adopting a no-tillage approach was unable to prevent a decrease in the carbon stock, although the loss was reduced to just 12 per cent. The authors suggest that a fallow period would be required to halt the decline in soil C at this site.

There are many different types of tillage system. Conservation tillage covers a range of practices-no-tillage, ridge-tillage, mulch-tillage. Mulch-tillage maintains higher levels of residue cover. With mulches, only a small fraction of the residue is in contact with the soil surface and the microbes it contains. Decomposition is slow, especially as oxygen availability is limited. The physical presence of crop residues on the soil surface also alters the microclimate of the upper soil layer, which tends to be cooler and wetter compared with conventional tillage.

The accumulation of residues also reduces the loss of CO_2 from the soil surface. Alvarez *et al.*, reported an increase in labile forms of organic matter under no-tillage in the Argentine rolling pampa, indicating a decrease in the mineralisation of the organic fraction. This study also noted that although organic C increased by 42-50 per cent under no-tillage compared with ploughing and chisel tillage, there was also a marked stratification in the distribution of C under the no-tillage regime that was not evident in the ploughed system.

Stratification of organic C is common with reduced or no-tillage. Zibilske, Bradford and Smart in semi-arid Texas, the United States of America, demonstrated that the organic carbon concentration was 50 per cent greater in the top 4 cm of soil of a no-tillage experiment compared with ploughing, but the difference dropped to just 15 per cent in the 4-8-cm depth zone. This is typical of organic carbon gains observed with conservation tillage in hot climates. Bayer *et al.*, working on a sandy clay loam Acrisol, also found that the increase in total organic C was restricted to the soil surface layers under no-tillage but that the actual quantity depended on the cropping system. An oat/vetch-maize/cowpea no-tillage system produced the largest quantity of crop residues and sequestered the most C: 1.33 tonnes C/ha/year in 9 years.

Reicosky has compared the results from many no-tillage trials. The data emphasise the effect that crop rotation and quantity of crop residue has on organic matter accumulation. Overall, rates of organic matter accumulation can be expected to be lower in the hotter climates. Nevertheless, even in the very sandy soils of in north of the Syrian Arab Republic, it has been possible to make modest increases in SOM with no-tillage. In western Nigeria, no-tillage combined with mulch application had a dramatic effect, increasing soil C from 15 to 32.3 tonnes/ha in 4 years.

Although no-tillage systems are an excellent tool for combating the carbon losses associated with conventional cultivation, they do have their own special problems. In temperate lands, the reduction in soil temperature commonly associated with plant residue accumulation on the soil surface can retard germination.

However, in drylands, where soil temperatures are frequently above the optimum for germination and plant establishment, such cooling is likely to be beneficial. No-tillage systems frequently suffer from an increased incidence of pests and diseases; the mouldboard plough and disc harrow are efficient weed controllers. Consequently, no-tillage systems generally rely upon extra herbicides and pesticides. These inputs have an economic price and they also incur a carbon cost.

However, in many dryland farming systems of the developing world, purchasing such products is not feasible, and quite often there is plentiful labour available for weeding. Application of N fertilizer can also be problematic when used on undisturbed, no-tillage soils. Where the soil is poorly drained, denitrification can occur and the reduced rate of evaporation increases the risk of nitrate leaching. In addition the native soil N has a lower rate of mineralisation in undisturbed soil.

Not all soils are suited to a reduced-tillage approach. Some soils in the Argentine pampa may actually lose more C under no-tillage (0.7-1.5 tonnes C/ha/year) compared with conventional ploughing and periodic ploughing is required to avoid soil compaction. Where no-tillage is used on the pampas, the physical status of the soil is a critical factor for the success of the system. Similarly, in the West African Sahel, the highest crop yields are obtained with deep ploughing, which is required to prevent crusting and alleviate compaction. In general, the success of reduced-tillage systems is often dependent on soil texture.

A particular advantage of the no-tillage system is that it favours multicropping; harvesting can be followed immediately by planting. Any cropping system that allows for continuous or near continuous plant growth should yield the maximum capacity to produce plant biomass and, consequently, has the potential to provide the greatest amount of organic mater for inclusion into the soil.

Considering the overall carbon budget, no-tillage systems have a lower energy requirement because tillage is very energy intensive. Phillips *et al.* have calculated that no-tillage systems in North America reduce the energy input into maize and soybean production by 7 and 18 per cent, respectively. Improved water-use efficiency means that the energy, and hence, carbon, cost of irrigation are reduced. However, the impact of energy savings is frequently offset by additional herbicide requirements. Kern and Johnson estimated that the manufacture and application of herbicides to no-tillage systems of the Great Plains is equivalent to 0.02 tonnes C/ha.

Reduced-tillage systems were adopted originally to help combat soil degradation. They were not intended as a means of sequestering C, which is a fortunate side-effect. Although the effectiveness of no-tillage at sequestering C will depend on the specific agricultural system to which it is introduced, there is no doubt that, as the intensity of tillage decreases, the balance between carbon loss and gain swings towards the latter.

ROTATIONS

The importance of rotation in agricultural systems has long been known and the procedure now forms an intricate part of many conservation tillage practices. The inclusion of rotations has many benefits such as countering the buildup of cropspecific pests and, thereby, lessening the need for 'carbon costly' pesticides and herbicides. Different crop species have a variety of rooting depths and this aids in distributing organic matter throughout the soil profile. In particular, deep-rooting plants are especially useful for increasing carbon storage at depth, where it should be most secure. The inclusion of N-fixing varieties in a rotation increases soil N without the need for energy-intensive production of N fertilizers.

The beneficial effects that rotations have for CS have been proved in many longterm field experiments. For example, Gregorich, Drury and Baldock made a comparison of continuous maize cultivation with a legume-based rotation. The rotation had a greater effect on soil C than did fertilizer. The difference between monocultured maize and the rotation was 20 tonnes C/ha while the effect of fertilization was 6 tonnes C/ha after 35 years. In addition, the SOM present below the ploughed layer in the legume-based rotation appeared to be more biologically resistant. This demonstrates that soils under legume-based rotations tend to preserve residue C. A positive effect on SOC (an increase of 2-4 tonnes/ha) was also found with legumes and alternate cattle grasing in semi-arid Argentina.

Rotations, especially legume-based ones, are generally regarded as extremely valuable for maintaining soil fertility and have a very good potential for sequestering C in dryland systems. Drinkwater, Wagoner and Sarrantonio estimate that their use in the maize/soybean-growing region of the United States of America would increase soil CS by 0.01-0.03 Pg C/year. The effectiveness of rotations for sequestering C is likely to be greatest where they are combined with conservation tillage practices.

FALLOWS

The role that fallows play in CS is varied. Where cropping is not taking place, it is important that vegetation cover is preserved. This is especially so in drylands where exposed soil is most likely to suffer from erosion and degradation. In addition to protecting the soil, cover crops can utilise solar energy that would otherwise be wasted. The CO_2 fixed is then available for sequestering into the soil as the plants senesce. The importance of vegetation cover can be illustrated with the results from an experiment conducted at a semi-arid site in Mediterranean Spain. Four and a half years after the vegetation cover was removed from one site, the SOC had decreased by 35 per cent compared with the control plots.

The type of fallow is important. In Nigeria, forest clearance caused a decline in soil C from 25 to 13.5 tonnes/ha in seven years, but 12-13 years of bush fallow restored the carbon content. Conversely, pigeon pea fallow was unable to sequester sufficient C on account of its low biomass production and rapid degradation. However, fallows can have a negative effect on carbon storage in many situations. The frequency of summer fallows in semi-arid regions has been suggested as one of the major factors influencing the level of soil C in agricultural systems. Reducing the summer fallow in the semi-arid northwest United States of America is reported to have had a more positive effect on soil carbon retention than that achieved by decreasing tillage intensity.

The loss of C in this region is believed to reflect the high rates of biological oxidation that occur here, which can only be offset by very large applications of manure. Consequently, yearly cropping and the associated organic additions is the recommended practice. Miglierina *et al.* also found that reducing summer fallow increased soil C, a consequence of the additional crop residue that was added. Using the Century agro-ecosystem model, Smith *et al* predicted that reducing summer fallow in wheat cropping systems (wheat-fallow to wheat-wheat-fallow) in the semiarid Chernozems of western Canada would reduce carbon losses by 0.03 tonnes/ha.

Elimination of fallows can be highly beneficial for soil C simply because most fallows are associated with small inputs of plant residue. The significance of fallows for CS in a given system will depend on whether or not the cropping cycle adds significant quantities of organic matter to the soil. Where it does, then the presence of fallows is unlikely to enhance carbon storage within the system. Conversely, where the cultivation practice is poor and little or no organic matter is added, fallow periods will serve to counter this situation.

SOIL INORGANIC CARBON

Not all soil C is associated with organic material; there is also an inorganic carbon component in soils. This is of particular relevance to drylands because calcification and the formation of secondary carbonates is an important process in the soils of arid and semi-arid regions where, as a result, the largest accumulations of carbonate occur. The dynamics of the inorganic carbon pool are poorly understood although it is normally quite stable. Sequestration of inorganic C occurs via the movement of HCO^-_3 into groundwater and closed systems. According to Schlesinger accumulation of calcium carbonate is quite low at 0.0012-0.006 tonnes/ha. However, Lal, Hassan and Dumanski believe that the sequestration of secondary carbonates can contribute 0.0069-0.2659 Pg C/year in arid and semi-arid lands.

Although soil inorganic C is relatively stable, it will release CO_2 if the carbonates become exposed through erosion. In addition, irrigation can cause inorganic C to become unstable if acidification takes place through inputs of N and sulphur. The release of CO_2 through carbonate precipitation is seen as a major problem if irrigation waters are used in any system that is trying to store C. Furthermore, Schlesinger has pointed out that the groundwater of arid lands often contains up to 1 per cent calcium and CO_2. This concentration is much higher than that which occurs in the atmosphere. Consequently, when these waters are applied to arid lands, CO_2 is released to the atmosphere and calcium carbonate precipitates. Schlesinger's calculations suggest that irrigation of some cropping systems would yield a net transfer of CO_2 from the soil to the atmosphere.

TRACE GASES

An important aspect of agricultural systems in relation to the global carbon balance is the production of trace gases, particularly CH_4 and N_2O. When CS by soils is being considered as a mechanism for offsetting greenhouse gas emissions, it is necessary to consider all the interacting factors that can influence global warming. Both CH_4 and N_2O are radiatively active gases and, like CO_2, contribute to the greenhouse effect. Although they are present in the atmosphere at much lower concentrations than CO_2, they are much more potent. CH_4 and N_2O are, respectively, 21 times and 300 times more active GHGs than CO_2.

Ruminants, composting, biomass burning and waterlogging produce CH_4, while N_2O is released from soils when N fertilizer or manure is applied. Manure usage is considered to be the major problem with regard to trace-gas emissions in agriculture. This is a potentially serious problem because the application of manure is a major tool for increasing soil C in drylands. Smith *et al* calculated that, for European soils, the effect of trace gases is sufficient to reduce the CO_2 mitigation potential of some no-tillage and manure-management practices by up to a half. Moreover, climate change is likely to amplify the problem as increased temperature is predicted to promote N_2O emissions.

CLIMATE CHANGE

Climate is a major factor involved in soil formation. Consequently, climate change will influence soils. Photosynthesis and decomposition will be affected directly and, hence, have an impact on soils. Whether soil carbon levels increase or decrease will depend on the balance between primary production and decomposition. Overall, productivity is predicted to increase as a consequence of rising CO_2 concentration and temperature, and this will lead to increased amounts of residue available for incorporation into the soil.

However, higher temperatures can be expected to increase mineralisation of SOM because this process is more sensitive to temperature increases than primary production. Kirschbaum predicts that SOC stocks will decline overall with global warming. However, Goldewijk *et al.* suggest that the effects of temperature and water availability on soil respiration will be smaller than those attributable to the CO_2 fertilization effect. The direction of change is not certain but the balance of change will most probably operate at the regional level. It has been argued that agricultural systems are to some extent buffered from environmental effects, while decomposition is not protected. Hence, increased rates of mineralization might be more significant than any enhancement of production.

However, the quality of plant organic matter is expected to decrease under elevated CO_2 owing to an increase in the C:N ratio. This would slow the rate of degradation. Globally, the drylands are expected to become moister, which should lead to an increase in productivity and decomposition. However, shifts in climate zones are dependent upon a complex array of variables. Predictions based on the Century agro-ecosystem model suggest that, overall, grasslands will lose soil C except in tropical savannahs, which should show a small increase. Experiments at elevated CO_2 have also shown that changes in soil C in agro-ecosystems are particularly dependent upon the crop species grown.

The full extent of the global rise in temperature associated with climate change may not be felt in many of the drylands because warming is predicted to be greatest at higher latitudes. With regard to the vegetation, some of the best-adapted plants for dryland regions use the C4 photosynthetic pattern. Because these species already have a CO_2-concentrating mechanism, they show little or no increase in productivity at elevated CO_2. However, they are still likely to receive some benefit from the increased water-use efficiency that accompanies a rising CO_2 concentration.

5

Manures in Drylands

RESEARCH

Most of the research and case studies on soil CS have been conducted in temperate zones. Much less work has been done in developing regions, including drylands. In order to realise the great potential for CS offered in drylands, efforts are needed to identify soil-specific practices that restore SOC in degraded soils. This will specific case studies in different representative agrosystems in drylands, where the potential for carbon storage is assessed under different land-use and landmanagement practices involving irrigation and biofertilizers.

MODELS FOR ANALYSING TROPICAL DRYLAND AGRICULTURAL SYSTEMS

RothC and CENTURY 4.0 are the most extensively used SOC simulation models. They have been tested against a variety of long-term agricultural field trials and have also been used in a variety of climate zones, including dryland regions. Both have also been adopted for use in major carbon-assessment projects. The two models vary in their complexity. RothC requires fewer data inputs and so is easier to parametise. However, it only deals with soil processes and, consequently, plant residue C is a required input.

The Century agro-ecosystem model has similar SOC pools to RothC but has the advantage of additional submodels. Although it is able to handle a great many more land-management options than RothC, it requires an increased array of input variables that require parametisation. This is important because the ability of any model to predict accurately depends on the accuracy and trustworthiness of the data used to parametise it.

APPROACH

Data for parametising the models can be divided into three areas: climate, soil and land management. Studies that contain data that are sufficiently detailed for modelling are few, particularly in dryland regions. Where investigations have been undertaken and detailed information collected, the primary data that are vital for modelling are often not readily available.

Climate parameters may be referred to by investigators reporting the effects of land management on soils, but complete data sets are rarely given. However, climate data are available independently, as from FAOCLIM 2, which contains a database of more than 28 000 weather stations worldwide.

The literature contains the results from many investigations analysing soil properties and the effect of various treatments and practices upon soils. However, there are far fewer studies that combine soil analysis with examination of land management, especially over the longer term. In particular, there has been little research on dryland systems.

For the case studies examined here, Century was parametised and run to equilibrium for between 2 000 and 5 000 years. Scenarios reflecting the recent past and present were then applied. Although Century can run many varied cropping practices, it can only handle one crop at a time. Consequently, intercropping, which is commonly practised in dryland farming systems, could not be incorporated into the scenarios.

RothC was run to equilibrium using the current soil carbon status after initially being run in reverse mode to calculate the necessary plant carbon inputs. In order to model some of the future scenarios for analysing the effects of land management on soil C, the appropriate plant residue inputs were obtained from the Century plant submodel and then used to parametise the RothC land-management files. The results in RothC frequently predict higher levels of soil C than Century. This has been noted before and has been attributed to the fact that SOC tends to turnover faster in Century than in RothC, and, consequently, that RothC requires lower carbon inputs to maintain the same organic carbon content. The Century plant submodel is quite basic. Therefore, where accurate estimations of plant production and crop yield are required, then alternative models, such as the fully mechanistic plant productivity model WIMOVAC, should be used.

SYSTEMS AND SOURCES

Data from four distinctly different dryland systems in Argentina, India, Kenya and Nigeria were used to model changes in soil C with a variety of farm practices and technologies. These systems had different precultivation stocks of soil C, and had lost different amounts during cultivation (*Table 5.1*). Additions of organic matter to the soil through use of FYM, green manures, legumes in rotations, vermicompost, or use of fallows in rotations, all increased soil C and increased agricultural yields. Trees as part of agroforestry systems further increase soil carbon stocks. Inorganic fertilizer used alone to increase nutrient supply for crops results in declines in soil C in all systems, or only small increases if used with no-tillage. No-tillage increases soil C, although again the accumulation is greatest where organic matter is added to the soil.

The scenarios show that CS in tropical drylands soils can be achieved at the different sites. The land-management practices have been chosen to be in accordance with the current farming systems. Thus, for example, application rates of organic matter are commensurate with quantities that should be available to local farmers. However, at the field level, important trade-offs may occur, preventing adoption of the best strategies for CS. Crop residues may be required for livestock feed or fuel rather than be returned to the fields, or may be sold in difficult times. Animal manures may be burnt for fuel. Many socio-economic factors will interact to determine which scenario or combination of scenarios is implemented in each growing season.

Some of the results predict that soil C can be restored to precultivation levels, or in certain circumstances to above them. The true 'native soil carbon level' is often difficult to establish in those systems where agricultural activity has been present for several centuries or millennia such as in the Nigeria and Kenya cases. To achieve quantities of soil C in excess of the 'natural level' implies that the agriculture system has a greater productivity than the native system, assuming that C is not being imported. The scenarios that predict the highest CS rates are often associated with the introduction of trees to the system. The inputs of C from trees are more resistant to decomposition than those from herbaceous crops and, consequently, can cause marked increases in the level of soil C.

Table 5.1 Summary of Findings on Carbon Stocks and Rates of Accumulation and/or Loss in Four Dryland Agrosystems

	Nigeria	India	Kenya	Argentina
Stocks of soil C before cultivation (tonnes/ha)	8-23	15-20	33-41	50-70
Current stocks of soil C after cultivation (tonnes/ha)	6-12	13-22	18-28	37-41
Effect of conventional tillage practices on soil C (tonnes/ha/year)	– 0.05 to – 0.01	– 0.07 to +0.06	– 0.3 to – 0.1	– 0.17 to – 0.19
Effect of FYM, organic additions, retained plant residues and fallows in rotations (tonnes/ha/year)	+ 0.1 to + 0.3	+ 0.2 to + 0.4	+ 0.4 to + 0.9	-
Effect of trees (tonnes/ha/year)	+ addition al 0.05 to 0.15	+ additional 0.5 to 0.7	-	-
Effect of using inorganic fertilizers as sole source of nutrients on soil C tonnes/ha/year)	– 0.12 to + 0.08	– 0.01	– 0.3	-
Effects of no-tillage (NT)				
NT alone				+ 0.02 +0.1 to 0.25

(*Cont...*)

NT + green manures or FYM				+0.04
NT + inorganic fertilizers				

Note: [1]Effects of conventional tillage are averages for the last 100 years for each site except Kenya where rates are calculated from when each settlement commenced (30-50 years).

Nigeria includes some of the most densely inhabited areas of semi-arid West Africa. This is not a recent phenomenon as indications of human activity can be traced back well over a thousand years. Consequently, the soils of this region have been subjected to long periods of cultivation. However, in the last 40 years the cultivated area of northern Nigeria has increased from 11 per cent to 34 per cent of the total land area. In particular, the level of agricultural intensity in the Kano Closed-Settled Zone (CSZ) is among the highest in semi-arid West Africa.

Investigations into the farming systems of this region and their effect on soil fertility have been conducted by the organisation Drylands Research, the United Kingdom. Its studies have found a close correlation between the intensity of farming and the adoption of soil-fertility management techniques. Plant production in the Sahel is generally limited by rainfall or nutrients. However, the economy and infrastructure of northern Nigeria is unsuited to high external inputs such as fertilizers. Consequently, the smallholder farming units operate as low-input systems, with cattle manure being the most common form of organic input.

PHYSICAL ASPECTS

This semi-arid region has a rainy season from May-July until September. However, rainfall is erratic and makes crop cultivation particularly difficult. The soils are principally ferruginous tropical soils that are sandy, with poor waterholding capacity and low levels of nutrients and organic matter. Nutrient balances can vary between years as crop growth fluctuates with rainfall. The natural vegetation is open forest savannah with a trend towards increasing open grassland where rainfall is lowest.

FARMING SYSTEMS

Northern Nigeria has been classified into three categories of farming system: intensive, less intensive and extensive. The intensive systems use permanent annual or biannual cultivation with a cropping intensity of more than 60 per cent. The low-intensity systems operate a shrub/short-bush-fallow regime and the cropping intensity is 30-60 per cent. The extensive system is one of long-bush-fallow and uncultivated areas, where the cropping intensity is typically less than 30 per cent. The major crops grown are millet, sorghum, groundnut, sesame and cowpea. As the systems are low input, grain yields are about 1 tonne/ha. Ridging ploughs are primarily used for cultivation and hoeing is commonplace. Applications of manure have to be made carefully to avoid "burning" the crops, and additions are 1-7 tonnes/ha. Crop residues are collected for fodder or left to be grazed in the fields.

Fallowing is practised in the less intensive systems although the land is still "harvested" through grasing and the collecting of wood and other products. Night-parking (or folding) of livestock is the most effective method of providing manure. Legumes such as cowpea are grown, primarily in higher-intensity systems, to provide nitrogen inputs. Inorganic fertilizers are scarce and seldom available at the optimal time.

STUDY

The study sites cover a range of population density and include the three categories of farming intensity. The soils and crops grown are similar across all categories. Initially, CENTURY was parametised with a natural system of grass, woodland and grasing. A medium-intensity fire was scheduled for every 10 years and a high-intensity fire event occurred every 30 years.

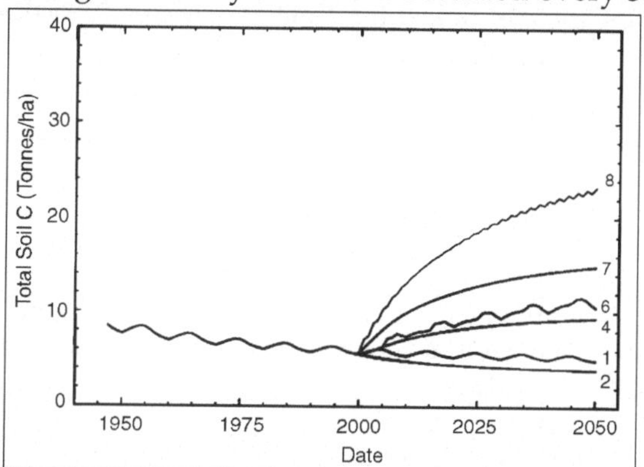

Fig 5.1 Total Soil Carbon for Futchimiram Settlement (Century)

One thousand years ago, slash and burn episodes were commenced and two seasons of millet cultivation incorporated, repeated every 60 years. In the nineteenth century, the frequency of cultivation events was increased to a 30-year cycle, and then once every 15 years by the commencement of the twentieth century.

FUTCHIMIRAM, BORNO STATE

This is a low-intensity, or extensive, agropastoral system practising shifting cultivation. Some land has now become degraded. Century was run for the last 60 years with alternate five-year cycles of grasing and millet cropping. Crop residues are grazed and there are no other inputs. This current practice produces a gradual and persistent decline in soil C (*Figure 5.1*). The estimated level is slightly above the measured value of soil C for cultivated soils that range between 3.5 and 4.4 tonnes/ha. RothC also predicts that the current practice will decrease soil C slightly over the next 50 years (Table 5.2). Figure illustrates the predicted average annual change in soil C over a 50-year period.

Table 5.2 Total Soil Carbon for Futchimiram Settlement

Scenario[1]	CENTURY			RothC		
	2000	2050	% change	2000	2050	% change
	(tonnes/ha)			(tonnes/ha)		
1	5.54	4.94	-10.8	5.38	5.18	-3.7
2		3.93	-29.1		3.72	-30.9
5		9.40	69.7		9.70	80.3
6		10.57	90.8		12.45	131.4

Table 5.3 Scenarios for Modelling Land Management Practices, Futchimiram Settlement

Scenario	Land Management
1	Current Practice
2	Continuous cultivation
3	Continuous cultivation, no grasing of residues, harvest only grain
4	Inorganic fertilizer only (100 kg/ha urea), no grasing
5	Plant residues average 0.5 tonnes/ha/year, no grasing of residues
6	5-year fallow, 5-year cultivation, 2 applications FYM 3 tonnes/ha, graze residues

(Contd...)

7	Continuous cultivation, FYM 1.5 tonnes/ha/ year, graze residues
8	Continuos cultivation, FYM 1.5 tonnes/ha/year Plant residues 0.5 tonnes/ha/year, no grasing

Effect of Loss of Fallow

Removing the fallow period only results in a greater decline in soil C over subsequent years, with both models predicting similar reductions. Preventing grasing of the crop residues under these conditions has very little effect on soil C.

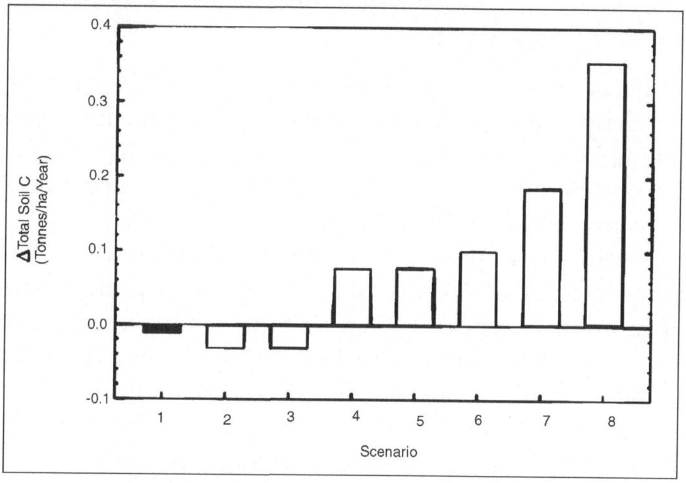

Fig 5.2 Average Annual Change in Total Soil Carbon for Futchimiram Settlement (Century)

Effect of Organic Inputs

The addition of FYM (two applications of 3 tonnes/ha in each five-year cropping cycle, average 0.6 tonnes/ha/year) has a positive effect on soil C, the two models indicating an increase of 5-7 tonnes C/ha over the next 50 years (0.08 tonnes C/ha/year). Figures 5.2 show the outcome of further scenarios using different combinations of fallow and organic inputs. The gradual increase in soil C occurs with FYM, retaining plant residues and no grasing after harvest. In this case, soil stocks rise from 6 to 24 tonnes C/ha over 50 years.

Effect of Inorganic Fertilizer

The use of inorganic fertilizer with no other organic inputs, and no grasing or fallow, leads to a modest increase in CS (0.08 tonnes C/ha/year).

Summary

This system will not yield a positive soil carbon balance without increased organic inputs. Although inorganic fertilizers can lead to CS, they bring with them a carbon cost that will result in an overall negative balance of the complete carbon budget.

KASKA, YOBE STATE

This is a low-intensity agropastoral farming system covering lowland, upland and some wetland areas. Only the lowland soils are modelled here. There is intercropping of legumes and grains, and crop residues are fed to livestock. Manure application to fields is low and long bush fallows are used.

Century was parametised for the last 50 years with a sevenyear cycle of 4 years of grasing and 3 years of millet-cowpea-millet cropping. FYM (0.75 tonnes/ha) was added in the first year of each cropping cycle. Cultivated soils have carbon contents of 4.5-7.0 tonnes/ha. The Century model calculates a current carbon content of 7.7 tonnes/ha (Figure), and RothC gives a similar result (Table). Both models suggest that with current practice the system is close to steady state.

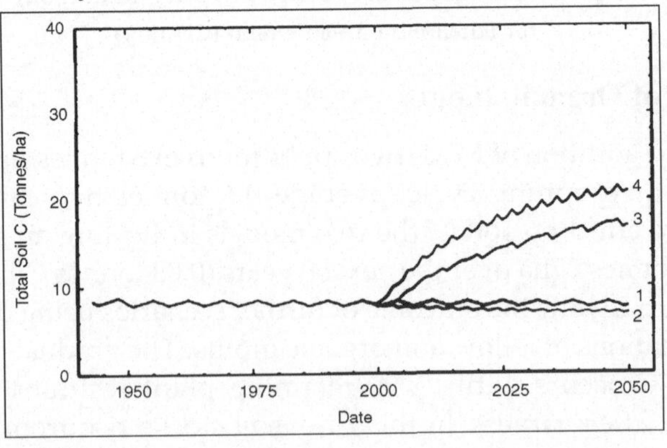

Fig 5.3 Total Soil Carbon for Kaska Settlement (Century)

Effects of Fallows and Organic Inputs

Removing the fallow from the current practice leads to a slight decline in soil C in subsequent years. Applying 3 tonnes/ha FYM to each millet crop (average 1.3 tonnes/ha/year over seven-year cycle) will produce a marked increase in soil C representing a CS rate of 0.18 tonnes/ha/year. This increase will be further enhanced if the fallow is removed, because the manure application rate will now average 2 tonnes/ha/year.

Summary

Table. Total Soil Carbon for Kaska Settlement

Scenario[1]	CENTURY			RothC		
	2000	2050	% change	2000	2050	% change
	(tonnes/ha)			(tonnes/ha)		
1	7.73	7.64	-1.2	7.33	7.87	7.4
3		16.94	119.1		15.57	112.4

Table 5.5 Scenarios for Modelling Land Management Practices, Kaska Settlement

Scenario	Land Management
1	Current practice
2	Continuous cultivation, millet-cowpea
3	Cultivation-fallow, FYM 3 tonnes/ha, to millet
4	Continuous cultivation, FYM 3 tonnes/ha, to millet

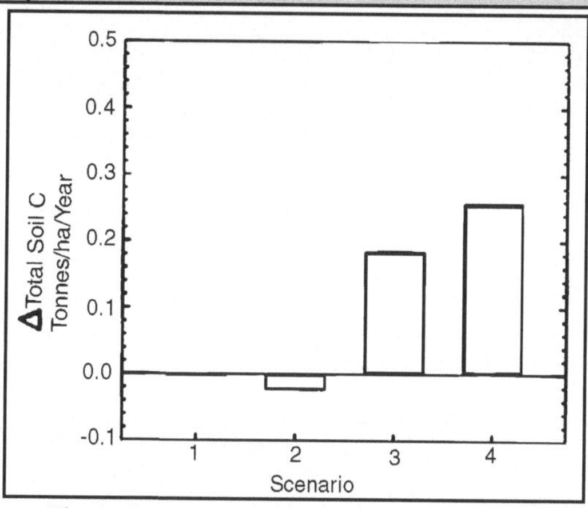

Fig 5.4 Average Annual Change in Total Soil Carbon for Kaska Settlement (Century)

The scenarios for Kaska illustrate the effect of fallow periods on stocks of soil C. Where the cropping regime is adding very little organic matter to the soil, fallows will often have a positive effect if correctly managed. However, if the cropping practice is accumulating significant organic matter in the soil, any interruption, such as fallowing, will decrease the overall potential for CS.

DAGACERI, JIGAWA STATE

This is a region undergoing rapid intensification. It is an agropastoral system with shrub or short-bush fallowing. The length of fallow has decreased as the area of arable land has expanded. Both legumes and grains are grown, but land degradation is a problem. As the fallow period shortens, farmers rely increasingly upon manures to maintain soil fertility.

Table 5.6 Total Soil Carbon for Dagaceri Settlement (Century and RothC)

Scenario[1]	CENTURY			RothC		
	2000	2050	%	2000	2050	%
	(tonnes/ha)		change	(tonnes/ha)		change
1	12.43	15 .00	20.7	14.69	20.43	39.1
5		22.22	78.8		29.55	101.2

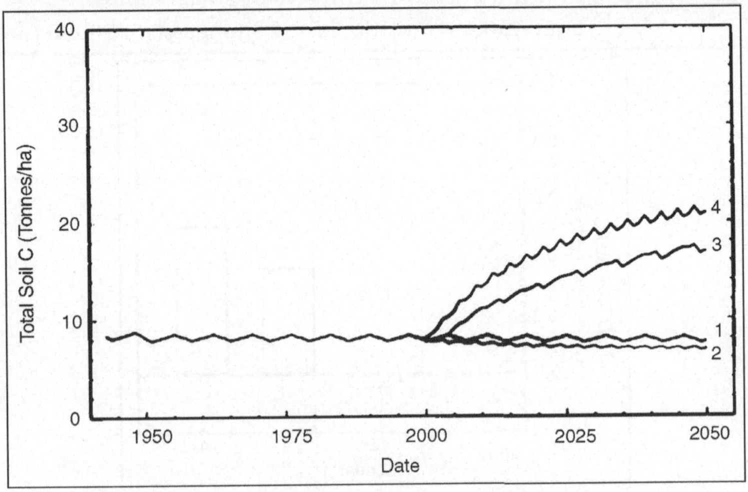

Fig 5.5 Total Soil Carbon for Dagaceri Settlement (Century)

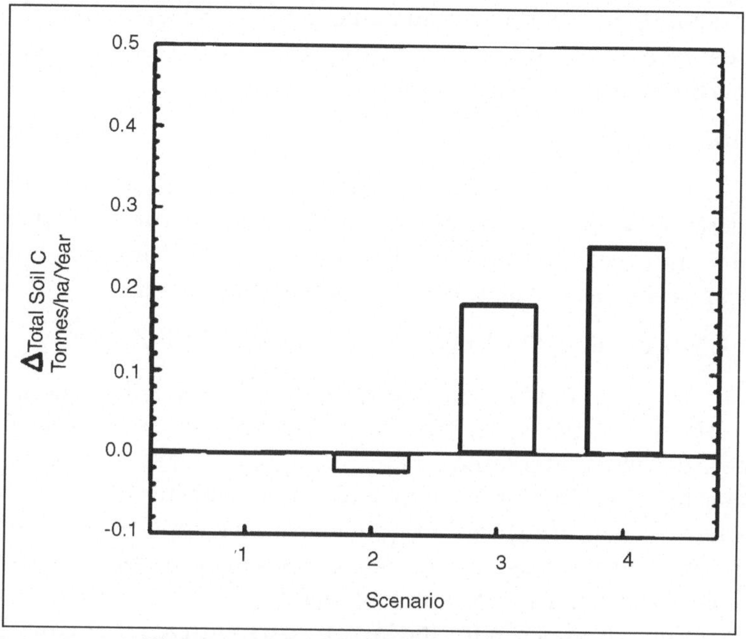

Fig 5.6 Average Annual Change in Total Soil Carbon for Dagaceri Settlement (Century)

The parametisation for Century was initially the same as for Kaska but then, 30 years ago, cropping was increased to five years out of seven. Millet and cowpea are cropped alternately with 1.5 tonnes/ha manure added to each millet crop (average 0.64 tonnes/ha over a seven-year cycle).

The additional manure input associated with the increase in cropping intensity results in an increase in soil C, predicted by both models, and this rise continues in subsequent years. Field measurements vary according to previous cropping intensity and range from 3 to 17 tonnes C/ha.

Effects of Fallows and Organic Inputs

The manure input to each millet crop is increased to 3 tonnes/ha in all scenarios. Carbon sequestration rates of 0.18-0.20 tonnes/ha can be achieved, with slight differences depending on whether the fallow is retained and crop residues grazed or ungrazed. However, if fallow elimination is accompanied by harvesting all aboveground material, CS is virtually halted even if manure application is maintained. The complete removal of trees from the system results in a net loss of soil C in spite of the increased application of manure.

Summary

This system shows that SOM can be maintained and increased even with intensification of cropping, provided there are legumes in the rotation. However, careful management of crop residues is vital as is the preservation of trees.

TUMBAU, KANO CLOSED—SETTLEMENT ZONE

This is a highly intensive agricultural area. All the land is cultivated although degradation reportedly affects less than 10 per cent of the land area. There is a highly integrated crop and livestock production system with intercropping of legumes, intensive manuring and inorganic fertilizer application. There is virtually no grasing land so animals have to feed on crop residues and fodder from nearby fields.

Century was run for the last 50 years with a millet-cowpea rotation, 6 tonnes/ha of manure applied to the millet (average 3 tonnes/ ha/year) and all aboveground plant material harvested. This system is now close to steady state with soil C stocks at 9.8 tonnes C/ha. This compares with an average of 10.5 ± 1.7 tonnes C/ha measured at cultivated sites. RothC calculates a value of 11.3 tonnes/ha for 2000 but predicts that a higher soil carbon level will be reached by 2050.

Table 5.7 Scenarios for Modelling Land Management Practices, Dagaceri Settlement

Scenario	Land Management
1	Current practice
2	Remove trees
3	No grasing of residues, harvest all aboveground
4	Continous cultivation, millet-cowpea
5	FYM average 1.29 tonnes/ha year,fallow, graze residues, harvest only grain
6	No grasing of residues, harvest only grain

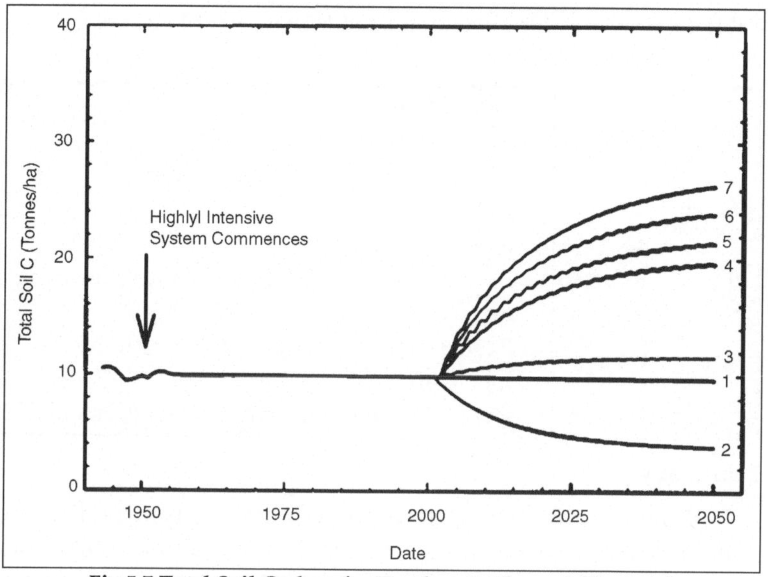

Fig 5.7 Total Soil Carbon for Tumbau Settlement (Century)

Effects of Organic Inputs

Additional FYM inputs have a marked impact on soil C, especially when they approach the maximum (7 tonnes/ha) normally applied in this region, *i.e.*, an annual input of 6.75 tonnes/ha (Table 5.9) will result in the sequestration of 0.20 tonnes C/ha/year over the next 50 years. Although adding Nfixing trees and plant residues to the fields will further increase soil C, the requirement of the former for livestock feed may exceed the capacity of the current farming system.

Effect of Inorganic Fertilizer

Replacing the manure input to this system with inorganic fertilizer results in a large reduction in soil C, with stocks falling by more than 0.1 tonnes C/ha/year.

Table 5.8 Total Soil Carbon for Tumbau Settlement (Century and RothC).

Scenario	CENTURY			RothC		
	2000	2050	%	2000	2050	%
	(tonnes/ha)		change	(tonnes/ha)		change
1	9.82	9.64	-1.8	11.3	13.39	18.5
3		11.54	17.5		14.96	32.4
6		23.9	143.4		31.7	180.5

Table 5.9 Scenarios for Modelling Land Management Practices, Tumbau Settlement

Scenario	Land Management
1	Current practice
2	Inorganic fertilizer (110 kg/ha urea)
3	FYM 3.75 tonnes/ha/year
4	FYM 6.75 tonnes/ha/year
5	FYM 3.75 tonnes/ha/year, add nitrogen-fixing trees
6	FYM 6.75 tonnes/ha/year, plant residues 2 tonnes/ha
7	FYM 6.75 tonnes/ha/year, harvest only grain

Summary

Provided that adequate organic matter is returned to the soil, these intensive-farming systems should maintain soil C and there is also scope for CS. These results are in agreement with findings in the field that provide no evidence for a decline in SOM in spite of increased cultivation pressure. However, the ability to realise future CS will depend on a careful balance between cropping and livestock husbandry and the overall capacity of the system. Maintaining crop yields through the application of inorganic fertilizer alone will probably result in substantial losses of SOM.

Conclusions

The modelling of farm data for the drylands of northern Nigeria shows that soil carbon stocks can be increased from a low base with a variety of technologies and practices already available to farmers.

The total amounts of C that can be sequestered with the use of legumes, fallow periods, FYM and retention of plant residues varies between 0.1 and 0.3 tonnes C/ha/ year. This amount rises when trees are also cultivated.

Soil C is lost when only inorganic fertilizers are used to maintain soil fertility-some 0.1 tonnes C/ha/ year in the intense systems of the Kano CSZ. Continuous cultivation results in small year-on-year losses of C where there are no additional inputs of organic matter. In spite of considerable intensification of current systems (shortening of fallow periods), farmers are maintaining carbon stocks. The benefits of maintaining trees in the landscape are shown in these modelled scenarios.

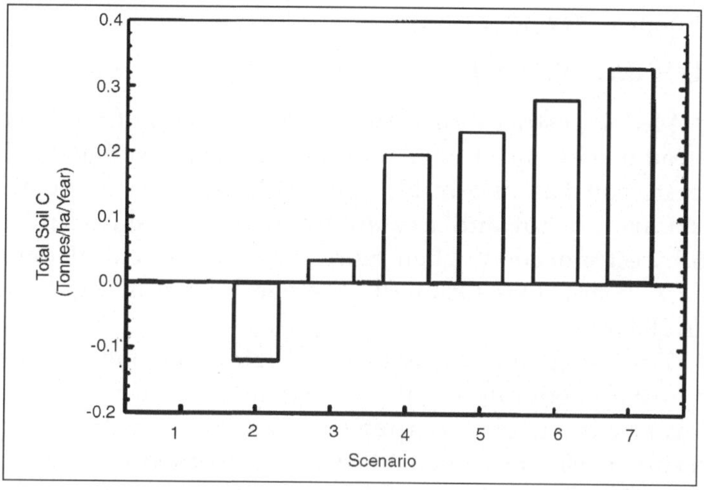

Fig 5.8 Average Annual Change in Total Soil Carbon for Tumbau Settlement (Century)

INDIAN CULTURE

More than half of India's farmers of India live in climate regions that can be described as semi-arid. Recent decades have seen increases in crop yields that have been attributed to the green revolution. However, the associated technologies, *e.g.*, irrigation and inorganic fertilizer are expensive, and not readily accessible to the rural poor. These practices may lead to declines in soil fertility, and are also dependent upon fossil-fuel energy. In fact, nearly two-thirds of the arable land in India remains dependent solely upon rainfall for agricultural production.

The Natural Resources Institute, the Deccan Development Society and the BAIF Institute for Rural Development (India) have studied soil fertility management in Medak District in Andhra Pradesh and in Tumkur District in Karnataka. They have shown that there is an increasing awareness about technologies for maintaining and improving soil fertility, identifying at least

14 different practices from legume cultivation to vermicompost production. Most involve maintaining and increasing the organic matter content of the soil. These studies provide an opportunity to investigate the effect that these soil-fertility improvement techniques may have on CS.

PHYSICAL ASPECTS

Medak District forms part of the tableland of the Deccan Plateau that extends from Andhra Pradesh into Karnataka. The climate consists of a mild winter period (rabi, November-February), a hot and dry summer (March-May) and the southwest monsoon, when more than 80 per cent of rainfall occurs (kharif, June-October). Average rainfall is slightly less than 900 mm.

The hottest month is May, just before the onset of rains, when the maximum daytime temperature can reach 40 °C. Conversely, night temperatures can drop to 6 °C in December. Moisture availability for crop growth ranges from 120 to 150° C.

The major soil types are Alfisols and Vertisols. The former include red lateritic soils comprising loamy sands, sand loams and sandy clay loams and are usually non-saline. The Vertisols, black cotton soils, are potentially more productive with a higher waterholding capacity, moderately alkaline and with a highly soluble salt content. They comprise clay loams, clays and silty clays.

The organic carbon content of soils in the area is usually 0.5-1 per cent. The land lies between 500-600 m above sea level, and very little natural vegetation remains. The tropical dry deciduous forest has mainly been felled except on protected government land.

FARMING SYSTEMS

The farming systems in this region have a high degree of integration between livestock, crops and tree. There is a huge agrobiodiversity that is combined with off-farm activities, particularly in Medak District. This situation makes for an efficient use of the limited land resources and acts as insurance against unpredictable weather conditions, a frequent problem in drylands. The average farm size is 2.6 ha. The small and marginal farmers can grow at least eight varieties of crops per half hectare. The cattle population has been falling continuously since, the 1980s. This has important implications for agriculture, not only because animal wastes are an important source of organic matter for soils, but also because bullocks make a vital contribution as draught animals, not least in the transport of FYM. Tillage is commonly performed with very basic implements. The greatest shift towards mechanised cultivation has been in Karnataka.

The predominant crops grown in Medak District are paddy, sorghum and maize while irrigated sugar cane is an important cash crop. The major crops grown in Karnataka are paddy, sorghum, finger millet, pearl millet, pigeon pea, green gram, and groundnut.

Farmers attach a high priority to maintaining soil fertility while inorganic fertilizers are ranked poorly in terms of maintaining soil quality. However, many farmers use them because organic alternatives are often unavailable and because the inorganic fertilizers are subsidised. The importance attached to soil fertility can have unforeseen consequences such as the sale of FYM by the poorest farmers to their more affluent counterparts. The ultimate effect of this will be an increase in the fertility and carbon content of some soils while degrading neighbouring areas.

MODELLING SOIL CARBON IN THE STUDY VILLAGES

The Century agro-ecosystem model was parametised using climate and soil data and run to equilibrium commencing with a grass/woodland system to represent the natural vegetation of this region. Low-intensity grasing and fires occurring every 30 years were included in the cycle. One thousand years ago, the effects of human interference were introduced with slash and burn events together with the cultivation of a grain crop.

The frequency of these events was increased slowly and by the start of the twentieth century, cultivation periods of four years out of ten were introduced. In the mid-twentieth century, one year of grazed fallow was followed by four years of cropping (sorghum-kharif, and cowpea-rabi). Cultivation consisted of hand or bullock ploughing and hand hoeing. Average annual applications of FYM were 2.1 tonnes/ha over the five-year cycle and all aboveground material was harvested. For the final 30 years of the twentieth century, cultivation was adjusted to reflect current practices.

The RothC model was run to equilibrium in the mid-twentieth century, and then parametised using current practice and plant residue quantities calculated by Century.

Data on five types of farm and location are presented below:

- Large mixed dryland farm (Lingampally);
- Small dryland farm, no livestock (Lingampally);
- Large farm using irrigation (Yedakulapaly);
- Small mixed drylands farm (Metalkunta);
- Small mixed drylands farm (Malligere).

ANALYSIS OF LAND MANAGEMENT BY A LARGE MIXED FARM, LINGAMPALLY VILLAGE, MEDAK DISTRICT

This is a holding of slightly more than 5 ha on predominantly Vertisols. Livestock are fed fodder and plant residues from the fields. Consequently, no plant material is returned to the soil. The animals are also grazed on local common land.

The livestock provide manure (2-3 tonnes/ha/year). In addition, inorganic fertilizer has been used in recent years (30-45 kg/ha of di-ammonium phosphate). Crops modelled are sorghum (kharif May-September) and cowpea (rabi October-January).

Century predicts that the current farming practice is resulting in a nearly stable soil carbon content of about 19 tonnes/ha declining to 2050 by nearly 1.5 tonnes/ha. RothC shows a lower total soil carbon content of 16 tonnes/ha, declining to 15 tonnes/ha by 2050. The scenarios in Figure compare current practices with additions of inorganic fertilizer, FYM, green manure, vermicompost, retained plant residues and cultivation of trees. Figure indicates the average annual change in soil C in a 50-year period.

Effect of Inorganic Fertilizer

If the application of inorganic fertilizer were halted and the quantity of FYM increased to replace the nitrogen input and maintain yields (increase manure application by 0.6 tonnes/ha), soil C would increase by only 0.85 tonnes/ ha by 2050 and there would be no net gain in soil C (Figure). Conversely, replacing all organic additions with inorganic fertilizer would result in a decrease in soil C of more than 4 tonnes/ha by 2050, a loss of 0.09 tonnes/ha/ year Thus, inorganic fertilizer results in a fall in soil C.

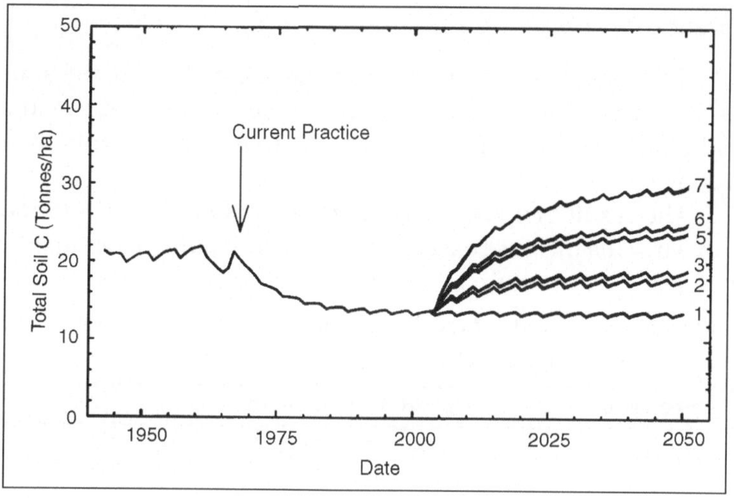

Fig 5.9 Total Soil Carbon For a Large Farm (5 ha), Lingampally Village (Cenury)

Effect of Farmyard Manure

Doubling the current annual input of FYM to 4-6 tonnes/ha without applying inorganic fertilizer has a marked effect on soil C: 0.27 tonnes/ha/year is sequestered in the next 50 years (Figure), with the system still not at a steady state. Similarly, RothC shows a continuing rise, reaching 28.3 tonnes/ha by the same date.

Table 5.10 Total Soil Carbon for a Large Farm Lingampally Village.

Scenario	CENTURY			RothC		
	2000	2050	%	2000	2050	%
	(tonnes/ha)		change	(tonnes/ha)		change
1	20.2	18.8	-7.2	18.3	17.9	-2.3
4		33.5	65.9		28.3	54.2
6		40.4	100		31.0	68.8

Effect of Other Organic Inputs

Adding only modest amounts of vermicompost (100 kg/ha) and green manure (250 kg/ha) in addition to the doubled FYM has a limited effect, while 2 tonnes/ha plant residues makes a bigger contribution, 0.4 tonnes/ha/year.

Effect of Trees

This farm has a capacity for introducing N-fixing trees such as *Glyricidia,* which creates Scenario 7 when added to the manure and plant residues. After 10 years, the trees are cut annually for wood.

The result is a very large increase in soil CS of 0.4 tonnes/ ha/year. This increase exceeds that which would be obtained by increasing the manure application by four times.

Table 5.11 Scenarios for Modelling Land Management Practices, Large farm Lingampally Village

Scenario	Land Management
1	Current practice
2	FYM 3 tonnes/ha/year
3	FYM 3 tonnes/ha/year, green manure 500 kg/ha/year, vermicompost 250 kg/ha/year
4	As current practice but incorporate crop residues into soil
5	FYM 3 tonnes/ha/year, leave plant residues
6	FYM 3 tonnes/ha/year, plant residues, green manure, vermicompost
7	FYM 6 tonnes/ha/year, plant residues, green manure, vermicompost

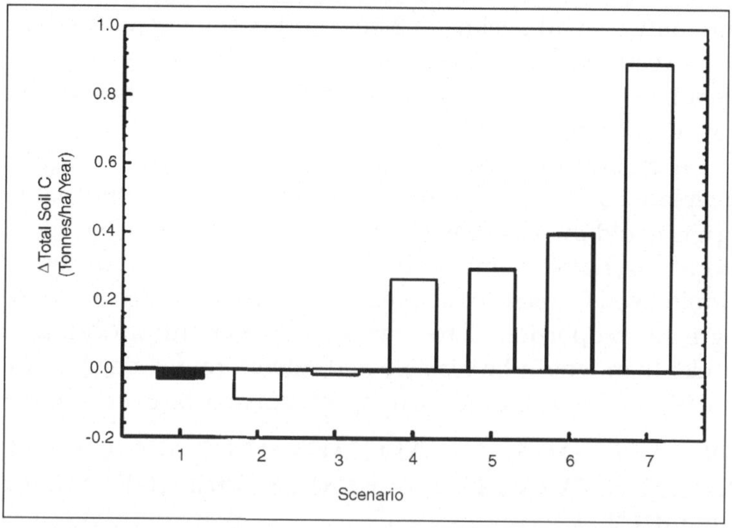

Fig 5.10 Average Annual Change (Over 50 Years) in Total Soil Carbon for a Large Mixed farm, Lingampally Village (Century)

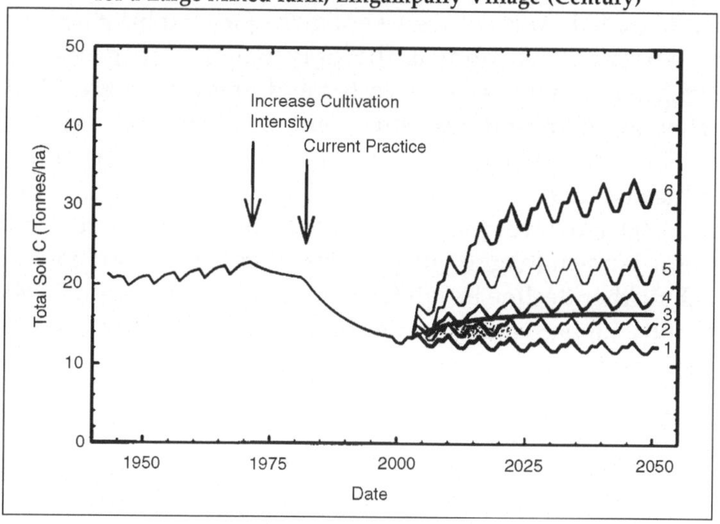

Fig 5.11 Total Soil Carbon for a Small Rainfed farm, Lingampally Village (Century)

Summary

The two soil carbon models are in fairly close agreement for this farming system. The current practice is nearly sustainable with only a small decline (< 2 per cent) in soil C predicted over the next 50 years. However, cattle are currently being grazed on other land and, consequently, some C is effectively being mined from elsewhere.

A modest increase in organic material would be required to replace the inorganic fertilizers currently used. Further organic inputs could increase soil CS substantially. Introducing trees is likely to have a marked effect on soil C and would simultaneously increase aboveground carbon storage. However, a greater proportion of trees may have been introduced to the model than would be feasible and, therefore, the degree of CS that is practicable for this farming system may be overestimated.

ANALYSIS OF LAND MANAGEMENT BY A SMALL RAINFED FARM, LINGAMPALLY VILLAGE, MEDAK DISTRICT

This holding is less than 1 ha and the Vertisol has become very degraded. Animals were kept in the past but have been sold and currently sorghum is the only major crop grown. All aboveground material is harvested and removed. Some FYM is applied at different times, equivalent to 3.9 tonnes/ha/year.

The Century model shows how current practices have produced a marked decline in soil C, reaching some 13 tonnes/ha in 2000. However the system is reaching steady state and the current land-management practice is not predicted to cause much further decline in soil C in the next 50 years. RothC yields a slightly higher carbon content in 2000 but predicts a slightly greater decline (1.8 tonnes/ha) by 2050.

Effect of Retained Residues

Harvesting only the grain and the returning crop residues to the soil would produce a positive carbon balance, sequestering 0.05 tonnes/ha/year.

Effect of Farmyard Manure

Increasing the input of FYM by 50 per cent to 6 tonnes/ha/year would increase soil C by 3.8 tonnes/ ha by 2050. RothC predicts a rise of 3.0 tonnes/ha.

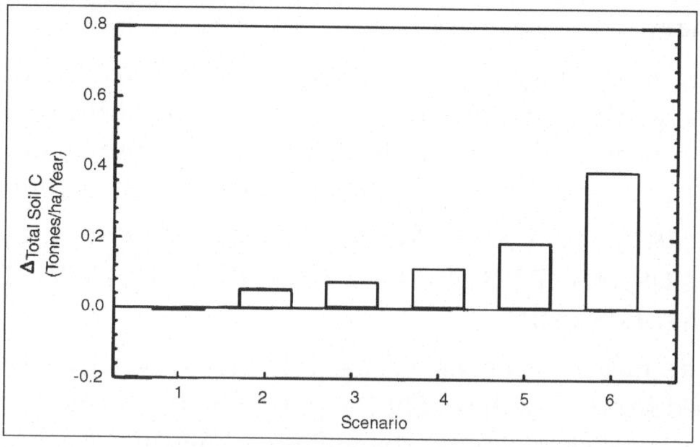

Fig 5.12 Average Annual Change in Total Soil Carbon for a Small Rainfed farm, Lingampally Village (Century)

Effect of Legume Crops

Adding cowpea the rotation would sequester 0.12 tonnes/ha/year. Introducing Nfixing trees (cut every 2 years after an initial 10 years) to the sorghum-only system with FYM at 4 tonnes/ha, would yield a sequestration rate of 0.19 tonnes/ha/year. Combining all treatments would lead to a soil CS rate of 0.39 tonnes C/ha/year.

Table 5.12 Total Soil Carbon for a Small Rainfed farm, Lingampally Village

Scenari	Century			RothC		
	2000	2050	% Change	2000	2050	% Change
	(Tonnes/ha)			(Tonnes/ha)		
1	12.77	12.41	-2.8	16.07	14.92	-7.2
3		16.58	29.8		19.11	18.9

Table 5.13 Scenarios for Modelling Land Management Practices, for a Small Rainfed farm, Lingampally Village

Scenario	Land Management
1	Current practice
2	Harvest only grain
3	FYM 6 tonnes/ha/year
4	Add legume (cowpea)
5	Add trees, *e.g. Glyricidia*
6	All additions

Summary

The modelling suggests that the loss of soil C can be reversed for this type of farm, even on degraded soil. In addition to direct organic inputs, this example illustrates the importance of a leguminous crop, and the inclusion of trees such as *Glyricidia*.

ANALYSIS OF LAND MANAGEMENT FOR A LARGE FARM USING IRRIGATION, YEDAKULAPALY VILLAGE, MEDAK DISTRICT

The farm comprises 4.5 ha of irrigated Vertisol. Water is pumped from a borehole. For the purposes of modelling, 5 cm of water is applied when the soil waterholding capacity is < 25 per cent during the vegetative growth stage of the crop. Livestock were originally kept but were sold some years ago because there was insufficient labour to collect fodder and tend to the cattle during grasing. Only inorganic fertilizers are now used-650 kg/ha di-ammonium phosphate and 150 kg/ha of urea annually. Crops are grown in all three seasons (summer-sorghum, kharif-legume, rabi-legume) and all aboveground material is harvested and removed. For the purposes of modelling, cowpea is used for the legume crop.

Century calculates that current practices have depleted soil C to 13.26 tonnes/ha and predicts no further reduction in the next 50 years.

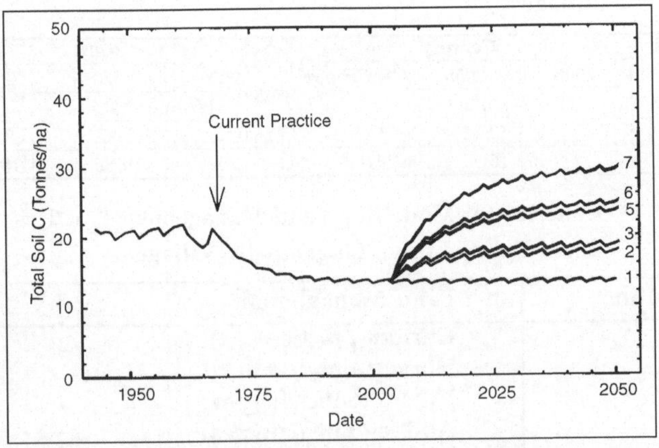

Fig 5.13 Total Soil Carbon for a Large farm Using Irrigation and Cultivating three Crops per Year, Lingampally Village (Century)

Effect of Organic Inputs

Adding 3 tonnes FYM/ha/year would increase soil C by 4.4 tonnes/ha to 2050, sequestering 0.09 tonnes/ha/year. Including 500 kg/ha/year of green manure and 250 kg/ha/year of vermicompost would increase soil organic C by a further 1 tonne, sequestering 0.11 tonnes/ha/ year.

A similar increase in soil C can be obtained with no extra organic additions if only the grain is harvested and the crop residues are returned to the soil. When 3 tonnes FYM/ha/year is applied and only the grain harvested, soil C increases by more than 10 tonnes/ha, equivalent to 0.20 tonnes/ha/year. Applying all the organic inputs and increasing the FYM component to 6 tonnes/ha would sequester 0.32 tonnes/ha/year.

Table 5.14 Scenarios for Modelling Land Management Practices, Large farm Using Irrigation Lingampally Village

Scenario	Land Management
1	Current practice
2	FYM 3 tonnes/ha/year
3	FYM 3 tonnes/ha/year green manure 500 kg/ha/year, vermicompost 250 kg/ha/year
4	As current practice but incorporate crop residues into soil
5	FYM 3 tonnes/ha/year, leave plant residues
6	FYM 3 tonnes/ha/year, plant residues, green manure, vermicompost
7	FYM 6 tonnes/ha/year, plant residues, green manure, vermicompost

Summary

A combination of leaving crop residues and adding manure could make a significant contribution to soil C in this kind of farming system, in which current practices have already caused a significant decline in soil carbon stocks. However, inorganic fertilizer and irrigation continue to have a carbon cost, resulting in smaller increases under the various scenarios. Additions of FYM can offset the nutrients applied in inorganic fertilizers. For example, removing inorganic fertilizer from Scenario 6 maintains yield without affecting soil C. Removing irrigation from the above scenario does not have a detrimental effect on soil C, but nor is there an apparent effect on yield.

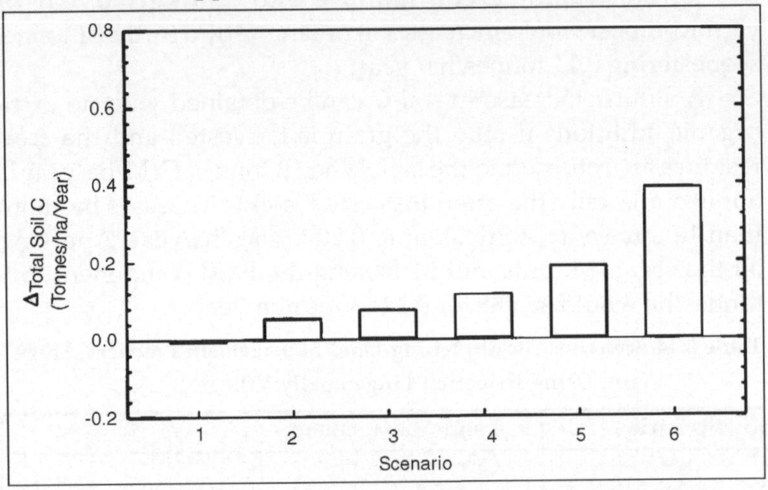

Fig 5.14 Average Annual Change in Total Soil Carbon for a Large farm Using Irrigation, Lingampally Village

ANALYSIS OF LAND MANAGEMENT FOR A SMALL MIXED CROP AND LIVESTOCK FARM, METALKUNTA VILLAGE, MEDAK DISTRICT

This landholding of 2.7 ha has a very large variety of crops on lateritic red soil. Livestock are kept, a good cultivation pattern is practised and there are also many trees present around the farm. All aboveground produce is harvested so that crop residues can be fed to the animals. Cattle are also grazed on nearby land and fodder is brought in. The average yearly manure application is 2 tonnes/ha, and vermicompost is added to the land.

Century was parametised with a sorghum-cowpea-millet-cowpea-maize-cowpea rotation to reflect the varied cropping pattern. The model was run with this scenario from the late 1960s. The model suggests that this system of land management would have approximately doubled the soil carbon content to nearly 25 tonnes/ha by 2000 and would reach 26 tonnes C/ha.

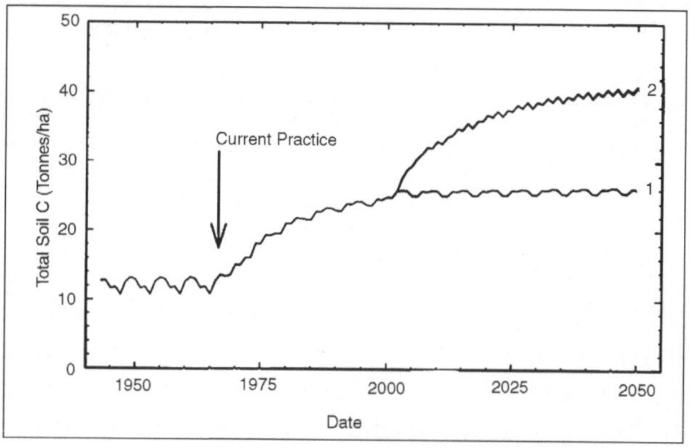

Fig 5.15 Total Soil Carbon for a Small Mixed Crop and Livestock farm, Metalkunta Village

RothC predicts 25 tonnes C/ha in 2000 rising to 29.1 tonnes/ha. This mixed cropping and livestock system has a substantial positive impact on soil C.

Table 5.15 Total Soil Carbon for a Small Mixed Crop and Livestock farm, Metalkunta Village

Scenario	Century			RothC		
	2000	2050	% Change	2000	2050	% Change
	(Tonnes/ha)			(Tonnes/ha)		
1	24.9	26.1	5.2	25.0	29.2	16.7
2		40.9	64.7		49.2	96.6

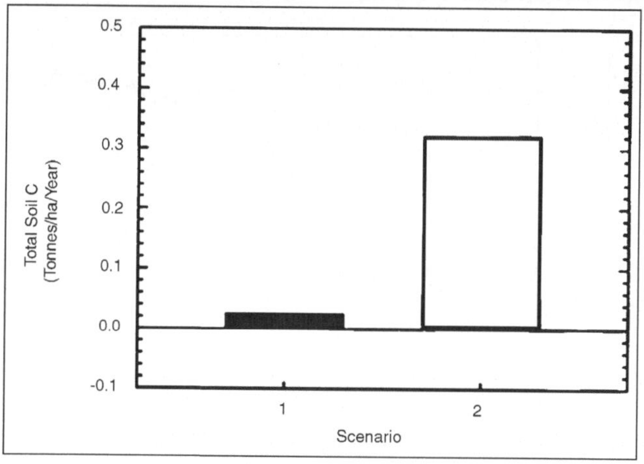

Fig 5.14 Average Annual Change in Total Soil Carbon for a Small Mixed Crop and Livestock farm, Metalkunta Village

Table 5.16 Scenarios for Modelling Land Management Practices, Small Mixed Crop and Livestock farm, Metalkunta Village

Scenario	Land Management
1	Current practice
2	Leave plant residues

Effects of Retaining Crop Residues

Returning crop residues to the soil would greatly increase the carbon content, sequestering 0.3 tonnes C ha/year in the next 50 years, with the soil carbon content reaching 40.9 tonnes/ ha by 2050. RothC calculates that leaving crop residues would increase soil C to 49.2 tonnes/ha.

Summary

The farmer is currently practising very good land management, and the models calculate that the soil carbon content has already been substantially increased. However, this is being accomplished in part by grasing cattle on other lands and bringing in fodder. This means that C is effectively being mined from elsewhere. Thus, although returning crop residues to the soil makes a further significant contribution to soil C, this would require importing more fodder to substitute for the plant residues, which again implies mining C.

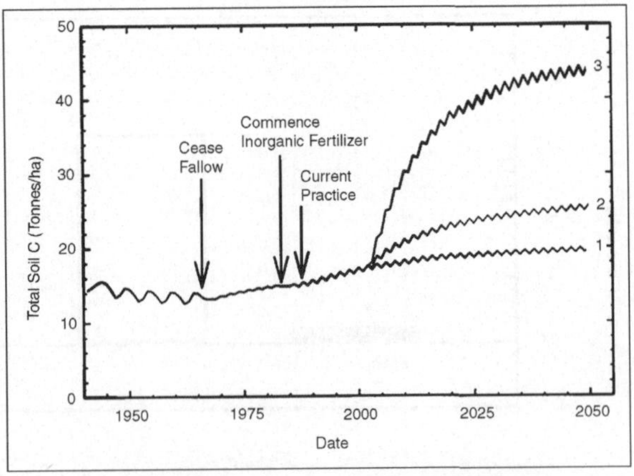

Fig 5.17 Total Soil Carbon for a Small farm, Malligere Village, Tumkur District

Table 5.17 Total Soil Carbon for a Small farm, Malligere Village, Tumkur District

Scenario	CENTURY			RothC		
	2000	2050	%	2000	2050	%
	(tonnes/ha)		change	(tonnes/ha)		change
1	17.24	19.97	15.8	19.82	24.32	22.7
2		25.73	49.2		34.2	72.6

Table 5.18 Scenarios for Modelling Land Management Practices, Small farm, Malligere Village

Scenario	Land Management
1	Current practice
2	Replace inorganic fertilizer with FYM
3	Add trees, *Glyricidia*

ANALYSIS OF LAND MANAGEMENT FOR A SMALL FARM, MALLIGERE VILLAGE, TUMKUR DISTRICT KARNATAKA STATE

This farm covers 2 ha on a red sandy soil. Tractors are hired for transport, livestock are kept and allowed to graze the crop residues, but additional fodder is brought in. The kharif crops modelled are sorghum and millet and the rabi crop is cowpea. On average, 3 tonnes/ha/ year FYM is applied. Inorganic fertilizers are also used: 75 kg/ha/ year of di-ammonium phosphate and 75 kg/ha/year of urea.

Modelling with Century shows that current practices are increasing soil C and that this will continue to rise by a further 2.7 tonnes/ha in the next 50 years, reaching almost 20 tonnes C/ ha in 2050. RothC also shows that the current practice is increasing soil C but shows an enhanced effect. Soil C in 2000 is predicted to be 19.8 tonnes/ha, rising to 24.3 tonnes/ha in 2050.

Effect of Organic Additions

Inorganic fertilizer has a carbon cost, so replacing the N supplied by the inorganic fertilizer with manure (annual addition 6.3 tonnes/ha) enhances the CS rate to 0.17 tonnes/ ha/year. The soil carbon level reaches 25.7 tonnes/ha by 2050. RothC predicts a much bigger effect on SOC of replacing the fertilizer with FYM: soil C is predicted to rise to 34.2 tonnes/ha by 2050.

Effect of Trees

Adding trees such as *Glyricidia* to the system, which are cropped annually for wood after ten years, makes a very large difference, increasing CS to 0.54 tonnes/ ha/year.

Summary

Both models show similar trends, with a switch from inorganic to organic fertilizer increasing soil C significantly. RothC predicts a larger increase. Cessation of inorganic fertilizer use would remove the negative carbon balance associated with its production, and the addition of trees may be sufficient to offset the inputs of C that arise from fodder grown outside the farm system. However, if tractors are used to transport fodder, the carbon budget for the system will probably be negative.

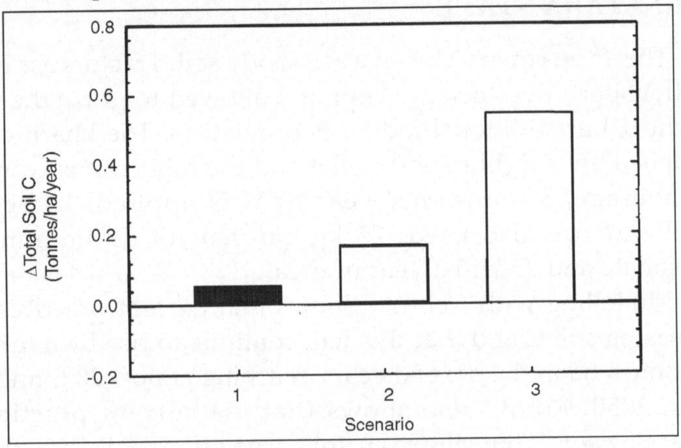

Fig 5.18 Average Annual Change in Total Soil Carbon for a Small farm, Malligere Village, Tumkur District

Conclusions from India Cases

The modelling of farm data for the drylands of India shows that soil carbon stocks can be increased with a variety of technologies and practices available to farmers. It also shows that some practices result in substantial declines in carbon stocks, particularly the use of inorganic fertilizer as the sole source of nutrients, and the continuous cultivation of cereals. In the large (5 ha) mixed farm, inorganic fertilizer results in the loss of 0.1 tonnes/ha/year, whereas the use of either FYM, green manures, vermicompost and/or plant residues produces increases of 0.2-0.4 tonnes/ha/year. The use of agroforestry substantially increases belowground CS to 0.9 tonnes/ha/year.

The models show substantial declines in soil C on the small farms that cultivate only sorghum and those that intensively cultivate three irrigated crops per year-a loss of 5 tonnes C/ha in a 25-year period. However, it appears that these falls can be reversed within 5-10 years with the adoption of legumes in rotations, the addition of FYM manure and cultivation of trees.

The small mixed cropping farm, with cereals and cowpea rotations and livestock, increases soil C from a stock of about 13 tonnes C/ha to 24.8 tonnes C/ha in 25 years. It can increase this to more than 40 tonnes C/ha in the next 50 years if plant residues are added to the soil. For full accounting of the C used or sequestered in these farms, it is important to consider the high energy cost of nitrogen fertilizer manufacture (65.3 MJ/kg for N, 7.2 MJ/kg for phosphorus, 6.4 MJ/kg for potassium), the use of mechanised operations on farms, the cost of irrigation and mechanical transport, and the issue of the transfer of C in feed or livestock themselves from one farm to another or from grasing areas to cropped fields. There are clear benefits for farmers and soil C if leguminous crops are included in rotations and in agroforestry systems.

CASE STUDY

Arid and semi-arid lands occupy about two-thirds of Kenya. The major factors limiting crop growth and production in these areas of Kenya are erratic rainfall, poor husbandry and declining soil fertility caused by continuous cultivation. Drylands Research has examined the sustainability of farming systems in semi-arid Kenya, recording physical aspects of the environment together with land-management practices in four villages of Makueni District. These span a range of settlement times from the 1950s to the 1970s. A major problem for farming in this region has been the frequency with which it has been affected by drought. Droughts reduce the returns that farmers receive and, consequently, provide little incentive for investment in soil fertility.

PHYSICAL ATTRIBUTES

The climate of this region is characterised by two rainy periods: the short rains, which deliver most precipitation in October-December; and the long rains of March-May. However, superimposed on the average annual rainfall (600-670 mm) is the periodic occurrence of drought. Annual mean temperature is in the range of 21-24 °C. Elevation is 800-1 600 m, and the natural vegetation is grassland and dense shrub-land or woodland. Fires have affected the area in the past and the grassland is used for grasing. The soils are mostly Ferralsols and are naturally low in phosphorus.

FARMING SYSTEMS

Annual or multiple cropping is practised with occasional incorporation of one-year fallows, although the latter is becoming less common. Each year covers two cropping seasons. The main crops are maize and pulses, with millet and sorghum recommended as drought crops. Yields vary considerably between years depending on rainfall; on average maize will yield 1 tonne/ ha, although some modern varieties yield 4 tonnes/ha of grain.

The animal population is not large because it is difficult to supply adequate feed during periods of drought. Consequently, manure is in short supply and highly valued. Scarcity means that its application is often rotated. Little investment is made in the grasing lands, and the animals are usually kept in pens during the wet season. Very little fertilizer is used, especially as drought causes "burning" of the crops. Crop residues are burnt, fed to animals or ploughed into the soil Tillage is accomplished by using simple ridging ploughs pulled by oxen; hand hoeing and digging are also common. Labour is in short supply and a constraint for farmers. A range of crop-residue management and tillage techniques are used to conserve moisture and to protect against soil erosion. Woodland is being cleared, although selective clearance is often practised to save those species that provide useful products. Most farmers also plant trees, especially fruit trees and others such as mulberry for silk production. The study villages lie along a gradient of precipitation, decreasing from Kymausoi through Kaiani and Darjani to Athi Kamunyuni. Century was run to equilibrium using a grassland-tree scenario with grass fires every ten years and major fires every 30 years.

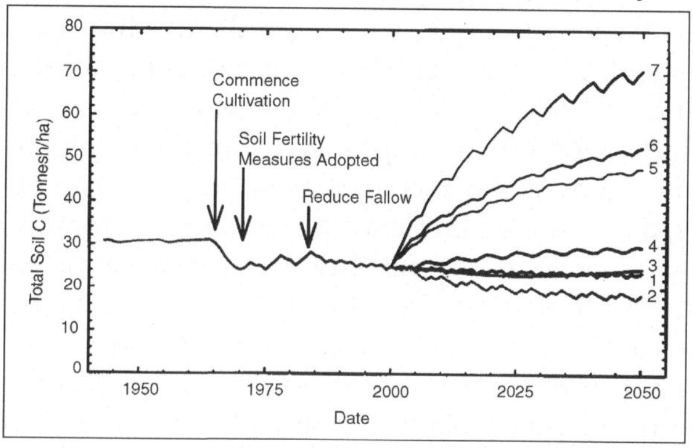

Fig 5.19 Total Soil Carbon for Darjani Settlement

Table 5.19 Total Soil Carbon for Darjani Settlement

Scenario	CENTURY			RothC		
	2000	2050	%	2000	2050	%
	(tonnes/ha)		change	(tonnes/ha)		change
1	25.04	23.74	-5.2	34.57	34	-1.6
5		47.92	91.4		59.3	71.5
6		52.79	110.8		65.67	90.0

Table 5.20 Scenarios for Modelling Land Management Practices, Darjani Settlement

Scenario	Land Management
1	Current practice
2	Remove fallow
3	Only inorganic fertilizer, burn residues, no fallow
4	Only inorganic fertilizer, burn residues, fallow
5	FYM 4.5 tonnes/ha/year, burn residues, fallow
6	FYM 4.5 tonnes/ha/year, do not burn residues, fallow
7	FYM 6.75 tonnes/ha/year, do not burn residues, fallow

DARJANI

The primary crops for this settlement are millet, sisal, cowpea and sorghum and the natural pasture can support low intensity grasing. Settlement took place in the 1960s. The average soil carbon content of bush soils is 37.6 ± 7.5 tonnes/ha, and for cultivated soils it is 33.7 ± 2.8 tonnes/ha. Once run to equilibrium, CENTURY gave a value for soil C of 31.0 tonnes/ha in 1964. This is just within the range expected for bush soils. The model was then run for a further 35 years, reproducing the current land management. This commenced with a six-year cycle of alternate maize and millet crops for four years followed by fallow for two years. Cultivation was accomplished using a steel ridging plough and hand weeding was included. Crop residues were burnt. In 1971, FYM additions commenced, averaging 1.5 tonnes/ha over the six-year cycle as soil fertility and conservation measures began to be adopted. In 1983, the fallow period was reduced to one year out of six, and by 2000 the modelled soil C was 24 tonnes/ha. This reduction of 7 tonnes/ha from the level modelled for the uncultivated bush soil is greater than the decline of 5 tonnes/ha measured in the field. Continuation of this landmanagement practice is predicted to lead to a further loss of 1.3 tonnes C/ha by 2050.

RothC was run to equilibrium using the current level of bush soil C and then used to predict the effect of land management using plant inputs calculated by CENTURY. RothC predicted soil C to be 34.6 tonnes/ha in 1999, which is within 1 tonne/ha of the measured value. In the next 50 years, RothC predicts a further decline of 0.6 tonnes C/ha.

Effect of Fallow Removal

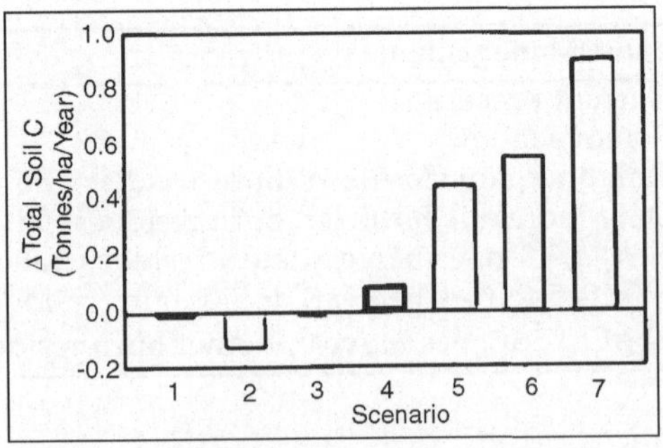

Fig 5.20 Average Annual Change in Total Soil Carbon for Darjani Settlement (Century)

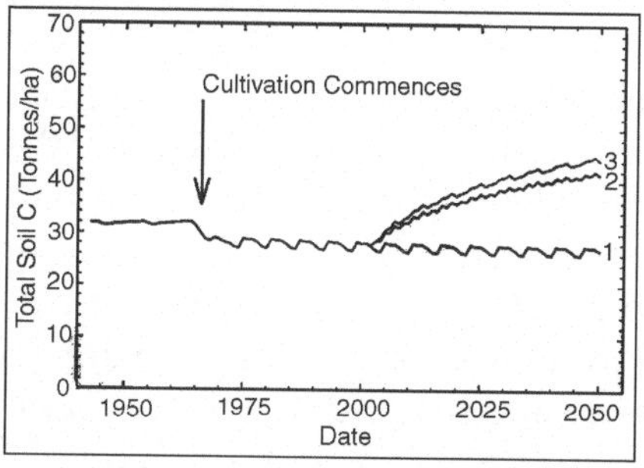

Fig 5.21 Total Soil Carbon for Kaiani Settlement

Century predicts that removing the fallow from the current practice will result in a reduction in soil C (6.6 tonnes/ha).

Effect of Organic Inputs

Adding an average 4.5 tonnes/ha/ year FYM over the 6-year croppingfallow cycle leads to a CS rate of 0.5 tonnes/ha/year. If the crop residues are returned to the soil rather than burnt, a further 4.9 tonnes C/ha can be accumulated by 2050, representing a sequestration rate of 0.6 tonnes/ha/year. RothC predicts similar increases. Increasing the FYM input to 6.75 tonnes/ha/year will increase the sequestration rate to 0.9 tonnes/ ha/year.

Effect of Inorganic Fertilizer

Replacing all organic inputs with inorganic fertilizer (100 kg N/ha/ year, Scenario 4) results in only a moderate increase in soil CS (0.09 tonnes/ha/year). However, the quantity of N applied is equivalent to about five times that which is added in FYM for the current practice scenario. If the fallow period is removed and only inorganic fertilizer added, the system behaves very much like the current practice scenario in spite of the additional N.

Summary

The importance of FYM as an organic input is demonstrated, as is the return of crop residues to the soil rather than burning them. Although addition of inorganic fertilizer can increase CS, the increase in C per unit of N added is much less efficient than if FYM is added. The indirect energy embodied in manufactured N fertilizer is an additional carbon cost.

KAIANI

The settlement of Kaiani has a farming system similar to that at Darajani. Century underestimated the current bush content of soil C, yielding nearly 32 tonnes/ha compared with measured values of 41.5 ± 3.1 tonnes/ha. Century was then run with a scenario to reflect the last 40 years of cultivation using a millet-cowpea system with grasing of plant residues and 4.5 tonnes/ha manure applied once in the six-year cycle.

Table 5.21 Total soil Carbon for Kaiani Settlement

Scenario	CENTURY			RothC		
	2000	2050	%	2000	2050	%
	(tonnes/ha)		change	(tonnes/ha)		change
1	28.07	26.81	-4.5	42.32	43.89	3.9
2		41.4	47.5		62.82	48.8
3		42.73	52.2		65.16	54.3

Table 5.22 Scenarios for Modelling Land Management Practices, Kaiani Settlement

Scenario	Land Management
1	Current practice
2	FYM 2 tonnes/ha/year
3	FYM 2 tonnes/ha/year, plant residues 0.3 tonnes/ha/year

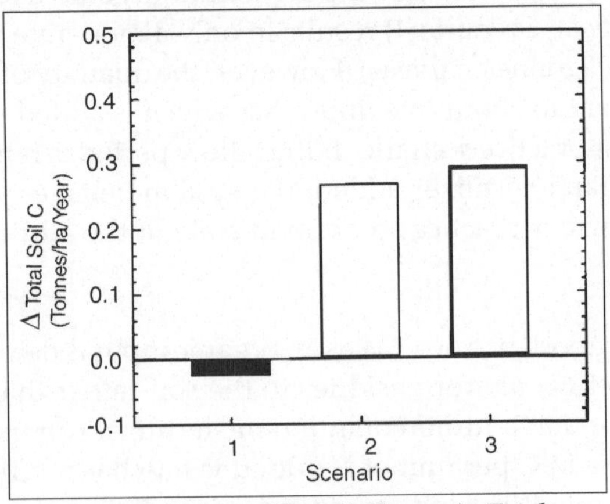

Fig 5.22 Average Annual Change in Total Soil Carbon for Kaiani Settlement

There was one year of fallow. Cultivation is calculated to have reduced soil C to 28.1 tonnes/ha by 2000, which compares with a measured value for cropped soil of 30.5 ± 4.8 tonnes/ha. Soil C is then predicted to decrease by slightly more than 1 tonne/ha in the next 50 years.

Table 5.23 Total Soil Carbon for Kymausoi Settlement

Scenario	CENTURY			RothC		
	2000	2050	%	2000	2050	%
	(tonnes/ha)		change	(tonnes/ha)		change
1	17.76	16.82	-5.3	35.69	34.79	-2.5
2		20.18	13.6		43.4	21.6
3		27.7	56.0		58.86	64.9

After parametisation with the carbon content for bush soils, RothC shows very little effect of cultivation when using plant inputs calculated by Century. Unlike Century, this model predicts a slight rise in soil C by 2050.

Effect of Organic Inputs

Modest increases in the application rate of FYM (0.75 tonnes/ha/year to 2 tonnes/ha/year) result in quite marked accumulation of soil C. Adding additional plant residues further increase the sequestration rate to 0.3 tonnes/ha/year. RothC predicts very similar proportional increases in soil C.

Summary

The models suggest that the current system is at or near steady state. It is possible to achieve reasonable rates of CS (0.3 tonnes/ha/year) with modest increases in organic manure inputs.

KYMAUSOI

Kymausoi is situated in a marginal cotton zone where maize, pigeon pea and sisal are also grown. Cattle ranching is practised and the village was settled in the 1950s. The average soil carbon content for bush soils here is 38.4 ± 4.8 tonnes/ha, while for cultivated soils the average is 33.5 tonnes/ha with a range of 17.4-38.9 tonnes/ha. The Century agro-ecosystem model was run to equilibrium and gave a bush soilcarbon level of 28.5 tonnes/ha in 1955, which is below the average concentration for soils in this area. The model was then run to reflect the farming system since, settlement commenced. This includes continuous maize cropping with grasing of the crop residues, and an average manure application rate of 0.75 tonnes/ha/ year. Soil conservation and fertility management commenced in the late 1960s, the average annual manure application rate being increased to 1 tonne/ha to reflect this. Century estimated soil C to be 17.8 tonnes/ha by 2000, which is at the lower end of measured values. A decline of less than 1 tonne C/ha is predicted to occur in the next 50 years.

Table 5.24 Scenarios for Modelling Land Management Practices, Kymausoi Settlement

Scenario	Land Management
1	Current practice
2	Plant residues 0.3 tonnes/ha/year
3	FYM 1.5 tonnes/ha/year, plant residues 0.6 tonnes/ha/year
4	FYM 1.5 tonnes/ha/year, plant residues 0.6 tonnes/ha/year, legume (cowpea)
5	FYM 2 tonnes/ha/year, plant residues 0.6 tonnes/ha/year, legume (cowpea)
6	FYM 4 tonnes/ha/year, plant residues 0.6 tonnes/ha/year, legume (cowpea)

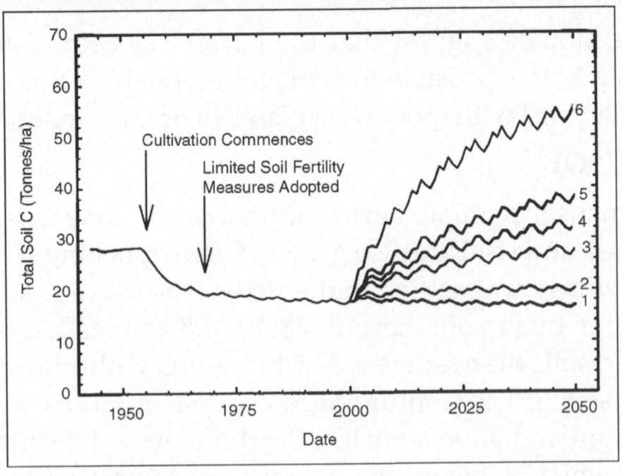

Fig 5.23 Total Soil Carbon for Kymausoi Settlement

Table 5.25 Total Soil Carbon for Athi Kamunyuni Settlement

Scenario	CENTURY			RothC		
	2000 (tonnes/ha)	2050 (tonnes/ha)	% change	2000 (tonnes/ha)	2050 (tonnes/ha)	% change
1	23.75	23.45	-1.3	29.68	28.29	-4.7
2		29.09	22.5		31.40	5.8
3		29.77	25.3		42.76	44.1

After being run to equilibrium for current bush soils and then parametised with plant inputs from Century, RothC calculated a reduction of 3.4 tonnes/ha in soil C resulting from cultivation. Like Century, it suggests a further decline of less than 1 tonnes/ha by 2050.

Effect of Organic Inputs

Adding additional plant residues and increasing the FYM application rate to 1.5 tonnes/ha/year will increase soil carbon levels by at least 50 per cent.

Effect of Legume Crop

Introducing a leguminous crop into the system, such as cowpea, can make a significant improvement in CS, increasing the rate from 0.2 to 0.3 tonnes/ha/year at the same rates of FYM application.

Summary

This example illustrates the advantage of including leguminous crops in the rotation. A farm system using 4 tonnes/ha/year of FYM, maintaining plant residues in the field, and with a legume in the rotation, can accumulate 0.7 tonnes/ ha/year. The current practice is reducing soil carbon stocks.

ATHI KAMUNYUNI

This village is situated in a lowland agro-ecological zone. Ranching will only support a very low grasing density and the area is at the limit for rainfed production of millet, cowpea and sisal. The village was established in the 1970s. Century was parametised for the commencement of cropping/grasing during the last 30 years. Millet was grown and an average of 0.75 tonnes/ha manure applied during the last six years.

The value for soil C modelled by Century matched the current bush level (33.2 ± 3.2 tonnes C/ha). When settlement commenced, Century calculated a decline in soil C of some 9 tonnes/ha over 25 years. Again, this is close to the actual measurements that show cultivated soils on average contain 24.0 ± 3.0 tonnes C/ha. Continuing this scenario into the twenty-first century suggests that the system has almost reached a new steady state. RothC calculates a smaller effect of cultivation on soil C, predicting a value of 29.7 tonnes C/ ha, and a slight decline over the next 50 years.

Table 5.26 Scenarios for Modelling Land Management Practices, Athi Kamunyuni Settlement

Scenario	Land Management
1	Current practice
2	Grasing
3	FYM 1.25 tonnes/ha/year
4	FYM 2.25 tonnes/ha/year
5	FYM 2.27 tonnes/ha/year, fallow reduced to 1 year
6	FYM 3.3 tonnes/ha/year
7	FYM 3.9 tonnes/ha/year, plant residues 0.3 tonnes/ha

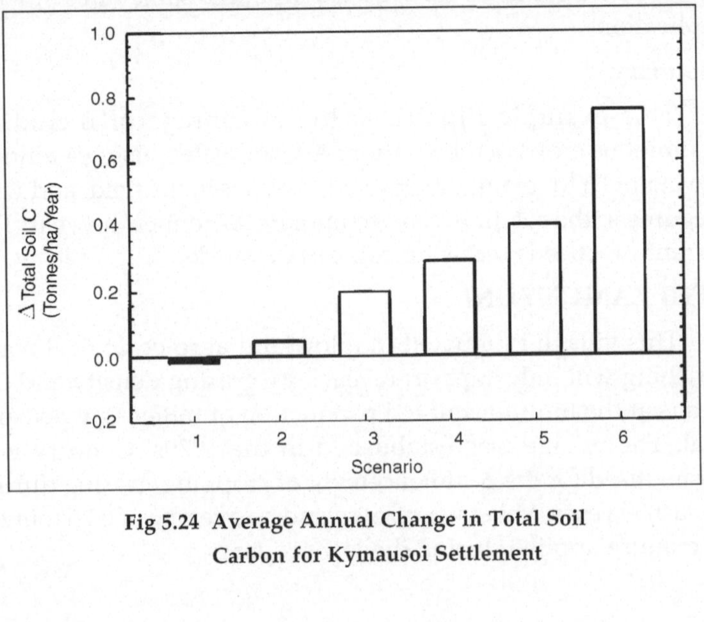

Fig 5.24 Average Annual Change in Total Soil Carbon for Kymausoi Settlement

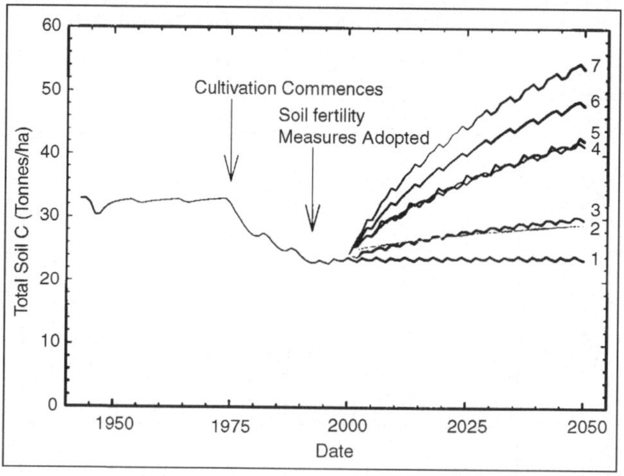

Fig 5.25 Total Soil Carbon for Athi Kamunyuni Settlement (Century)

Effect of Organic Inputs

Increasing the current average application rate of FYM from 0.75 tonnes/ha/year to 1.25 or 2.25 tonnes/ha/year increases rates of CS by 0.12-0.37 tonnes/ha/year. Further additions of organic inputs, if available, could yield an increase in CS rates of up to 0.6 tonnes/ha/year.

Effect of fallows

Reducing the fallow period from two years to one year has very little effect on soil C providing the organic inputs are maintained. Using this location solely for ranching would result in an increase in soil C as the system returned to similar conditions that existed before cultivation commenced. The rate of CS is very similar to Scenario 3, where an average of 1.25 tonnes/ha FYM was added annually. RothC predicts a much smaller increase in soil C on return to ranching. This reflects the fact that this model initially calculated a much smaller decline in total soil C following the commencement of cultivation.

Summary

The level of soil C in this recently settled system could be restored to pre-settlement levels and then raised higher by the addition of FYM. Conditions at this location are not ideal for cropping and a return to a grasing-only system should also restore soil C to its pre-settlement level.

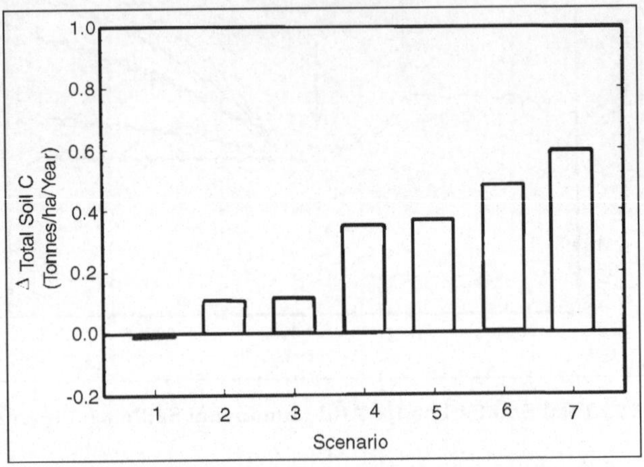

Fig 6.13 Average Annual Change in Total Soil Carbon for Athi Kamunyuni Settlement

Conclusions

The modelling of farm data from four communities in the semi-arid Makueni District again shows that carbon stocks can increase when a variety of technologies and practices already available to farmers are used. Modest inputs of organic material in the form of FYM and plant residues can lead to CS, particularly where systems are currently at or near steady state for soil carbon stocks.

Removal of fallow periods from existing systems results in losses of 0.1 tonnes C/ha/year. Inorganic fertilizers are again an inefficient choice for plant nutrients when soil C is a concern. Burning plant residues is not desirable. The combination of legumes in rotations, 2-4 tonnes/ha/year of FYM in addition to 0.6 tonnes/ha/year of plant residues, results in the highest rate of CS in all the dryland cases—0.7 tonnes C/ha/year. At lower levels of FYM but with maintenance of fallows, combined with legumes in rotation, increases in soil C of 0.3-to 0.4 tonnes/ha/year can be achieved.

6

Manure Management

INTRODUCTION

The quantity, composition, and consistency of manure influence the selection and the design of manure-handling facilities. In its strictest definition, animal manure refers only to feces and urine. However, bedding, feed wastage, rain, soil, milk-house wastes or wash, and more are mixed with the feces and urine on many farms. This results in a manure that has properties considerably different from fresh manure. To minimize confusion, the term fresh will be added to manure when talking only about feces and urine mixtures.

FRESH MANURE

Table 6.1 lists fresh manure (feces and urine) production and its characteristics by livestock types, weights, and production levels. Values in the table are averages for individual animals being fed according to National Research Council Guidelines. Variations of 20 per cent can occur and are highly dependent on feed digestibility and nutrient feeding levels of the animal. Recent studies have shown nitrogen (N), phosphorus (P), and potassium (K) can be reduced in many feeding programmes without reducing animal productivity.

The result is manure with N, P, and K levels lower those given in Table 6.1. Laboratory analysis of fresh manure is the most reliable way to determine its chemical content. Procedures for sampling manure are discussed.

The first part of Table 6.1 gives the ratio of fresh manure weight generated daily per animal body weight, along with moisture and dry solids level. Also included are ash, N, P, and K concentrations as a per centage of dry solids (all water removed). Results show that manure production per unit of body weight varies with production level (dry *vs.* lactating), diet (high energy vs. high roughage), sex, age, and stage of production, as well as with species. Also, N, P, and K concentrations vary with these same factors.

Thus, the quantity and properties of manure depend on:

- Animal species, age, productivity.
- Levels of nutrients fed and ration digestibility.

Two properties of fresh manure are relatively constant, namely water content and density. For fresh manure, water content is consistent at 88 to 92 per cent for non-poultry species and 73 to 75 per cent for poultry. Thus, unless an animal is sick or is being fed excessive levels of salt (in which case, moisture increases), these moisture ranges can be expected. Manure in the 88 to 92 per cent range should be handled as a liquid, while manure in the 73 to 75 per cent range should be handled as a solid. Figure 6.1 shows graphically how manure moisture affects its handling characteristics.

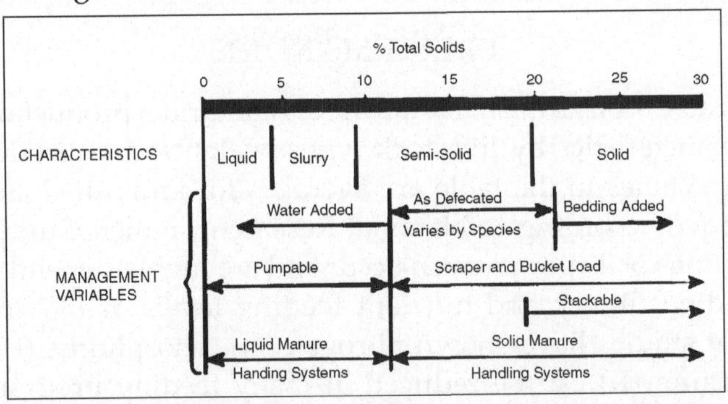

Fig 6.1 Physical Manure Characteristics and Handling Requirements

Density of fresh manure is similar for all species at 62 to 65 lb/ft^3 (water has a density of 62.4 lb/ft^3). At these densities, a gallon of manure would weigh approximately 8.3 lb. Therefore, to convert fresh manure weights to gallons, divide weights by 8.3.

USING MANURE AND COMPOST AS NUTRIENT SOURCES FOR FRUIT AND VEGETABLE CROPS

Manure is a valuable fertilizer for any farming operation and has been used for centuries to supply needed nutrients for crop growth.

The use of manure has generally declined on many farms over the past 50 years due to:

- Farm specialisation with increasing separation of crop and livestock production,
- Cost of transporting manure, which is a bulky, relatively low analysis nutrient source, and
- Increased availability of high analysis synthetic fertilizers that usually provide a cheaper source per unit of nutrient than manure. Despite these limitations, manure (and other organic nutrient sources) produced on or near a vegetable farm provide many benefits and should be beneficially utilised whenever possible.

Manure and compost not only supply many nutrients for crop production, including micronutrients, but they are also valuable sources of organic matter. Increasing soil organic matter improves soil structure or tilth, increases the water-holding capacity of coarse-textured sandy soils, improves drainage in fine-textured clay soils, provides a source of slow release nutrients, reduces wind and water erosion, and promotes growth of earthworms and other beneficial soil organisms. Most vegetable crops return small amounts of crop residue to the soil, so manure, compost, and other organic amendments help maintain soil organic matter levels.

Proper use of manure and compost is essential from both a production and environmental standpoint. Applying rates that are too low can lead to nutrient deficiency and low yields. On the other hand, too high a rate can lead to nitrate leaching, phosphorus run-off, accelerated eutrophication of lakes, and excessive vegetative growth of some crops. Thus, understanding how to manage manure is important for any farming operation with livestock that relies on manure as a major source of nutrients, as well as for vegetable producers who have access to an economical supply of manure, compost, or other organic nutrient sources. This discussion addresses differences between the composition of fresh and composted manure, nutrient availability from manure/compost, and calculation of how much manure/compost to apply. Although focussed on manure or composted manure, much of the discussion and the methods for calculating rates are generally applicable to effective use of different types of compost, biosolids, and similar organic nutrient sources.

Nutrient Composition of Manure and Compost

Many different types of manure are available for crop production. For this discussion, it is assumed that most vegetable growers will be using solid manure with or without bedding. Similar principles will apply to the use of liquid manures. The nutrient content of manures varies with animal, bedding, storage, and processing. The approximate nutrient composition of various solid manures, including some composted manures, is presented in Table.

While this table provides a general analysis of manure or compost nutrient content, it is strongly recommended that if routine applications are made for crop production the specific manure being used should be tested by a laboratory for moisture and nutrient content. Nutrient analysis should include: total nitrogen (N), ammonium-N, phosphate (P_2O_5), and potash (K_2O). Accurate manure or compost analysis requires that a representative sample be submitted; so several subsamples should be collected and composited to make up the sample. If manure or compost is being purchased, request a nutrient analysis from the seller for N, P_2O_5, and K_2O content.

Fresh *vs.* composted manure. Fresh, non-composted manure will generally have a higher N content than composted manure (Table). However, the use of composted manure will contribute more to the organic matter content of the soil. Fresh manure is high in soluble forms of N, which can lead to salt build-up and leaching losses if over applied.

Fresh manure may contain high amounts of viable weed seeds, which can lead to weed problems. In addition, various pathogens such as *E. coli* may be present in fresh manure and can cause illness to individuals eating fresh produce unless proper precautions are taken. Apply and incorporate raw manure in fields where crops are intended for human consumption at least three months before the crop will be harvested. Allow four months between application and harvest of root and leaf crops that come in contact with the soil. Do not surface apply raw manure under orchard trees where fallen fruit will be harvested.

Heat generated during the composting process will kill most weed seeds and pathogens, provided temperatures are maintained at or above 131°F for 15 days or more (and the compost is turned so that all material is exposed to this temperature for a minimum of 3 days). The microbially mediated composting process will lower the amount of soluble N forms by stabilising the N in larger organic, humus-like compounds. A disadvantage of composting is that some of the ammonia-N will be lost as a gas. Compost alone also may not be able to supply adequate available nutrients, particularly N, during rapid growth phases of crops with high nutrient demands. Composted manure is usually more expensive than fresh or partially aged manure.

Heat-dried manure/compost. Drying manure or compost to low moisture content reduces their volume and weight, which lowers transportation costs, but it also requires energy inputs. Dried products can be easier to handle and apply uniformly to fields, especially those that have been processed into pellets. Heat drying also reduces pathogens if temperatures exceed 150 to 175°F for at least one hour and water content is reduced to 10 to 12 per cent or less.

The significant energy costs to heat-dry manure or compost at high temperatures are in contrast to the self-heating generated by microbial respiration during the composting process. Heat-dried composts vary widely in the degree to which they are composted before drying.

Many are only partially composted and have higher amounts of soluble (inorganic) N forms than mature, stable compost. This readily available N gives these products some characteristics that are similar to soluble N fertilizers, such as ammonium nitrate. Heat drying of manure and immature compost may increase volatilisation of ammonia-N and reduce the total N content of the finished product. In addition, composted or partially composted material that is dried at high temperature rather than going through a curing phase at ambient temperatures is not as biologically active as mature compost. The disease suppressive properties of some composts depends upon recolonisation of the compost by disease suppressing organisms during the curing phase.

Nutrient Availability from Manure and Compost

The analysis of manure or compost provides total nutrient content, but availability of the nutrients for plant growth will depend on their breakdown and release from the organic components. Generally, 70 to 80 per cent of the phosphorus (P) and 80 to 90 per cent of the potassium (K) will be available from manure the first year after application. Numbers from a table or from an analysis report should to be multiplied by these factors to obtain the amount of P_2O_5 and K_2O available to crops from a manure or compost application.

Calculating N availability is more complex than determining P and K availability. Most of the N in manure is in the organic form and essentially all of the N in compost is organic. Organic N is unavailable for uptake until microorganisms degrade the organic compounds that contain it. A smaller fraction of the N in manure is in the ammonium/ammonia or inorganic form. The ammonium-N form is a readily available fraction. Other inorganic forms such as nitrate and nitrite can also exist, but their quantities are usually very low. Estimated levels of ammonium-N and total N in fresh and composted manure are shown in Table.

When applied to soil, manure, compost, and other organic amendments undergo microbial transformations that release plant-available N over time. Volatilisation, denitrification, and leaching result in N losses from the soil that reduce the amount of N that can be used by crops.

The steps of N transformation in manure, compost, and other organic amendments, and the plant-available N forms, are as follows:

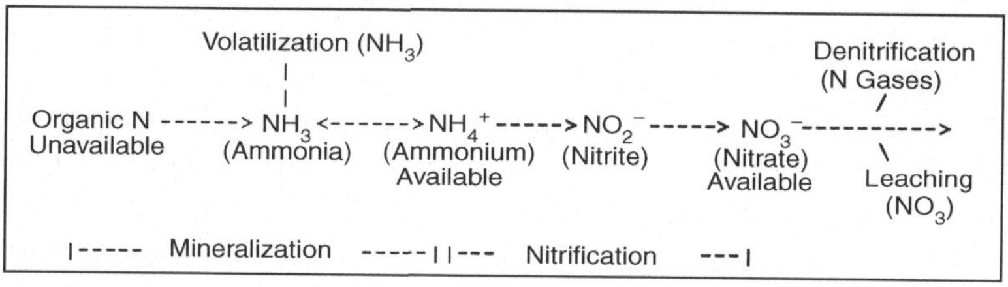

Table 6.1 Approximate Nutrient Composition of Various Types of Animal Manure and Compost (All Values are on a Fresh Weight Basis).

Manure Type	Dry Matter	Ammonium-N	Total N[a]	P_2O_5	K_2O
	%	lb/ton			
Swine, no bedding	18	6	10	9	8
Swine, with bedding	18	5	6	7	7
Beef, no bedding	52	7	21	14	23
Beef, with bedding	50	8	21	18	26
Dairy, no bedding	18	4	9	4	10
Dairy, with bedding	21	5	9	4	10
Sheep, no bedding	28	5	18	11	26
Sheep, with bedding	28	5	14	9	25
Poultry, no litter	45	26	33	48	34
Poultry, with litter	75	36	56	45	34
Turkey, no litter	22	17	27	20	17
Turkey, with litter	29	13	20	16	13
Horse, with bedding	46	4	14	4	14
Poultry compost	45	1	17	39	23
Dairy compost	45	<1	12	12	26
Mixed compost: Dairy/Swine/Poultry	43	<1	11	11	10

Note: [a]Total N = Ammonium-N plus organic N

Table provides estimates of N availability from manure the first growing season after application. The actual amount available is dependent on manure type, bedding, and whether the manure has been composted. Usually 25 to 50 per cent of the organic-N in fresh manure is available the first year. In addition to the organic fraction, N availability from manure also has to take into account the amount of ammonium-N present. This form of N is readily available for plant uptake, but is prone to losses as ammonia if not incorporated within 12 hours after application. Assuming direct manure incorporation after application, 45 to 75 per cent of the total N (organic-N + ammonium-N) is available the first year. Note that for composted manure, the per centage of the organic N available in the first year following application is much lower than it is for fresh manure. Because there is very little ammonium-N in composted manure, the organic N fraction is basically the same as the total N fraction.

Bedding or litter will usually decrease nutrient content by dilution. If materials high in carbon (C) like straw or wood shavings are used as bedding, N availability may be reduced by the larger C/N ratio of the product. High C relative to N will lead to a tie-up of N, potentially causing N deficiency in the crop. A C/N ratio of 25/1 or greater will lead to N tie-up in the soil. A C/N ratio of less than 25/1 will release N to the crop. The C/N ratio is also an important consideration in the use of various composts, as well as a controlling factor in the composting process itself.

Table 6.2 Estimated Organic N Availability (Km) from Manure and Composted Manure the First Season After Application

Manure Type	Organic N (per cent available)
Swine, fresh	50
Beef, no bedding	35
Beef, with bedding	25
Dairy, no bedding	35
Dairy, with bedding	25
Sheep, solid	25
Poultry, no litter	50
Poultry, with litter	45
Horse, with bedding	20
Composted poultry	30
Composted dairy	14

Manure and Compost Application

As discussed above, some of the N in fresh manure will be lost to the atmosphere during application in the form of ammonia gas. The higher the ammonium-N fraction is in manure, the more prone it is to ammonia volatilisation. Manure should be incorporated within 12 hours of application to avoid excessive ammonia losses.

Unincorporated manure will supply the organic N fraction and at most 20 per cent of the ammonium-N fraction. Incorporation of composted manure is not as critical, because the N is stabilised in organic compounds with little free ammonium present. However, in order to obtain full benefit from compost, incorporation is recommended whenever possible. Manure and compost are often high in soluble salts, so to avoid salt injury seeding operations should take place about 3 to 4 weeks after application.

Residual Nutrients in Soil from Manure and Compost Application

The residual effects of the manure and compost are important. Some benefit will be obtained in the second and third years following application. When manure and compost are used to fertilize crops, soil organic matter will increase over time and subsequent rates of application can generally be reduced because of increased nutrient cycling. Continuous use of manure or compost can lead to high levels of residual N, P, and other nutrients, which can potentially be transported to lakes and streams in run-off or leach and pollute the groundwater. Taking into account residual release of N in subsequent years should help to avoid excessive applications. General rules of thumb for N are that organic N released during the second and third cropping years after initial application will be 50 per cent and 25 per cent, respectively, of that mineralised during the first cropping season.

Remember that some manures and composts contain high levels of P, so if organic nutrient sources are regularly applied at rates to meet crop N demands, the amount of P in the soil can build up to excessively high levels. Use of soil tests, plant tissue tests, and monitoring of crop growth will help in determining the amount of residual N and other nutrients in the soil and the need for further applications.

Calculating the Amount of Manure or Compost to Apply

Methods for calculating the amount of manure or compost to apply have been adapted and summarised from *Livestock Waste Facilities Handbook*, 2nd ed., 1985, Midwest Plan Service. Composts can be thought of as similar to manure, but with little or no ammonium-N present. The amount of compost required to meet crop nutrient demands can be very large. For these situations, more readily available nutrients from other sources may be required to supplement compost additions, especially early in the growing season.

Use the following steps to determine the manure or compost rate needed for a particular crop:

Step 1

- Determine the nutrient needs of the crop – Base nutrient needs on soil test recommendations.

Step 2

- Determine the total nutrient content of the manure or compost– Chemical analysis of the actual product is strongly recommended; a general estimate can be obtained from Table above.

Step 3

- Determine the available nutrient content– Use 80 per cent availability for P_2O_5 and 90 per cent availability for K_2O. Calculate N availability using the following equation:

Available N = (Organic N x Km) + Ammonium-N*

Where:

- Organic N = Total N – Ammonium-N (lb/ton) (from manure or compost analysis or Table)
- Km = Fraction of organic N released (per cent available/100, from Table)
- Ammonium-N* = Ammonium-N in lb/ton (from manure analysis or Table)

Note:

*if manure is not incorporated within 12 hours after application, reduce the value for ammonium-N using Table to account for volatilisation losses; reduce ammonium-N in the Available N equation, but use the full value in the equation for Organic N

Table 6.3 Per cent of the Ammonium-N Available to a Crop When the Time between Application and Incorporation is More than 12 Hours

Days Until Incorporation	per cent of Ammonium-N Available to Crop
0.5-2	80
2-4	60
4-7	40
>7	20

Step 4

- Calculate the rates of application needed to supply the recommended amounts of N, P_2O_5, and K_2O– Divide the recommended nutrient needs from Step 1 by the pounds of available nutrients per ton of manure or compost determined in Step 3.

Step 5

- Select the rate of manure or compost to apply– Frequently, manure and compost application rates are based on the N need of the crop. If manure or compost is applied on a regular basis, you may need to base rates on P to avoid excessive buildup of P in the soil, and supplement with other N sources to meet the total crop N requirement. For legumes, either P_2O_5 or K_2O can be used as a basis for rates, depending on crop needs and soil test levels.

Step 6

- Determine the amount of available nutrients applied with the manure or compost– multiply the application rate of manure or compost determined in Step 5 (in tons/A) times the estimated available nutrients (in lb/ton) determined in Step 3. The amounts calculated can be compared with crop needs to determine if supplemental nutrients are needed (next Step).

Step 7

- Determine whether application of additional nutrients is needed– Subtract the amount of nutrients needed by the crop from the amounts of available nutrients applied with the manure or compost. If the number obtained for a nutrient is zero or negative, then no further application is necessary. A positive number indicates the amount of that nutrient (in lb/A) that needs to be applied from another nutrient source to meet crop demands.

Example Calculation

The following steps provide an example manure rate calculation for the following situation:

- Crop – sweet corn.
- Nutrient source – turkey manure with litter.
- Soil test results.
  - pH = 6.3.
  - Organic matter = 4.8 per cent.
  - Available P (Bray-P1) = 8 ppm.
  - Available K = 70 ppm.

***Step 1*—Determine the nutrient needs of the crop**

- Yield goal = 9 tons/acre.
- Previous crop = pumpkin.
- NPK soil test recommendations.
  - 120 lb N/A.
  - 60 lb P_2O_5/A.
  - 100 lb K_2O/A.

***Step 2*—Determine the Total Nutrient Content of the Manure**

- Chemical analysis of the manure is strongly recommended for efficient nutrient use.
- For this example, we will use the general estimates in Table (all values on a wet weight basis).

— Ammonium-N – 13 lb/ton.
— Total N – 20 lb/ton.
— P_2O_5 – 16 lb/ton.
— K_2O – 13 lb/ton.

Step 3—Determine the Available Nutrient Content

- We will calculate available N first
- The equation is: Available N = (Organic N x Km) + Ammonium-N.
  — Organic N = Total N – Ammonium-N, so Organic N = 20 – 13 = 7 lb/ton.
  — Km = Fraction of organic N released the first season after application; get the per centage available from Table and then convert to a decimal fraction, so Km = per cent available/100 = 0.45.
  — Substituting into the original equation: Available N = (Organic N x Km) + Ammonium-N, so Available N = (7 x 0.45) + 13* = 16.2 lb/ton.

Note: *we are assuming the manure is incorporated within 12 hours after application; if it is more than 12 hours before incorporation, reduce the value for ammonium-N using Table; reduce ammonium-N in the Available N equation, but use the full value in the equation for Organic N.

- Next we can calculate available P_2O_5.
  — Using the 80 per cent availability factor (from Step 3 above) the equation is:
  — Available P_2O_5 = 0.80 x Total P_2O_5.
  — Available P_2O_5= 0.80 x 16 = 12.8 lb/ton.
- Finally, we can calculate available K_2O.
  — Using the 90 per cent availability factor the equation:
  — Available K_2O = 0.90 x Total K_2O.
  — Available K_2O = 0.90 x 13 = 11.7 lb/ton.

Step 4—Calculate The rates of Application Needed to Supply the Recommended Amounts of N, P_2O_5, and K_2O

- Divide the nutrient recommendations by the pounds of available nutrient per ton of manure.

- To meet the N requirement
  - 120 lb N/A divided by 16.2 lb available N/ton = 7.4 tons/A
- To meet the P_2O_5 requirement
  - 60 lb P_2O_5/A divided by 12.8 lb available P_2O_5/ton = 4.7 tons/A
- To meet the K_2O requirement
  - 100 lb K_2O/A divided by 11.7 lb available K_2O/ton = 8.5 tons/A

Step 5—Select the Rate of Manure to Apply

- Decide whether to base the application rate on the N, P_2O_5, or K_2O requirement
- For this example, we will use the N requirement
  - The application rate will be 7.4 tons of manure/A

Step 6—Determine the Amount of Available Nutrients Applied with the Manure

- Multiply the application rate of manure times the amounts of available nutrients (calculated in Step 3)
- We decided to meet the N requirement and are applying 120 lb N/A
- P_2O_5 application rate
  - 7.4 tons of manure/A x 12.8 lb available P_2O_5/ton = 94.7 lb P_2O_5/A
- K_2O application rate
  - 7.4 tons of manure/A x 11.7 lb available K_2O/ton = 86.6 lb K_2O/A

Step 7—Determine Whether Application of Additional Nutrients is Needed

- Subtract the amounts of nutrients needed by the crop from the amounts of available nutrients applied with the manure
- The N requirement is met
- P_2O_5 requirement
  - 60 – 94.7 = – 34.7
  - Excess of 34.7 lb P_2O_5/A
  - This field has a medium soil test P level (8 ppm Bray-P1), so a single application of excess P should not cause a problem; however, continued manure applications

based on crop N requirements will build up soil test P to levels that eventually could cause water quality problems

- K_2O requirement
  - 100 – 86.6 = 13.4
  - Shortage of 13.4 lb K_2O/A
  - Supplemental K_2O could be applied in starter fertilizer

BEDDING AND WATER ADDITIONS

Bedding should be considered in many manure-handling systems. An estimate of the amount of bedding used can be obtained by measuring the amount used for a small number of animals and expanding it to the whole herd. Table provides characteristics of common bedding materials as related to water absorption and fertilizer nutrients. This information can be used in calculating nutrient value of fresh manure and the bedding when laboratory analysis is unavailable.

Table 6.4 Bedding Characteristics

Type	Water Absorbing Capacity	Density	Water	Solids	Nutrient Concentrations		
					N	P_2O_5	K_2O
	lb/lb, bedding	lb/ft³	% wb	% wb	% db	% db	% db
Straw[a]							
Wheat, Oat	2.2	5 to 8	10.0	90.0	0.55	0.20	1.00
Cornstalks[a]							
Shredded	2.5	4 to 5	10.0	90.0	0.75	1.40	0.90
Hardwood[a]							
Shavings or Sawdust	1.5	9 to 12	10.0	90.0	0.20	0.10	0.20
Sand[b]							
Clean Sand (dry)	0.16	80.6	6.2	93.8	0.00	0.00	0.00
Clean Sand (wet)	0	91.6	19.4	80.6	0.00	0.00	0.00

a Adapted from Ohio State University Extension Bulletin 604, 1992 Edition. Material wetted from 10% moisture to 65 to 70% moisture.

b Unpublished Ohio Agricultural Research and Development Center (OARDC) data.

Bedding, water additions, handling and storage losses alter manures characteristics; therefore, the data given in Tables are only the place to begin for analysing nutrient loading rates on farms and calculating the value of manure.

VOLUME OF MANURE

Estimating the total volume of manure produced is accomplished by adding the volume of fresh manure from the animal, plus half the volume of the dry bedding used, plus the volume of water additions. Only half the volume of bedding is used to allow for void spaces in the bedding which are filled with the fresh manure during mixing.

MOISTURE AND COMPOSITION

Figure 6.2 shows the ratio of bedding to fresh manure needed to achieve a specific moisture ratio of manure. For example, free-stall fresh manure (88 per cent moisture, liquid) would require about 0.05 lb of dry bedding at 10 per cent moisture to be added per 1.0 lb of fresh manure to produce a semi-solid manure with a moisture of 84 per cent. For a dairy cow producing 90 lb of milk per day, this would be about 7.7 lb per day of bedding (153 lb manure per day × 0.05).

If the bedding was wheat straw, this would have added 0.038 N, 0.014 P_2O_5, and 0.069 K_2O lbs per day of nutrients or a 3.8 per cent, 4.7 per cent, and 12 per cent increase above fresh manure values, respectively.

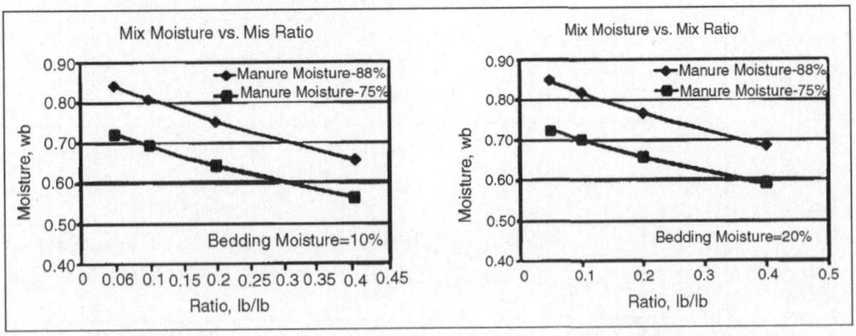

Fig 6.2 Expected Manure Moisture Based on Ratio of Bedding Added to Fresh Manure

When bedding with straw or corn stalks, nutrient values should be considered for nutrient management planning (NMP) on a farmstead. However, for sawdust or sand bedding, nutrient additions will generally be less than 3 per cent for N, P_2O_5, and K_2O.

SAND BEDDING

Sand-bedded dairy free-stall barns have become increasingly popular because of cow comfort and hygienic improvements over organic bedding and mats. Sand usage averaged about 53 lb per stall per day in Michigan State University studies. The sand significantly increases the solids content of the manure and its volume. However, since, sand does not readily absorb water, the manure will continue to behave as a slurry or semi-solid.

Other materials often get added to fresh manure. Feed wastage and soil can add considerable nutrients, while water additions from washing equipment and buildings, leaking waterers inside buildings, rain from building roofs and outside lots, and rainfall into open storage structures can add considerable volume and weight. Conversely, manure in open lots or well-ventilated buildings will often lose water.

Thus, the quantity and the properties of manure depend on:

- Quantity of added bedding, feed wastage, soil, surface water, washwater, etc.
- Environment wet or dry climate, housing ventilation, handling and storage losses.

HANDLING AND STORAGE LOSSES

Nutrient losses occur in the handling, storage, and spreading of manure. The major nutrient lost is nitrogen through volatilisation of ammonia and can range as high as 80 per cent or more of the total nitrogen. Also, phosphorus can be lost due to its accumulation in the unrecovered sludge in the storage system. Because nutrient losses are highly variable, the information on fresh manures and bedding given in Tables should not be relied upon once manure is available for sampling and analysis.

Sampling is also recommended because of uncontrolled water additions or losses (drying) that can occur. Thus, to accurately predict manure properties, sampling and testing manure from storage is critical.

SAMPLING, TESTING, AND EVALUATING MANURE NUTRIENTS

Sampling

To make the most appropriate and environmentally responsible use of manure, it is necessary to test the manure to accurately determine its nutrient concentrations. Furthermore, for the test results to be meaningful, it is important to obtain an adequate number of samples that are representative of the bulk manure. The number of samples needed will depend on the variability of the manure. The more variable the manure, the more samples are required. Variability of liquid manures is usually less than for solid manures, especially if the liquid manure can be mixed prior to sampling.

Manure from different storage systems should be sampled differently. For solid manures, the sample can be taken while loading or during spreading. For poultry, the sample can come from within the house or from a stockpile of litter. Liquid manure can be sampled from storage or during the time of application. Liquid manure in storage should be agitated two to four hours before taking the sample.

Testing: Select a reputable testing laboratory. In selecting a laboratory, determine if the laboratory is knowledgeable in testing manure and belongs to a manure proficiency testing programme. Obtain the laboratorys appropriate sampling kit and read the corresponding instructions thoroughly. Manure samples should be identified regarding the farm, animal species, and date of sampling. The samples should be kept frozen until shipped to a laboratory. It is best to ship early in the week.

The laboratory analyses required on manure are moisture, total nitrogen (N), ammonia-N (NH_3-N), phosphorus (generally reported as phosphate [P_2O_5]), and potassium (generally reported as potash [K_2O]). Other useful analyses include pH, electrical conductivity, calcium (Ca), magnesium (Mg), and sulphur (S). The nutrients manganese (Mn), copper (Cu), and zinc (Zn) may also be important, especially if these nutrients are included in the animal diet.

Evaluation of Test

Most laboratories design their test reports to meet the needs of their customers. However, there may be differences from laboratory to laboratory in the reporting format, reporting units of the test values, conversion factors, and the estimate of the nutrient availability. The test report usually involves three types of information. The first type is the descriptive information about the sample and the customer, including sample identification, sample description, and date of analysis.

The second type of information is the actual analytical results. Careful attention should be paid to the units associated with the test values. Typically, the laboratory will report the test values in parts per million (ppm) or per centage (per cent), and then convert them to the units needed by the customer to calculate application rates. Examples are lb per 1,000 gal for liquid manure and lb per ton for solid manure. Laboratories may also report the analysis on an as-is basis and a dry-matter basis. The as-is basis is used to calculate the application rates. Most laboratories report the results only on an as-is basis. However, the dry-matter basis, if it is needed, can be calculated from the moisture determination. The dry-matter basis is used to compare the nutrient concentrations of one manure with those of another manure.

The third type of information is interpretive and includes estimates of nutrient availability and fertilizer value. Since, the laboratory may be using estimates of nutrient availability from other sources, it is important to verify that the labs nutrient availability factors are the same as reported in this bulletin for Ohio conditions. The fertilizer value is often assigned to the manure by taking into account the current local fertilizer prices for the nutrients in the manure. However, the fertilizer value may be less when not all nutrients are needed due to already high soil-test levels. Manure application costs vary between fields and can be more than the fertilizer value of the nutrients.

NUTRIENT BUDGET

Over application of manure is a major concern for water quality and soil health. Nitrogen and phosphorus are two nutrients that can hurt the quality of our groundwater and surface water. Nitrogen leaching out of the root zone may enter a tile and be transported to surface water, or it may leach to the groundwater.

Phosphorous leachate or run-off entering the surface water contributes to excessive algae growth which causes low oxygen levels in surface water. This, in turn, impairs aquatic life. Proper management of manure is critical to protecting water quality and to sustaining the livestock and poultry industry.

The key to preventing manure nutrient overload is to balance manure nutrients with crop needs. However, as livestock and poultry operations get larger, the manure nutrients generated often exceed the nutrient needs of the crops on the farm. When more manure nutrients are applied to the crops than the crops can use, nutrient levels built up in soil, leading to a higher risk of nutrient run-off or leaching to surface and groundwater.

The purpose of this chapter is to provide an understanding of the flow of nutrients on the farm and to help the livestock producer determine if his or her farm:

- Has a nutrient balance;
- Has an excess of manure nutrients;
- Has a shortage of nutrients.

In addition, strategies will be discussed to deal with excess nutrients.

NUTRIENT IMBALANCES

Nutrient imbalances can occur on a single field, an individual farm, or on a regional basis.

Single-field nutrient imbalances: are common on any livestock farm. Easy access fields, fields close to the barn, loafing areas, and pasture fields often accumulate excess manure nutrients. Spreading manure based on convenience and not the crops nutrient requirements may result in excessive nutrient concentrations and water-quality problems. *Individual farm nutrient imbalances*: Livestock farms import significant quantities of nutrients as animal feeds. Livestock utilise only 10 to 30 per cent of these nutrients, excreting the remainder as manure. This results in a concentration of nutrients on the livestock farm. This is a common challenge in the Corn Belt states where producers tend to concentrate either on grain production or livestock production.

Regional nutrient imbalances: have developed in the past 30 years as livestock/poultry production and feed-grain production have concentrated in specific, but separate, regions of the state and the country. Nutrient excesses on a regional scale involve townships, counties, or multiple counties with high concentrations of livestock or poultry that produce more manure nutrients than the crop base in the geographical area can utilise. Several top livestock-producing areas have accumulated high concentrations of nutrients where more nutrients are available from the manure produced than can be utilised by the crops grown.

The primary question a livestock farmer must ask is: Am I building up nutrients (producing more nutrients than can be utilised on the farm)? To answer this question, the farmer needs to understand the flow of nutrients into the farm, the nutrient needs of the farm, and the flow of nutrients off the farm. The primary nutrients to track for the farm nutrient balance are nitrogen, phosphorus, and potash (N-P_2O_5-K_2O).

The main nutrient inputs on a livestock or poultry farm are commercial fertilizer, purchased feed, animals, irrigation water and rainfall, and legume nitrogen fixation. Figure 6.3 illustrates the flow of nutrients onto, and off, a farm.

Within the boundaries of the farm, a recycling of nutrients occurs between the livestock and the crops. Manure nutrients are recycled, at least in part, for crop production. Feed crop nutrients are recycled as animal feed for livestock or poultry production. Nutrients exit a livestock operation preferably as managed outputs including animals and crops sold and possibly other products moved off farm (*e.g.*, milk, eggs, or manure sold or given to a neighbouring crop producer). Some nutrients exit the farm as losses to the environment (nitrates in groundwater, ammonia volatilised into the atmosphere, and nitrogen and phosphorus into surface water).

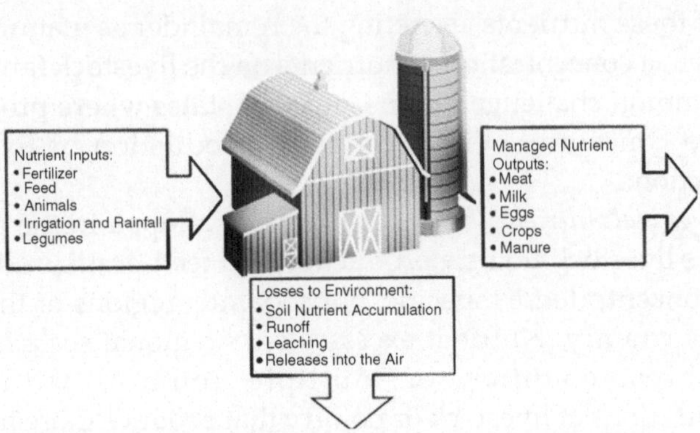

Fig 6.3 Typical Livestock and Poultry Nutrient Flows. Adapted from the Livestock and Poultry Environmental Stewardship Curriculum, MidWest Plan Service (MWPS)

Nutrients (especially phosphorus) also accumulate in large quantities in the soil. Although not a direct loss to the environment, a growing accumulation of nutrients in the soil adds to the risk of future environmental losses.

Nutrient Inputs Managed Nutrient Outputs = Losses to Environment

The loss to environment is the difference between the inputs and the managed outputs. This imbalance accounts for both the direct environmental loss and the accumulation of nutrients in the soil. Livestock operations with a significant imbalance are concentrating nutrients, resulting in increased risk to water quality and are fundamentally unsustainable. In contrast, livestock farms that have achieved a balance represent a sustainable production system.

The goal of the livestock or poultry operation is to achieve a balance of inputs with managed nutrient outputs. On some farms, a farm nutrient balance can be managed on the farm itself; in other cases, manure needs to be moved to other farms to achieve a nutrient balance. Evaluating the Whole Farm Nutrient Balance for Livestock or Poultry Operations

There are two primary methods for estimating the whole nutrient balance on your farm.

- Whole Farm Nutrient Balance review assesses nutrient input content of the feed purchased, the fertilizer purchased, the legume nitrogen produced on the farm, animals purchased, and an estimate of the nutrients added as a result of irrigation and/or rainfall. The second phase of this budget involves estimating the nutrient content of all the nutrients flowing out by way of crops, meat, milk, eggs, animals sold, and manure transported off the farm. This method is scientifically based, but time consuming, and requires extensive records to calculate.

- A second method provides an easier, but factual, estimate of your whole farm nutrient balance. It involves measuring or estimating total manure nutrient production compared to whole farm crop nutrient utilisation. An excess of manure nutrients for crop production suggests a likely whole farm nutrient imbalance.

ESTIMATING MANURE NUTRIENT CONTENT

One of the best ways to determine manure nutrient content is to obtain a manure analysis of the different types of manure produced on the farm. An annual manure analysis should be taken for each different manure storage on the farm.

The manure analysis will provide information on the amount of nitrogen, phosphorus, and potash in the manure. For solid manures, the amounts are expressed as pounds of N (nitrogen), P_2O_5 (phosphate), and K_2O (potash) per ton. For liquid manure, the amounts are expressed in pounds of N, P_2O_5, and K_2O per 1,000 gallons of manure.

In addition to knowing the concentration of nutrients, the quantity of the manure that coincides with the respective manure analysis must be determined. For example, a typical manure analysis may indicate 20 lbs of nitrogen (N), 14 lbs of P_2O_5, and 17 lbs of K_2O per 1,000 gallons. If this represents 1 million gallons of manure, then the total nutrient content of the liquid manure is 20,000 lbs of nitrogen, 14,000 lbs of P_2O_5, and 17,000 lbs of K_2O. Note: Software programmes are available at the local USDA, Natural Resources Conservation Service, and Soil and Water Conservation district offices to do Whole Farm Nutrient Budgets.

If manure analyses are not available, a second method to determine manure nutrient content involves using book values to determine volumes of manure and pounds of manure nutrients produced. Table 6.5 provides estimates of the nutrients and volumes of manure produced for various types of livestock and poultry. Using Table, lets look at an example for a swine operation with 500 grower-finishers averaging 150 lbs. The manure is stored in an underground pit and handled as a liquid.

Table 6.5 Estimated Nutrient Content and Volumes of Manure Production (As Excreted)

Animal Type Group Size	Size Lbs	Estimated Nutrient Content						Amount of Manure Produced	
		Lbs/Ton			Lbs/1,000 Gallons			Tons Per Year	1,000 Gal. Units Per Year
		N	P_2O_5	K_2O	N	P_2O_5	K_2O		
Col. 1*	Col. 2*	Col. 3*	Col. 4*	Col. 5*	Col. 6*	Col. 7*	Col. 8*	Col. 9*	Col. 10*
Dairy Cattle									
Heifer	150	5.8	1.5	6.2	21.8	5.8	23.3	2.4	0.6
Heifer	250	5.7	1.9	6.7	21.6	7.2	25.2	3.8	1.0
Heifer	750	5.3	2.2	6.8	20.1	8.1	25.6	11.9	3.1
Dairy Milk 40 lbs/day	NA	9.7	3.7	7.2	35.2	13.3	26.0	22.1	6.3
Dairy Milk 50 lbs/day	NA	9.8	3.9	7.2	35.2	14.0	26.0	23.3	6.5
Dairy Milk 60 lbs/day	NA	9.8	4.0	7.2	35.2	14.4	25.9	24.5	6.9
Dairy Milk 70 lbs/day	NA	9.8	4.2	7.2	35.1	14.8	25.9	25.7	7.2
Dairy Milk 80 lbs/day	NA	9.8	4.3	7.2	35.0	15.2	25.8	26.8	7.5

(Contd...)

Dairy Milk 90 lbs/day	NA	9.9	4.4	7.2	35.3	15.7	26.1	28.0	7.8
Dry Cow	800	6.6	3.0	6.8	23.7	10.8	24.6	12.2	4.1
Dry Cow	1,000	6.6	3.0	6.8	23.6	10.8	24.7	15.0	4.7
Dry Cow	1,200	6.6	3.0	6.9	23.5	10.8	24.9	18.1	5.3
Dry Cow	1,400	6.5	3.0	7.0	23.5	10.8	25.1	21.0	5.8
Veal	250	6.7	6.7	13.3	24.0	24.0	48.1	1.6	0.5
Beef Cattle									
Calf	450	8.1	7.7	8.5	29.6	28.2	31.0	4.7	1.3
High Forage	750	9.9	4.5	8.1	36.3	16.5	29.5	11.3	3.1
High Forage	1,100	9.9	4.6	7.8	35.9	16.5	28.2	16.8	4.7
High Energy	750	10.6	5.2	8.1	38.0	18.7	29.4	9.9	2.7
High Energy	1,100	10.1	5.3	8.0	36.5	18.9	28.8	14.6	4.1
Cow	1,000	7.4	6.0	8.3	27.0	22.1	30.2	11.5	3.1
Swine									
Nursery	25	11.1	7.4	7.4	40.1	26.7	26.7	0.5	0.1
Grow-Finish	150	12.6	10.5	8.4	45.5	37.9	30.4	1.7	0.5
Gestating	275	10.0	10.7	10.7	36.0	38.4	38.4	1.4	0.4
Lactating	375	12.0	11.6	12.4	44.0	42.3	45.6	4.1	1.1
Boar	350	10.4	11.1	11.1	38.2	40.7	40.7	1.3	0.4
Sheep									
Sheep	100	15.0	10.0	20.0	54.9	36.6	73.3	0.7	0.2

(Contd...)

Poultry									
Layer (per 1000)	4	20.2	20.8	12.3	76.3	78.5	46.5	47.5	12.6
Broiler (per 1000)	2	19.2	15.6	12.2	70.2	57.0	44.8	32.9	9.0
Turkey (per 1000)	20	21.0	24.0	12.0	76.9	87.9	44.0	164.3	44.8
Duck (per 100)	6	20.9	23.0	17.0	75.4	83.0	61.2	6.0	1.7
Horse									
Horse	1,100	7.4	4.5	4.4	27.1	16.5	16.0	10.2	2.8

Notes: * Column Number (*e.g.*, col. 1) will help users find the correct values in the following example.

1. Values do not include bedding or additional water that may be added.
2. The actual values can very + or n 30 per cent (recommend actual manure analysis).
3. Estimated nitrogen assumes a 25 per cent loss during storage and handling prior to land application.

Estimate Manure and Nutrient Production for Each Animal Type

- Using the book values in Table, determine the total manure output.

- 500 grower/finishers × 0.5 thousand gallons/year (Col. 10) = 250 thousand gallon units/year
- Then, calculate the total nutrient output for the manure produced:
- 250 × 36.0 lbs of N per 1,000 gal. (Col. 6) = 9,000 lbs N/ year
- 250 × 38.4 lbs P_2O_5 per 1,000 gal. (Col. 7) = 9,600 lbs P_2O_5/year
- 250 × 38.4 lbs K_2O per 1,000 gal. (Col. 8) = 9,600 lbs K_2O/year

Add the Nutrient Amounts for Each Animal Type

- Round the total nutrients calculated in Step 1 and complete the table shown here:

AnimalPhase/Type	Nitrogen	P_2O_5	K_2O
Grower/Finishers	9,000	9,600	9,600
Total	9,000	9,600	9,600

Now we have a good estimate of the manure nutrients available on the farming operation. The next step is to determine the farms crop nutrient needs.

Determine Acres of Each Crop and Average Yield Per Acre

Example:

- 100 acres of corn grain 140 bushels/acre
- 100 acres of soybeans 40 bushels/acre
- 100 acres of wheat + straw... 60 bushels/acre

Determine Crop Nutrient Needs.

Using Tables to determine nutrient needs, complete the table shown here. (Note: P_2O_5 and K_2O amounts are for crop removal; results from soil tests may vary.)

Crop	Yield	Acres	Nutrient Needs = Yield × Acres × Crop Removal (Tables 5 and 6)		
			N	P_2O_5	K_2O
Corn, Grain	140	100	16,800**	5,180	3,780
Soybeans	40	100	0*	3,200	5,600
Wheat + Straw	60	100	6,600	4,320	7,680
Totals		**300**	**23,400**	**12,700**	**17,060**

Note: * UP to 150 lbs per acre of manure nitrogen could be budgeted if this acreage is needed to help balance excess nitrogen that cannot be utilised for the non-legume crops.

** (*e.g.*, N = 140 bu per acre × 1.2 lbs N per bu. × 100 acres = 16,800 lbs)

Table 6.6 Recommended Nitrogen

Crop	Yield Units	Recommended Nitrogen
Corn	Bu/Acre	1.2 lbs/bushel
Corn Silage	Tons/Acre	7.2 lbs/ton
Tobacco	Lbs/Acre	0.1 lbs/lb
Wheat	Bu/Acre	1.1 lbs/bushel
Oats	Bu/Acre	0.65 lbs/bushel
Grass Hay/Pastures	Tons/Acre	40 lbs/ton (max. 175 lbs/acre)

Table 6.7 Approximate Amounts of P_2O_5 and K_2O Removed by Harvested Crops

Crop	Nutrients Removed for the Given Unit Yield	
	P_2O_5	K_2O
Alfalfa and Grass Forages	13.0 lb/ton	50 lb/ton
Corn, Grain	0.37 lb/bu	0.27 lb/bu
Corn, Silage	3.3 lb/ton	8.0 lb/ton
Oats, Grain	0.25 lb/bu	0.20 lb/bu
Oats, Grain + Straw	0.40 lb/bu	1.20 lb/bu
Sorghum, Grain	0.39 lb/100 lbs	0.39 lb/100 lbs
Soybeans	0.8 lb/bu	1.4 lb/bu
Sugar Beets	2.0 lb/ton	10.0 lb/ton
Tobacco, Burley	1.3 lb/100 lbs	8.3 lb/100 lbs
Wheat, Grain	0.63 lb/bu	0.37 lb/bu
Wheat, Grain + Straw	0.72 lb/bu	1.28 lb/bu

Compare Manure Nutrients and Crop Needs

Comparison of Nutrients and Crop Needs.			
	N	P_2O_5	K_2O
Nutrient Available from Manure	9,000	9,600	9,600
Crop Nutrient Needs/Removal	23,000	13,000	17,000
Whole Farm Nutrient Balance (Available from Manure-Crop Needs)	-14,000	-4,400	-7,400

Note: * The actual amount available to the crop will depend on the storage method, and the time and method of application. The actual amount available may range from 25 per cent to 60 per cent. Figures from Nutrient Needs rounded to nearest 1,000.

Whole Farm Budget Analysis

With this particular example, the nutrients available from the manure are less than the recommended nitrogen needs and crop removal rates for P_2O_5 and K_2O (short 14,000 lbs of N, 4,400 lbs of P_2O_5, and 7,400 lbs of K_2O). Even though a deficit is shown, the farm may not need additional P_2O_5 or K_2O if soil-test levels are above the critical levels for P and K. Also, if soil test levels for P and K are low, more nutrients may be needed than indicated in the Whole Farm Nutrient Budget. What Is the Most Important Nutrient for the Whole Farm Nutrient Balance?

Table 6.8 Manure Production (As Excreted), Estimated Nutrient Content, and Acres to Utilize Nutrients

Animal Type and Size	Size lbs	Annual Nutrients Available for Application in lbs/Animal			Acres Needed per Animal Type and Size to Utilize Nutrients		
		N	P_2O_5	K_2O	@130 lbs/ac	@50 lbs/ac	@50 lbs/ac
					N	P_2O_5	K_2O
Dairy Cattle							
Heifer	150	13.7	3.7	14.6	0.11	0.07	0.29
Heifer	250	21.9	7.3	25.6	0.17	0.15	0.51
Heifer	750	63.0	25.6	80.3	0.48	0.51	1.61
Dairy Milk 40 lbs/day	NA	217.0	82.1	159.9	1.67	1.64	3.20
Dairy Milk 50 lbs/day	NA	228.0	90.2	168.3	1.75	1.80	3.37
Dairy Milk 60 lbs/day	NA	240.0	98.2	176.7	1.85	1.96	3.53
Dairy Milk 70 lbs/day	NA	251.0	106.2	185.1	1.93	2.12	3.70

(Contd...)

Dairy Milk 70 lbs/day	NA	251.0	106.2	185.1	1.93	2.12	3.70
Dairy Milk 80 lbs/day	NA	263.0	114.2	193.5	2.02	2.28	3.87
Dairy Milk 90 lbs/day	NA	274.0	122.3	202.6	2.11	2.45	4.05
Dry Cow	800	89.0	32.0	91.0	0.68	0.64	1.82
Dry Cow	1,000	98.6	45.0	102.2	0.76	0.90	2.04
Dry Cow	1,200	118.0	54.0	124.0	0.91	1.08	2.48
Dry Cow	1,400	137.0	63.0	146.0	1.05	1.26	2.92
Veal	250	11.0	11.0	21.9	0.08	0.22	0.44
Beef Cattle							
Calf	450	38.3	36.5	40.2	0.29	0.73	0.80
High Forage	750	112.2	51.1	91.3	0.86	1.02	1.83
High Forage	1,100	167.0	76.7	131.4	1.28	1.53	2.63
High Energy	750	104.0	51.1	80.3	0.80	1.02	1.61
High Energy	1,100	147.8	76.7	116.8	1.14	1.53	2.34
Cow	1,000	84.9	69.4	94.9	0.65	1.39	1.90
Swine							
Nursery	25	5.5	3.7	3.7	0.04	0.07	0.07
Grow-Finish	150	21.9	18.3	14.6	0.17	0.37	0.29
Gestating	275	13.7	14.6	14.6	0.11	0.29	0.29
Lactating	375	49.3	47.5	51.1	0.38	0.95	1.02
Boar	350	13.7	14.6	14.6	0.11	0.29	0.29

(Contd...)

Sheep							
Sheep	100	11.0	7.3	14.6	0.08	0.15	0.29
Poultry							
Layer (per 1000)	4	1,000.0	985.5	584.0	7.69	19.71	11.68
Broiler (per 1000)	2	629.6	511.0	410.5	4.84	10.22	8.21
Turkey (per 1000)	20	3,449.3	3,942.0	1,971.0	26.53	78.84	39.42
Duck (per 100)	6	1,259.3	1,387.0	1,022.0	9.69	27.74	20.44
Horse							
Horse	1,100	75.3	45.8	44.5	0.58	0.92	0.89

Notes: Values do not include bedding or additional water that may be added.

The actual values can vary + or-30 per cent (recommend actual manure analysis).

Estimated available nitrogen assumes a 25 per cent loss during storage and handling prior to land application. Rotation corn, soybeans, and wheat.

In general, it requires fewer acres to balance the available manure nutrients for the farms nitrogen needs. However, applying manure nutrients at the nitrogen needs rate generally over applies P_2O_5 by two to four times the crop needs. This poses an environmental risk due to the high application of P_2O_5 at one time and the build up of phosphorus in the soil. As phosphorus soil-test levels approach 300 pounds or 150 ppm (Bray-Kurtz P1), the risk of phosphorus run-off in the dissolved and particulate form begins to increase substantially. Also, applying manure nutrients at a nitrogen needs level can very rapidly increase soil-test potassium levels, which can contribute to animal-health problems. A farm can sustain itself for a short time by balancing for nitrogen, but this will rapidly increase soil-test phosphorus and potassium levels. The goal is to operate a livestock enterprise in a manner that can sustain the cycling of manure nutrients indefinitely while minimizing the risk of nitrogen and phosphorus leaching and run-off.

Table 6.8 provides a quick reference to determine the number of acres needed to utilise manure nutrients. When using Table 6.8, read the assumptions made in the notes area.

STRATEGIES TO IMPROVE NUTRIENT BALANCE

Evaluating a livestock systems nutrient balance from a whole farm perspective provides a more complete picture of the driving forces behind nutrient-related environmental issues. The original sources of these nutrient inputs are clearly identified, which in turn suggests management strategies for reducing excess nutrient accumulations. The management strategies presented here should help to reduce nutrient imbalances:

Strategy 1. Efficient Use of Manure Nutrients in Crop Production

By accurately crediting manure nutrients in a cropping programme, the purchase of commercial fertilizer can be reduced or eliminated and the risk to the environment reduced. This practice is especially important to livestock operations with significant crop production and substantial commercial fertilizer nutrient inputs. It may offer greater benefit for nitrogen-related issues due to common use of commercial nitrogen fertilizers as insurance on manure-applied fields.

Strategy 2. Alternative Livestock Feeding Programmes

Opportunities are available for reducing both nitrogen and phosphorus inputs by alternative livestock feeding programmes.

Feeding certain rations can also increase the nutrient content of the manure produced. A Nebraska study observed a greater phosphorus imbalance when high phosphorus rations were used in feedlot feeding programmes. Ethanol and corn processing by-products, attractive feed alternatives for some cattlemen, are typically high in phosphorus concentrations, resulting in finished cattle rations with excess phosphorus levels. Participating operations that used these by-products experienced substantially greater phosphorus imbalance as compared to those operations not utilising these by-products.

Both groups had similar nitrogen balance. Feeding programme choices are likely to impact whole farm nutrient balance, especially for farms purchasing significant quantities of feed from off-farm sources.

In addition to changes in feed rations, some additional options that may reduce purchased feed nutrient inputs include:

- Alternative crops or crop rotations that result in a greater on-farm production of livestock protein and phosphorus requirements.
- Harvesting and storage practices that improve the quality of animal feed and reduce losses.

Strategy 3. Marketing of Manure Nutrients

Marketing of manure creates an additional managed output similar to the sale of crops or livestock products. Several farms throughout Ohio and the United States are now marketing their manure to other farms and for other beneficial uses. Some farms sell their manure based on its nutrient content to other farms needing nutrients. Some livestock and poultry producers have manure-spreading agreements with neighbouring farms to apply manure nutrients on their farms at no cost. Still others market their manure products to non-farm individual users as well as commercial firms, such as landscapers.

***Strategy 4.* Manure Treatment**

In some situations, it may be necessary for animal production systems to consider manure-treatment technologies similar to municipal and industrial-waste treatment systems. Some manure-treatment systems focus on disposal of nutrients with modest environmental impact. For example, treatment systems commonly dispose of wastewater nitrogen as a gas (no environmental impact) or ammonia (some environmental impact).

Other treatment systems enhance the value of manure (*e.g.*, solids separation or composting) to allow alternative uses of the nutrients. Complementary manure-treatment and manure-marketing strategies can contribute to improved nutrient balance. For example, some producers are successfully combining composting (for odour control and volume reduction) with marketing of manure to crop farms and urban clients.

Strategy 5. Changing Crop Rotations

Table 6.9 Nutrient Removal Rates for Specified Rotation and Yield

Rotation/Yields	Average Phosphate (P_2O_5) Removed/Acre/Year	Average Potash (K_2O) Removed/Acre/Year
Corn (140 bu/ac) Soybeans (40 bu/ac)	42	47
Corn (140 bu/ac) Soybeans (40 bu/ac) Wheat (60 bu/ac) with Straw Removed	47	57
Corn (140 bu/ac) Soybeans (40 bu/ac) Wheat (60 bu/ac) with Straw Removed plus three years of Alfalfa (4 tons/ac)	49	128

Changing rotations should include crops that can utilise more nutrients such as wheat/straw removed and forage crops compared to corn and soybeans. Corn and soybeans generally use fewer pounds of phosphate and potash per acre than do wheat with straw removed or hay crops. Table 6.9 illustrates the additional amounts of phosphate and potash that can be utilised by adding more wheat or hay crops to the farming system. This strategy diversifies the cropping system on the farm and better utilises nutrients from the manure produced on the farm.

SUMMARY

Sustaining the livestock and poultry industry requires achieving a balance between environmental concerns and production goals. Manure nutrients must be balanced on the field scale, the farm scale, and the regional scale.

Whole farm nutrient balancing requires management of:

- Nutrient inputs, including fertilizer, feed, animals, irrigation and rainfall, and legumes, with feed and fertilizer usually being the largest contributors.
- Managed nutrient outputs, including meat, milk, eggs, crops, and manure, with the goal of recycling as many manure nutrients through crops as possible.
- Unmanaged nutrient outputs, including soil nutrient accumulation, run-off, and leaching, all of which lead to environmental concerns that can negatively impact an individual operation and, potentially, the entire livestock and poultry industry.

A single strategy will not fit all situations. In many cases, farms will need to implement multiple strategies to achieve whole farm nutrient balance. For farms with sufficient cropland, utilising manure nutrients on the crops is usually best. This strategy should focus on preventing manure nutrient losses and reducing commercial fertilizer inputs to achieve a nutrient balance and gain the greatest benefit from manure.

When the land base is insufficient, livestock dietary options for reducing manure nutrients may be an important strategy for attaining nutrient balance. If neighbouring crop farms or other nutrient users are in the vicinity of livestock operations, manure treatment and marketing of manure nutrients to off-farm customers may be an important alternative.

In recent years, Argentina has experienced a rapid growth in the adoption of reduced and no-tillage systems, especially in dryland regions. This change has been brought about by a deterioration in soil quality and associated crop yields. Many local soils are not suited to the heavy tillage and cropping practices introduced by European settlers.

The Argentine Pampa now has very little natural vegetation. Xerophitic vegetation such as *Prosopis algarrobilla* and *Larrea divaricata* can still be found in the most arid areas. Agricultural practices commenced with the arrival of colonists in the sixteenth century. Ungulates were introduced to graze the grasslands, which have now been mostly re-sown. Very few trees remain except around farmsteads. Wheat was initially cultivated and row-crop production has increased with time. In many parts, grazed pasture was dominant until the 1990s but since, then there has been a marked increase in the cultivation of summer annuals, such as maize, sunflower and soybean. The Argentine Pampa has been recognised as a region with potential for increased production, if soils can be improved.

Crop yields have declined in many areas. These declines have been correlated closely with a reduction in SOM content. This has prompted the need for change in existing land-management practices. The negative effects of heavy tillage on SOM led to the commencement of no-tillage experiments in the 1960s, in an attempt to produce a more sustainable agricultural system. Now some 13 million ha, or about half of the agricultural area in Argentina, is under some form of reduced-tillage system. Fertilization of crops is primarily achieved through the use of inorganic fertilizers, with organic material tending to be conserved for use in horticultural farming systems.

NO-TILLAGE MODELLING STUDIES

Three case studies are reviewed to model soil C under a variety of conventional and no-tillage systems in Tucuman, Catamarca and Cordoba Provinces.

MONTE REDONDO, TUCUMAN PROVINCE

This is a semi-arid area that naturally supports xerophitic vegetation. The agricultural practices include grazed prairie lands and row cropping, the two systems often being rotated. The studied site consists of cropping for seven years followed by four years of prairie grassland. The crop sequence is wheat/ soybean, maize, soybean, wheat/ soybean, maize, soybean, wheat, and four years of prairie. Both conventional tillage and no-tillage cultivation are practised. In the tillage system, disc and chisel plough are used for soil preparation, while the no-tillage system uses the same cropping sequence without tillage.

After an equilibrium phase of grassland and trees, with fire every 60 years, CENTURY was parametised to run with improved prairie grassland from the midnineteenth century. The model predicts that the prairie system is losing C at the rate of 0.06 tonnes/ha/year under the current regime, but at stocks of 55.4 tonnes C/ha, it is overestimating the current measured level of 48.8 tonnes C/ha. Cultivation is scheduled to commence in the 1950s. Fertilizer applications of 110 kg/ha urea begin in 1980. Two scenarios compare the effect of conventional tillage with that of no-tillage. The model predicts a consistent difference between the two systems of less than 3 tonnes C/ha.

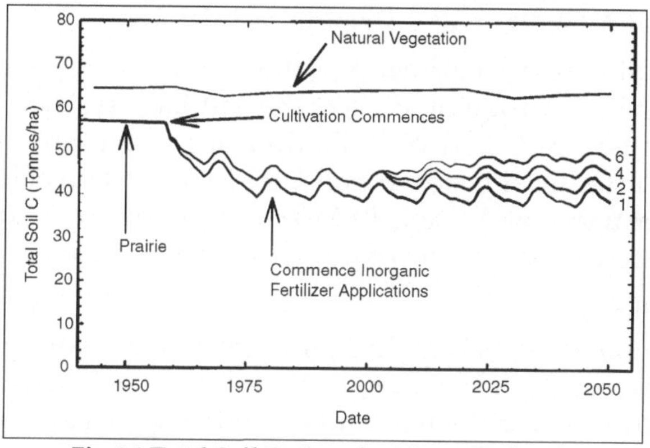

Fig 6.4 Total Soil Carbon for Monte Redondo

This is less than the difference of 6 tonnes C/ha currently measured in the field. Century predicts that this difference between the two systems will be maintained into the future, although both systems continue to lose soil C. The pattern of fall and rise in the soil C curve occurs because the crop part of the rotation results in soil C loss, while the return to prairie increases soil C.

Table 6.10 Total Soil Carbon for Monte Redondo

Scenario	CENTURY			RothC		
	2000	2050	% change	2000	2050	% change
	(tonnes/ha)			(tonnes/ha)		
Prairie	55.40	54.50	-1.6	43.95	43.21	-1.7
Tillage	40.43	39.27	-2.9	32.57	27.58	-15.3
No-tillage	43.64	42.23	-3.2	35.33	33.58	-5.0
5		48.23	4.4		41.89	18.6

Table 6.11 Scenarios for Modelling Land Management Practices, Monte Redondo

Scenario	Land Management
1	Conventional tillage, inorganic fertilizer
2	No-till, inorganic fertilizer
3	No-till, FYM 1.5 tonnes/ha/year, inorganic fertilizer

(Contd...)

4	No-till, green manure 10 tonnes/ha/crop, inorganic fertilizer
5	No-till, FYM 1.5 tonnes/ha/year, green manure 10 tonnes/ha/crop, no inorganic fertilizer
6	No-till, FYM 3.3 tonnes/ha/crop, no inorganic fertilizer

Effect of No-tillage and Organic Additions

Additions of green manure (10 tonnes/ha/crop) or FYM (1.5 tonnes/ha each cropping year) to the no-tillage system both lead to increases in CS. A combination of these inputs without inorganic fertilizer yields a similar result. Cessation of inorganic fertilizer usage and using FYM as a replacement source of N results in the highest rate of CS, 0.1 tonnes/ha/year.

Summary

Both models register the improvement that no-tillage has on soil carbon content. However, if the decline in soil carbon content is to be reversed, additional inputs of organic matter are required—either from FYM or use of green manures in the rotation. An increase in prairie in the rotation will also increase soil carbon stocks.

Santa María River Valley, Catamarca Province

This is an arid region, with mean annual rainfall of 400 mm and temperatures in the ranging of 7-32°C. The native vegetation is xerophitic consisting of creosote bush scrub (*Larrea divaricata*) and trees such as *Prosopis algarrobilla.* In cultivated areas, vines are grown and crops include alternate plantings of red pepper and barley. Measured soil carbon stocks are high in this district at 3.9 per cent.

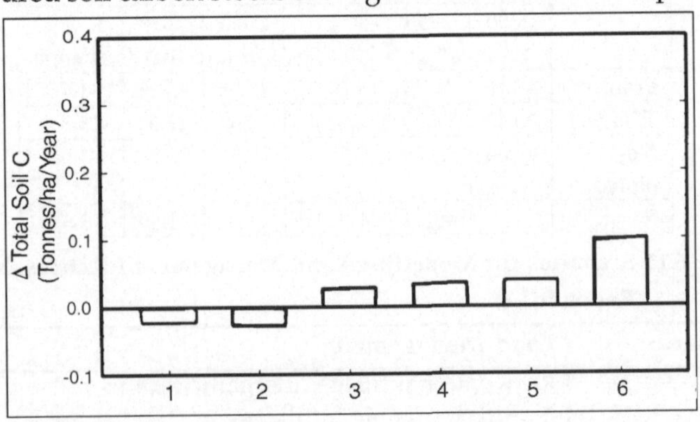

Fig 6.5 Average Annual Change in Total Soil Carbon for Monte Redondo

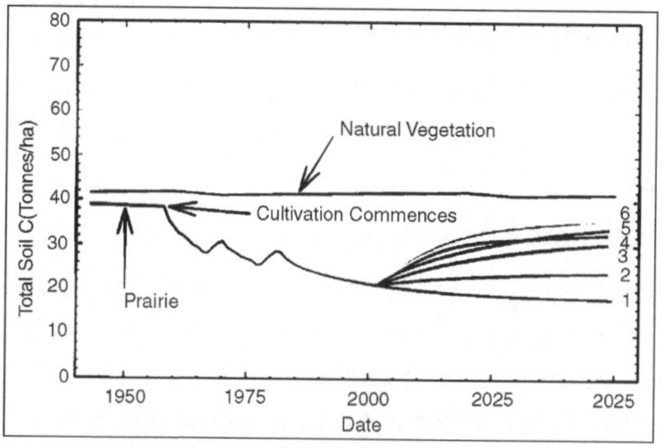

Fig 6.6 Total Soil Carbon for Santa Maria

Table 6.12 Total Soil Carbon for Santa Maria

Scenario	CENTURY			RothC		
	2000	2050	% change	2000	2050	% change
	(tonnes/ha)			(tonnes/ha)		
Prairie	37.11	35.75	-3.7	70.68	74.71	5.7
Tillage	21.39	18.11	-15.3	51.46	47.36	-8.0
No-tillage		24.00	12.2		53.53	4.0
3		30.49	42.5		58.71	14.1

After reaching equilibrium with natural vegetation, Century was run with a prairie scenario from the mid-nineteenth century and cultivation commenced in the late 1950s using conventional tillage (disc plough). A cotton-barley rotation commenced in 1980. Century calculates that soil C had decreased to two-thirds of its initial value by 2000. Measurements in the region confirm declines in soil C in cultivated areas of 33-66 per cent. Therefore, the model estimate is at the top of this range. However, the system is predicted to reach a new steady state and the decline in soil C is estimated to be 3 tonnes/ha over the next 50 years.

RothC, parametised with the higher, measured level of soil C and using quantities of plant inputs calculated from Century shows a proportionately smaller effect of the current cultivation practice on soil C.

Effect of No-tillage

Adopting a no-tillage system not only halts the loss of soil C predicted by Century. It also leads to a low sequestration rate of 0.05 tonnes/ha/ year in the next 50 years. The RothC model is less sensitive to this scenario.

Effect of Organic Additions

Additions of FYM and green manure both lead to marked increases in CS rates of 0.18-0.25 tonnes/ha/year. RothC again shows a smaller effect.

Effect of Inorganic Fertilizer

Replacing inorganic fertilizer with FYM promotes CS (0.22 tonnes/ha/year). Combining the green manure and FYM applications gives the best carbon accrual rate, 0.29 tonnes/ha/year. Inorganic N fertilizer is inefficient owing to the high energy cost of manufacture.

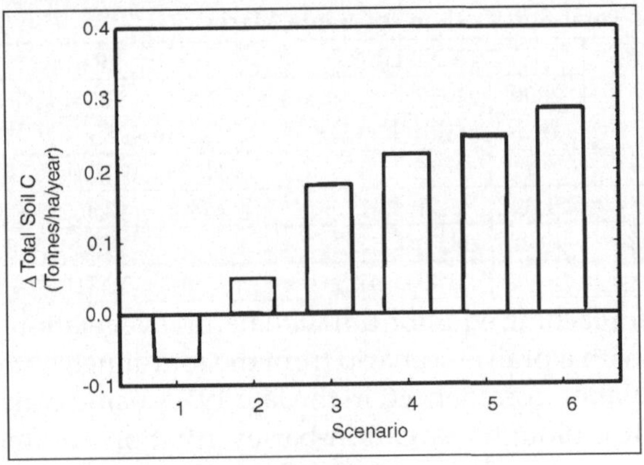

Fig 6.7 Average Annual Change in Total Soil Carbon for Santa Maria

Table 6.13 Scenarios for Modelling Land Management Practices, Santa Maria

Scenario	Land Management
1	Conventional tillage, inorganic fertilizer
2	No-till, inorganic fertilizer
3	No-till, FYM 1.5 tonnes/ha/year, inorganic fertilizer
4	No-till, FYM 3.3 tonnes/ha/crop, no inorganic fertilizer
5	No-till, green manure 10 tonnes/ha/crop, inorganic fertilizer
6	No-till, FYM 1.5 tonnes/ha/year, green manure 10 tonnes/ha/crop, no inorganic fertilizer

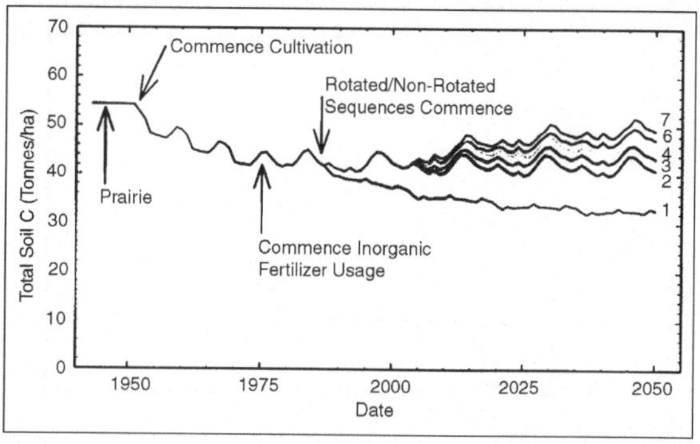

Fig 6.8 Total Soil Carbon for Rotated and Non-rotated Plots

Summary

Both models suggest that adopting no-tillage will halt the decline in soil C. However, to increase CS, higher organic additions are necessary (green manures and FYM), which can be used to replace the inorganic fertilizer applications.

Cordoba Province, Buenos Aires Province, and La Pampa Province

Following an equilibrium period with natural vegetation and subsequent prairie conditions from the mid-1800s, CENTURY was parametised with a cultivation regime commencing in the 1950s. This included a fouryear cropping (wheat-soybean-maize-soybean) and a four-year prairie cycle with inorganic fertilizer applications (100 kg/ha urea) starting in 1985. In 1987, a rotated and a non-rotated cropping system was applied that is similar to cultivation practices occurring in the field. The rotated crop sequence was winter forage-soybean-maize-soybean-wheat-soybean-maize-four years of prairie and winter forage-wheat-soybean-maize-soybean-maize-prairie. The non-rotated crop sequence was similar but without the prairie interludes. Modelled results for the non-rotated crop system show an initial steep fall in soil C to 37 tonnes/ha in 2000 and further losses over subsequent years. RothC estimates a proportionately larger fall from a higher base.

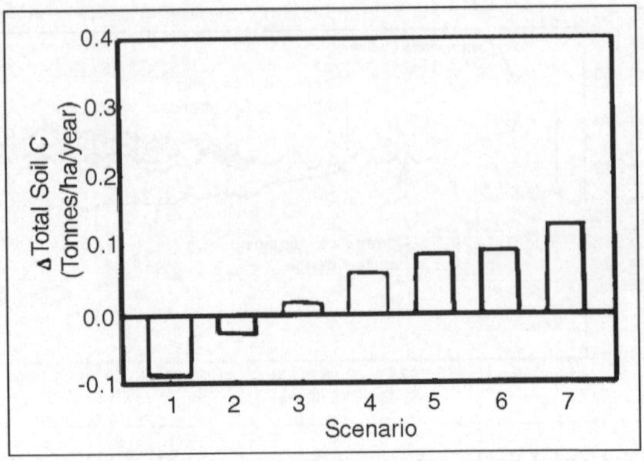

Fig 6.9 Average Annual Change in Total Soil Carbon for Rotated and Non-rotated Plots

The rotated crop-prairie system does not show the same sharp decline in soil C as the non-rotated system did and oscillates around a level of slightly more than 40 tonnes/ha. However, RothC estimates a slightly larger proportionate decline in C for the rotated crop system. Both models calculate smaller differences between the rotated and non-rotated cropping systems in 2000 compared with the difference of 8.5 tonnes/ha measured in the field.

Table 6.14 Total Soil Carbon for Rotated and Non-rotated Plots, Modeled With Century and RothC.

Scenario	CENTURY			RothC		
	2000	2050	% change	2000	2050	% change
	(tonnes/ha)			(tonnes/ha)		
Non-rotated plots	37.22	32.74	-12.0	50.61	41.17	-18.7
Rotated plots	42.47	40.91	-3.7	54.62	49.53	-9.3
4		45.54	7.2		62.86	15.1

Table 6.15 Scenarios for Modelling Land Management Practices.

Scenario	Land Management
1	Non-rotated plots, inorganic fertilizer
2	Rotated plots, inorganic fertilizer
3	Rotated plots, no-till, inorganic fertilizer

(Contd...)

4	Rotated plots, no-till, FYM 1.5 tonnes/ha/year, green manure 10 tonnes/ha/crop, no inorganic fertilizer
5	No-till, FYM 1.5 tonnes/ha/year, inorganic fertilizer
6	No-till, green manure 10 tonnes/ha/crop, inorganic fertilizer
7	No-till, FYM 3.3 tonnes/ha/crop, no inorganic fertilizer

Effect of No-tillage

The adoption of a no-tillage regime for the rotated-plots system increases soil C by 2.5 tonnes/ha in the next 50 years, representing a CS rate of 0.02 tonnes/ha/year. The rate increases to about 0.1 tonnes C/ ha/year if green manures and FYM are used instead of fertilizers.

Effect of Organic Inputs

Additions of green manure and FYM with or without inorganic fertilizer can lead to CS rates of 0.06-0.13 tonnes/ha. Organic material can replace inorganic fertilizer successfully.

Summary

The inclusion of prairie interludes in the cropping system is an important factor for reducing the decline in soil C. However, the models show that no-tillage and organic inputs are required if C is to be sequestered in this system.

Conclusion

The modelling of farm data from three dryland provinces of Argentina shows that carbon stocks have fallen substantially since, the prairies were opened up for cultivation. At all three locations, there have been sharp falls in soil carbon stocks, with losses of about 15 tonnes/ha. However, the adoption of no-tillage systems in recent years has halted these declines and, on their own, resulted in small annual increases in soil C of the order of 0.02 tonnes/ ha/year. Rotations with significant periods for return to prairie grassland (*e.g.*, 4 years in 11) result in further increases in soil C.

The highest rates of sequestration (0.1-0.25 tonnes/ha/year) occur when no-tillage systems also include cultivation of green manures and additions of FYM.

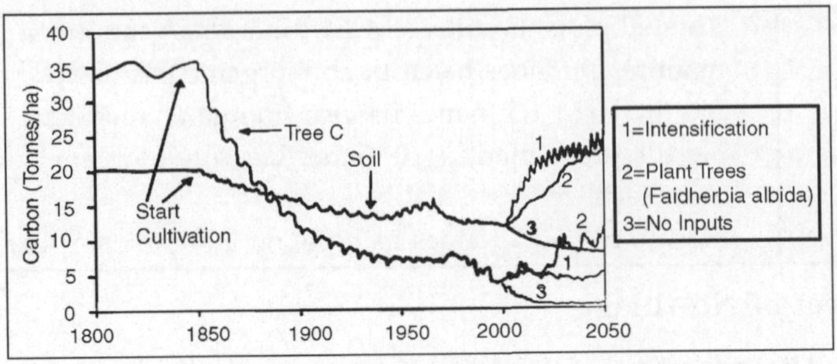

Fig 6.10 Century Model Simulation with a Historic Scenario Based on Undisturbed Savannah Grasslands to the Current Condition and the Impact of Selected Management Practices

The Senegal study area, the "Old Peanut Basin", is located in the west-central part of the country. The climate is semi-arid with annual precipitation ranging of 350-700 mm. Almost all arable land is used for rainfed agriculture, with millet, groundnuts, sorghum and cowpea as major crops.

The rainy season usually lasts from July to September/ October. However, both spatial and temporal variation in rainfall are high and episodic crop failures are not uncommon. The natural vegetation, including *Faidherbia albida* and various other tree species, has become heavily degraded, primarily because of a long agricultural history and increasing population pressure.

As described in Tschakert, CENTURY model simulations suggest that soil C in the study area decreased from 20.1 tonnes C/ ha under a native savannah environment in 1851 to 11.9 tonnes C/ ha in 2001. This indicates an annual loss of soil C of 0.055 tonnes C/ ha/year. Tree C declined from 33.6 tonnes/ha to 4.2 tonnes/ha, corresponding to an annual decrease of 0.2 tonnes C/ha/year.

Under improved management conditions (assuming a 50-year period), soil C could increase by 0.3-13.5 tonnes/ha, or 0.006-0.27 tonnes/ha/year. C gains in trees could be tripled (from 4.2 to 11.8 tonnes/ha), assuming a conversion of croplands to grassland-tree plantations. Given the fact that most of the C gains are achieved in the first 25 years, annual increases for this time period range from 0.02 to 0.43 tonnes C/ha/year, which is higher than the estimates provided by Lal, Hassan and Dumanski.

Under poor management, in this case an annual millet-sorghum rotation with no inputs and permanent browsing and pruning of tree resources, both soil and tree C continue to drop, reaching an absolute minimum level of 7.9 tonnes/ha and 0.6 tonnes/ ha, respectively.

Table lists the various improved management practices with the anticipated changes in soil C over two time periods as discussed by Tschakert. As illustrated, considerably higher gains in soil C can be achieved in the first 25 years, except for the tree-plantation scenario.

However, in some cases, these gains cannot be sustained in the second twenty 25-year period, and losses would have to be expected if no additional inputs occurred. This is particularly true for the fallow scenarios.

Table 6.16 Effects of Land Management Practices or Land Use on Carbon Sequestration Potential in the Old Peanut Basin, Senegal

Technological Options	Change in soil C (tonnes/ha/year) 2001- 2026 (first 25 years)	Change in soil C (tonnes/ha/year) 2027 2050 (second 25 years)
Compost (2t)	0.02	-0.01
Conversion of croplands to grasslands + grazing	0.06	0.02
3-year fallow + 2 tonnes manure in rotation with 4 years cropping	0.14	-0.05
Cattle manure (4 tonnes)	0.10	0.01
Conversion of croplands to grasslands	0.17	0.04
Cattle manure (4 tonnes) + min. fertilizer (250kg on millet; 150kg on groundnuts)	0.12	0.01
Sheep manure (5 tonnes)	0.13	0.01
3-year fallow + Leucaena prunings (2 tonnes) in rotation with 4 years cropping	0.18	-0.05
Conversion of croplands to grasslands with tree protection	0.10	0.04
Sheep manure (10 tonnes)	0.17	0.01
10-year fallow + 2 tonnes manure in rotation with 6 years cropping	0.25	-0.04

10-year fallow + Leucaena prunings (2 tonnes) in rotation with 6 years cropping	0.25	-0.04
Conversion of croplands to grasslands + tree plantation (*Faidherbia albida*)	0.23	0.21
Agricultural intensification (improved millet, manure, Leucaena prunings, min. fertilizer, animal traction, 1-year fallow)	0.43	0.11

The study was undertaken in Northern Kordofan Province in the Sudan, an area dominated by coarse-textured soils of Aeolian origin, locally named *Qoz*. The study site is representative in terms of soils, climate and vegetation type for a large region stretching from the Atlantic coast to the Ethiopian highlands.

The climate is semi-arid with annual rainfall ranging from less than 200 mm in the north to about 350 mm in the south. Land use can be characterized as a gradual increase in intensity with rainfall. In the northern part, only very extensive grasing by camels is possible owing to the lack of permanent water sources. Cultivation of mainly millet and to a lesser extent sesame and groundnuts predominates where rainfall and water resources increase towards the south. Grasing by cattle, sheep and goats is also an important factor in the cultivated parts of the area.

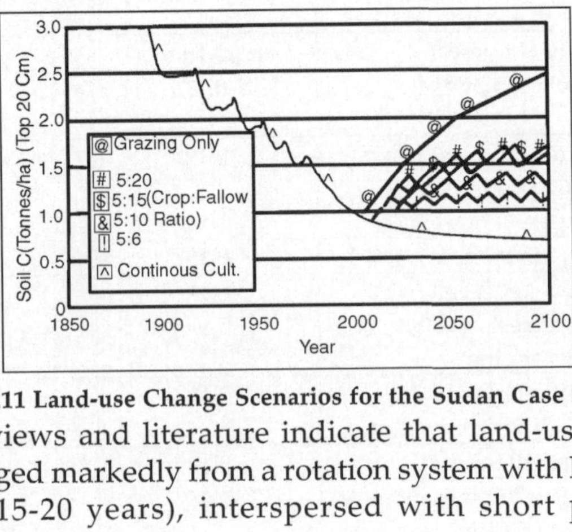

Fig 6.11 Land-use Change Scenarios for the Sudan Case Study

Interviews and literature indicate that land-use practices have changed markedly from a rotation system with long fallow periods (15-20 years), interspersed with short periods of cultivation (4-5 years), to more continuous cultivation in the last three to four decades. In the same period, crop yields have decreased, mainly because of a marked decline of rainfall but to some extent also due to the abandonment of fallow periods. Increased demand for food (as a result of population increase) combined with decreasing yields has forced farmers to extend their cultivated area primarily by reducing fallow periods.

In order to investigate the potential for increasing the soil carbon content through land-management changes, a number of future scenarios were simulated. First, the equilibrium level was established by running the model for 2 000 years with no land use, and then six different land-management scenarios were simulated for the period 2000-2100. The land-management scenarios were: continuous cultivation, crop-tofallow ratios of 5:6, 5:10, 5:15, 5:20, and no cultivation but only grasing.

While the results in Figure come from model simulations, the results in Figure show the result of empirical research, using soil sampling, linking fallow periods to increased levels of SOC. In order to investigate the role of the length of fallow periods, fields in different stages of the crop rotation were sampled and their corresponding SOC levels were determined. The graph verifies to a large extent the model results and shows that there is significant potential for increasing SOC even in these dry sandy soils.

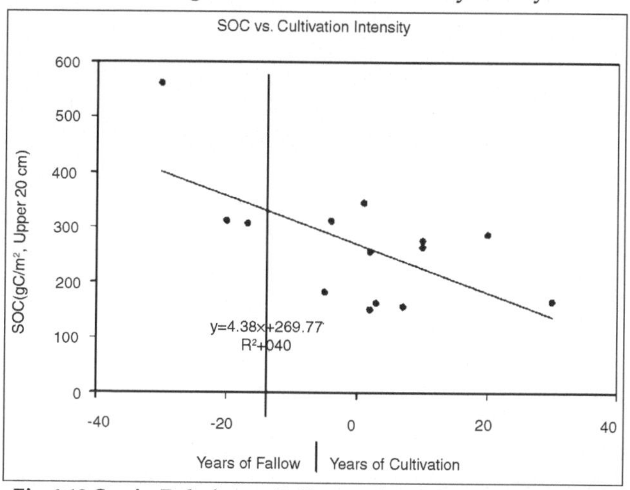

Fig 6.12 Soc in Relation to Fallow and Cultivation History in Fields in Northern Kordofan Province in the Sudan

Figure 6.12 shows that increasing the length of the fallow periods, *i.e.*, decreasing the crop-fallow ratio, causes an increase in the soil carbon content proportional to the ratio (*i.e.*, longer fallow more soil C). A landuse change from millet cultivation to grasing is estimated to increase the soil carbon content from about 1.5 tonnes/ha to 2.5 tonnes/ha in 100 years. This is 82 per cent of the equilibrium phase prior to millet cultivation. If millet cultivation is continued into the future, a further decrease in the soil carbon content is expected to 0.68 tonnes/ha in 2100. Changing the continuous cultivation to crop-fallow ratios of 5:6, 5:10, 5:15 and 5:20 will increase the soil carbon content.

7

Application of Manure

INTRODUCTION

Manure is a valuable resource that needs to be managed effectively and efficiently. Land application of manure should not be considered simply a disposal system. Manure provides nutrients for crops and helps build and maintain soil fertility. Manure can also improve soil tilth, increase water-holding capacity, lessen wind and water erosion, improve aeration, and promote beneficial organisms.

There are three principal objectives in applying animal manure to land:

- Ensure maximum utilisation of the nutrients in the manure by crops.
- Minimize environmental hazards.
- Minimize neighbourhood complaints and concerns.

Available land for manure application is an important consideration for all livestock operations. When planning a new operation or expanding an existing operation, adequate land area for manure application must be included in the plan. A conservative approach in determining the amount of land required is to consider the removal of the nutrient by the harvested crop.

This will ensure that enough land area is available in future years to prevent nutrient buildup in the soil beyond recommended agronomic and environmental levels. In addition to balancing nutrients, best management practices (BMPs) for applying manure to crops must be used. To maximize manure nutrients while minimizing potential environmental impacts and neighbours concerns, manure application must consider nutrient losses during handling and storage, run-off and preferential flow, and timing and rate of application.

NUTRIENT LOSSES DURING HANDLING AND STORAGE

Nitrogen (N) is the nutrient most likely to be lost during handling and storage of manure. Table provides a comparison of N losses due to storage and handling. Nitrogen lost to the atmosphere through volatilisation can be reduced by applying manure when soil and air temperatures are less than 50F and by incorporating manure into the soil within 24 hours of application.

The amount of N available from the manure also depends on the method of application. Injecting, chiseling, or knifing liquid manure into the soil minimizes odors and nutrient losses to the air or as surface run-off.

Table 7.1 Estimated Nitrogen Losses During Storage and Handling

System	Nitrogen Lost in %
Solid Systems	
Daily Scrape and Haul	25–35
Manure Pack	20–40
Open Lot	40–55
Deep Pit (poultry)	25–50
Litter	25–50
Liquid Systems	
Pit under Floor*	15–30
Above-Ground Tank*	10–30
Holding Pond	20–40
Lagoon	70–85

Note: *Indicates losses due to agitation

Table 7.2 Gives Approximate Manure Nutrient Values for Land-applied Manure, Taking into Account Handling and Storage Losses

Animal Type and Storage Type	Estimated Nutrient Content[1]					
	Lbs/Ton			Lbs/1000 Gallons		
	N	P_2O_5	K_2O	N	P_2O_5	K_2O
Dairy Heifer						
Manure Pack	4.2	1.7	5.6			
Open Lot	3.0	1.7	5.6			
Holding Pond				12.1	5.0	16.1
Pit				22.7	8.2	26.6
Dairy Lactating Cow						
Manure Pack	6.9	5.1	5.2			
Open Lot	4.9	5.1	5.2			
Holding Pond				18.9	13.9	14.4
Pit				28.6	18.5	19.1
Dairy Dry Cow						
Manure Pack	5.4	2.4	6.0			
Open Lot	3.9	2.4	6.0			
Holding Pond				14.7	6.4	16.4
Pit				22.1	8.4	21.5
Veal						
Pit	6.2	5.8	11.6			
Manure Pack				3.9	4.1	8.3
Beef Cattle						
Manure Pack	7.9	4.4	6.6			
Open Lot	5.6	4.4	6.6			
Holding Pond	20.0	11.1	17.0			
Pit				29.1	14.1	21.5
Swine						
Manure Pack	6.6	5.9	4.8			
Open Lot	4.7	5.9	4.8			
Holding Pond				18.0	16.0	13.1
Pit	31.8	24.8	20.3			
Lagoon[2]				1.4	3.6	2.9
Sheep						
Manure Pack	6.3	4.5	9.0			
Poultry[3]						
Manure Pack	52.0	72	38			
Horse						
Manure Pack	6.6	3.7	7.7			

IRRIGATION OF LIQUID MANURE AND WASTEWATER

Additional issues need to be considered when applying liquid manure and wastewater. To minimize the risk of run-off or preferential flow, site inspection and preparation are important. The use of manure or wastewater for true irrigation is seldom accomplished because of the relatively small volumes applied and annual application-rate restrictions. Those who desire to irrigate in addition to spreading manure must be certain of an adequate supply of water available for irrigating. Liquid manure from below-ground storage, earth basins, or above-ground storage should not be used to irrigate growing crops as the manure is usually high in ammonia and solids, which can coat and/or burn vegetation. However, wastewater in the second stage of a two-stage lagoon may be dilute enough for irrigation on growing crops.

ADVANTAGES OF IRRIGATING WITH LIQUID MANURE

- Large amounts of effluent can be spread in a relatively short time.
- Waste effluent can be used to supplement irrigation water and to supply plant nutrients where regular crop irrigation is practical.
- Irrigation may cost less than other land-application methods to install, usually is cheaper to operate, and requires less labour for equivalent volumes of application.
- A high degree of automation is possible with some types of irrigation equipment.
- Manure guns (nozzles) can handle slurry directly from confinement and wash-down operations.
- Disposal can often be accomplished when moist soil conditions prohibit conventional hauling. However, do not irrigate on saturated soil, as run-off will occur.
- Less soil compaction occurs with irrigation than with tank wagons.

DISADVANTAGES OF IRRIGATING WITH LIQUID MANURE

- An adequate application area may not be within economical pumping distance of the waste source.
- Odors and spray drift (aerosols) are possible, depending on location and management.

- Additional water supply and/or large storage basins may be required for dilution, flushing the equipment, and safe efficient use of wastewater.
- Run-off is a potential pollution hazard.
- Without good management, annual application of nutrients may be excessive and cause nitrate pollution in ground water. Operator error or mismanagement is often a cause of liquid manure flowing through subsurface drains to surface waters of the state.
- Over-application or a too-high application rate may result in irrigated wastewaters entering the drainage tile and surface water supplies. See section on Preferential Flow for best management practices to prevent liquid manure in subsurface drains.

RUN-OFF AND PREFERENTIAL FLOW

Excess nutrients in soil may impact the environment when they are dissolved or eroded and transported to surface or ground water supplies. Excess phosphorus (P) in surface waters can result in eutrophication and a decrease in oxygen levels in the water that leads to loss of animal life. Nitrogen compounds may harm human health and are toxic to fish. In addition, erosion of manure may contaminate water supplies with pathogens such as *E. coli* or *Cryptosporidium*. Minimizing these environmental risks requires using best management practices when applying manure to cropland. While most transport of P occurs with the erosion of soil sediment, it can also leach if soil P levels are too high. Phosphorus accumulates in soils if applied in quantities greater than those removed by crops. Accumulation of P in the soil can be measured by soil-testing.

To minimize potential N run-off, manure applications should not provide more available N than what is needed by the succeeding crop. For corn, the determination of total available N should include credits for any contributions of the present or preceding crop, any N fertilizer added, and available N provided by previous manure applications.

MINIMIZING RUN-OFF

Run-off potential is affected by numerous factors, some of

which are fixed by the nature and location of the field, while other factors can be altered through management.

Run-off potential must be determined on a site-by-site basis by evaluating:

- *Location of receiving stream*: Run-off to streams is more likely when the field selected for manure application is bordered by a stream or other surface water rather than separated from surface water by a field, pasture, wooded area, or other suitable buffer strip.
- *Slope steepness and complexity*: Run-off is more likely from fields sloping steeply and evenly towards a stream than fields with a gentle or no slope. Priority areas for land application of manure should be on gentle slopes located as far as possible from waterways. When manure is applied on more steeply sloping land or land adjacent to waterways, other conservation practices should be installed to reduce run-off potential.
- *Soil and weather conditions*: Run-off is more likely when applied on frozen, saturated, or compacted soils.
- *Soil type*: Soils with low infiltration rates and/or soils with limited water-holding capacity are more likely to promote run-off than soil types that absorb and retain large quantities of water.

Management factors that can alter the potential for manure run-off into a stream include:

- *Buffer strips*: Properly designed buffer strips along stream banks adjacent to sites with high-run-off potential can absorb the run-off, reducing the amount of manure entering a stream.
- *Soil surface condition*: A rough or covered soil surface reduces run-off compared with soil surfaces that are smooth or have very little residue cover.
- *Manure characteristics, application rate, and application method:* Liquid manure applied at rates greater than the soil infiltration rate or water-holding capacity can promote run-off. Injection or incorporation of applied manure reduces chances of run-off.
- *Pre-existing nutrient status of the soil*: Greater quantities of nutrients are likely to move off fields when soils have

a high soil test level rather than lower soil test levels.

- *Surface and subsurface drainage*: Proper installation and routine maintenance of surface and subsurface drainage systems can reduce the potential for run-off or direct discharge of manure from land application.
- *Setback distances*: To protect the environment and minimize neighbour complaint, manure should not be applied adjacent to sensitive areas. Table specifies these minimum setback distances. Consider additional application setback distances from neighbours and environmentally sensitive areas such as sinkholes, wells, gullies, ditches, surface inlets, or rapidly permeable soil areas. Setback distances may need to be increased due to local conditions such as a pond or lake used for a water supply or recreational area or a stream that is already impaired by excess nutrients.

Table 7.3 Minimum Recommended Setback Distances from Sensitive Areas

Minimum Setback Distances for the Application of Manure and Other Organic By-Products.			
Type of Sensitive-Setback Area	**Setbacks Based on Methods of Manure Application**		
	Surface Application	**Winter Application Frozen or Snow-Covered Soils**	**Surface Incorporation Within 24 Hours OR Direct Injection**
Residences/Private Wells down slope from the application area.	100 ft.	200 ft.	100 ft.
Sinkholes	300 ft.	300 ft.	100 ft.
Pond or Lake	35-ft. Vegetative Barrier, with the remaining 100-ft. setback	35-ft. Vegetative Barrier, with the remaining	35-ft. Vegetative Barrier

	in non-vegetative setback	200-ft. setback in non-vegetative setback	
Streams Ditches Surface Inlets	35-ft. Vegetative Barrier, OR 100-ft. setback in non-vegetative setback, OR 35 ft. in non-vegetative setback	200 ft.	None
Grassed Waterway	35 ft.	200 ft.	None
Field Surface Drains	35 ft.	200 ft.	None
Public Wells	300 ft.	300 ft.	100 ft.
Developed Springs	300 ft. upslope	300 ft. upslope	300 ft. upslope
Public Surface Drinking-Water Intake	300 ft.	300 ft.	300 ft.

MINIMIZING PREFERENTIAL FLOW

Liquid manure applied to fields that are tile drained presents a risk of the liquid manure following preferential flow paths, such as worm holes, cracks, old root channels, directly to subsurface (tile) drains. Some of these channels connect directly to subsurface drains and are a direct route to surface water. Anything that promotes good drainage will increase the risk of preferential flow of liquid manure to subsurface drains. The greatest area of concern is two to three feet horizontally from the tile line.

Most problems occur with liquid manure having a low solids content. As the per centage of solids in the manure decreases (high water content), viscosity (stickiness) decreases, and the manure flows more easily to tile lines. Typically, liquid swine manure from a lagoon is 95 per cent water, 5 per cent solids, and liquid dairy manure is 97 to 98 per cent water and only 2 to 3 per cent solids. Milkhouse wastes and egg wash are highly diluted and have even less solids. However, gray water from all these systems may have very high BOD (biological oxygen demand), ammonia, and soluble phosphorus levels that can be deadly to fish and aquatic organisms if it reaches surface water without treatment.

Injection of the liquid manure can actually make the situation worse, especially if sweep-type shovels are used on the injection equipment. Ideally, the liquid manure should be applied at low rates, under low pressure, evenly across the soil, and either at or slightly below the soil surface to allow the liquid manure to infiltrate the soil, be absorbed by the soil, and be treated.

Strategies to minimize the movement of liquid manure to subsurface drains include:

- Avoid applying manure before or after a heavy rain. Monitor manure storage capacity to prevent applying when conditions are not acceptable. Applicators have a limited number of days to apply manure when environmental conditions (soil, wind, rain, moisture) are optimal, so it is advisable to contact custom applicators up to a year in advance of the anticipated manure application. Use crop rotations that will allow timely manure applications throughout the growing season.
- Reduce liquid manure application rates. No more than 13,000 gallons or 0.5 inch of liquid manure per acre should be applied in one application. Multiple smaller applications of 7,000 gallons or 0.25 inch of liquid manure per acre allow for more effective absorption by the soil than one large single application. Reduce manure application rates if wet soil conditions exist. Do not apply a greater volume (gallons per acre) than the upper eight inches of soil can hold.

- Maintain subsurface drainage lines and drainage outlets. Do not apply liquid manure if subsurface (tile) lines are flowing with water. In areas with springs, subsurface lines flow continually, and soil moisture conditions should determine application. Monitor drainage outlets before, during, and after manure applications for signs of discharge. If manure is in the tile flow, plug the outlets or capture the flow immediately. Provisions for tile plugging or the capture of tile flow must be planned and available prior to application. Follow emergency manure spill procedures if a spill occurs.
- Minimize preferential flow by tilling the soil at least three to five inches when large macropores like cracks, earthworm burrows, or root channels exist. If manure is injected, use straight points spaced closely to reduce the volume of liquid manure coming out of each knife point. For soils with cracks more than six- to eight-inches deep at the time of application, till before application or do not apply until adequate moisture seals the cracks.
- Calibrate manure application equipment before application. Over application of liquid manure is a major cause of liquid manure in surface water.
- Maintain minimum setback distances from surface water. Minimum Recommended Setback Distances from Sensitive Areas. Minimum suggested setback distances vary depending on weather, soil conditions, and time of year. For winter manure application, setback distances are doubled.
- Install in-line tile flow controls that can plug tile flow or have inflatable tile plugs available during application. Control structures allow for easy monitoring and cleanup of manure in tile lines but need to be installed properly to prevent leaching around the control structure. Allow enough time for the liquid manure and surface water to absorb into the surrounding soil before removing the plug.

Record keeping is important in preventing manure in subsurface (tile) lines. Document application rates, set-back distances, weather and soil conditions, subsurface drain lines and outlets, broken tile, sink holes, and other potential problems to help prevent environmental problems in the future. Have emergency equipment (backhoe, bales of straw, pumps, etc.) available if a liquid manure spill occurs.

RATE AND TIMING OF APPLICATION

Using best management practices to determine the rate and timing of manure application will optimize crop production, reduce environmental risks, and minimize neighbours concerns. The factors that most often limit the amount of manure that should be applied to cropland are existing soil-fertility levels, manure nutrient content and concentration, crop nutrient needs, run-off potential, slope, leaching potential, and site limitations.

Hauling distances, distance to surface water, distance to neighbours, distance to water wells, the potential for manure leaching to tile lines, and other factors can also limit how and when manure is applied.

ASSESSING NUTRIENT NEEDS

Manure application rates must balance manure nutrients with crop nutrient requirements as discussed. In general, only about one-third of the organic nitrogen in animal manure is available to crops during the year it is applied, and the remaining two-thirds, residual organic nitrogen, becomes part of the soil organic matter over time (Table). Phosphorus and potassium from manure application are considered as available as commercial fertilizer during the first growing season. The limiting nutrient, usually nitrogen (N), phosphorus (P), or potassium (K), will determine the amount of manure applied. The limits on the amount of phosphorus that can be applied are those that most often limit any further manure applications. Since, it is difficult to balance manure nutrients, additional fertilizer applications may be needed to balance the crops nutrient needs.

Table 7.4 Estimated N Availability of Manure Based on Time and Application Method

Available Nitrogen Per cent		Time of Application	Days Until Incorporated
NH_4	Organic N	Date	Days
50	33	Nov-Feb	< 5
25	33	Nov-Feb	> 5
50	33	Mar-April	< 3
25	33	Mar-April	> 3
75	33	April-June	< 1
25	33	April-June	> 1
75	15	July-Aug	< 1
25	15	July-Aug	> 1
25	33	Sept-Oct	< 1
15	33	Sept-Oct	> 1

Notes:
a. The calculations are for all animal manures. It is assumed that 50% of the organic N in poultry manure is converted to NH_4 rapidly and is therefore included in the NH_4 column for calculating available N.
b. Incorporation is the mixing of manure and soil in the tillage layer. Disking is usually enough tillage for conserving nitrogen availability.
c. The 75% available nitrogen (NH_4) is based on the nitrogen being used in the year it is applied. If the nitrogen is carried over to the following year, then 25% available nitrogen should be used.

Evaluation of nutrients is needed to determine accurate manure application rates. Plant tissue analysis should be done on a regular basis to monitor the nutrient balance of the crop. Soils receiving manure should be tested for plant-available nutrients before manure application. Also, the manure should be tested. Application rates of manure are determined by using the results of these tests. Soil should be tested at least every five years. If the grower has applied P and K over the years, soil-test levels may be in the adequate to high range. It is important to note that manure contains more K than magnesium (Mg) and after many years of continued manure application, the ratio of K to Mg may be too high for optimum crop growth. To adjust the ratio, additional Mg may have to be added as dolomitic limestone, if the soil pH indicates an acid soil. Adding high levels of manure may also increase soluble salts in the soil and reduce plant stands.

APPLICATION RATES

Accurate application rates for manure should consider soil

moisture to reduce the risk of run-off, and equipment should be calibrated to obtain the desired application rate. In addition, understanding the effects of manure application practices on nutrient levels in the soil and methods to minimize nutrient buildup is essential to minimizing environmental impacts.

The manure utilisation and cropping systems used on a particular field should maintain Bray-Kurtz P1 soil-test P levels at no greater than 80 pounds per acre or 40 ppm of P in the top eight inches of soil. Special precautions should be taken if manure is applied where Bray-Kurtz P1 levels already exceed this level.

If manure must be applied to fields with levels greater than 80 pounds per acre or 40 ppm P, the following recommendations should be considered:

- No additional phosphorus fertilizer should be used on such fields.
- Crops should be monitored for nutrient deficiencies and nutrient imbalances using plant-tissue analysis.
- Manure should be applied in quantities such that the long-term P level at the soil surface does not increase appreciably. If the manure is surface-applied or incorporated to a shallow depth (within the tillage depth), ensure that applications supply no more N than will be removed by the crop in the following year and no more P than will be removed in the next one to three years.
- Adequate soil and water conservation should be practiced to control soil erosion and minimize run-off.
- Manure application is not recommended for crop production where the Bray-Kurtz P1 level in the top eight inches of soil exceeds 300 pounds per acre or 150 ppm P.
- If more than 250 pounds of P_2O_5 are applied at one time from manure, the manure should be incorporated within 24 hours to a minimum depth of 4 inches.

One approach to planning manure application rates is to apply two or three years of P or K in one year. Often the goal with manure applications is to meet the nitrogen needs of the crop first. However, with this goal, phosphorus and potassium needs are often exceeded.

Table 7.5 Multiple-Year Manure Nutrient Applications

Applying 2-3 Years P_2O_5 or K_2O Crop Requirements with one application of manure.	
Due to the nutrient composition of most livestock manure, one can usually apply two or three years worth of P_2O_5 and K_2O while not over applying nitrogen for the succeeding crop. Applying manure on a two- to three-year cycle also reduces the risk of soil compaction and reduces the acres needed in any one year. The following example demonstrates how one can apply enough manure in one application to meet the P_2O_5 and K_2O crop needs while not over applying nitrogen for the succeeding crop:	
EXAMPLE:	
•	CornSoybean Rotation. Manure injected in soybean stubble in November prior to Corn.
•	Crop Fertility Needs: Nitrogen Corn 1 year (145 lbs/ac); 3 years P_2O_5 (152 lbs/ac); 3 years K_2O (152 lbs/ac).
•	Swine Pit Manure Analysis: N = 34.7 lbs/1,000 gal; P_2O_5 = 33 lbs/1,000 gal; K_2O = 27 lbs/1,000 gallons.
Apply enough manure to meet P_2O_5 needs for three years:	
•	Applying 5,000 gallons per acre will provide: Nitrogen @ 130 lbs/acre (application losses deducted); P_2O_5 @ 165 lbs/acre, and K_2O @ 135 lbs/acre.
Results:	
*	Additional nitrogen will need (15-20 lbs/ac) to be applied to meet the corn yield goal; no additional P_2O_5 will be needed for three years; and 15-20 lbs/ac of K_2O will be needed during the three-year period.

Multiple year applications of P_2O_5 may be applied at a rate equal to the recommended P_2O_5 application rate or estimated P_2O_5 removal in harvested plant biomass in a single application.

When such applications are made, the application rate should:

- Not exceed the recommended nitrogen application rate for the succeeding crop, or:
- Not exceed the estimated nitrogen removal in harvested plant biomass (for legumes) during the year

of application when there is no recommended nitrogen application, or:

- Not exceed a phosphate (P_2O_5) application rate of 250 lbs/ac per year, or:
- Not exceed the potash (K_2O) application rate of 500 lbs/ac per year.

Applications of P_2O_5 above 250 lbs per acre are not recommended. However, if P_2O_5 concentrations in the liquid manure exceed 60 lbs P_2O_5 per 1,000 gallons or 80 lbs P_2O_5 per ton for solid manure or other bio-solids rates higher than 250 lbs per acre may need to be applied due to limitations of the application equipment. P_2O_5 applications should not exceed 500 lbs per acre of P_2O_5 during one year from manure or other bio-solids.

When P_2O_5 applications exceed 250 lbs per acre, the following are recommended:

- Do not apply to fields with a soil test exceeding 100 ppm P, Bray-Kurtz P1 test or equivalent.
- Immediately inject or incorporate manure three to five inches deep.
- Do not apply on either frozen or snow-covered soil.
- Do not apply additional P_2O_5 for a minimum of three years on land below 40 ppm P, Bray-Kurtz P1 test or equivalent, and for a minimum of five years above 40 ppm P, Bray-Kurtz P1 test or equivalent.
- Apply P_2O_5 at rates that meet application rate criteria for both nitrogen and potash.

Other limitations to manure application include volume limitations relating to how much manure can physically be applied to the soil at one time. With low nutrient concentrations in liquid manure, large volumes of liquids may be applied and yet the crop nutrient needs may not be met simply because the liquid is mostly water and has low concentrations of nutrients. Application of liquid manure above the available water capacity of the soil can create a run-off risk and leaching to tile or underground water Manure application equipment on wet soils can cause significant soil compaction.

APPLICATION RATE CONSIDERATIONS FOR LIQUID MANURE AND WASTEWATER

To prevent run-off or preferential flow, hourly application rate should be matched to the infiltration rate and permeability of the soil. The design application rate should be conservative and usually lower than the maximum allowable rate in the Ohio Irrigation Guide, because the soil intake rate may be reduced over time by the solids and salt content in some wastes. When recommended application rates vary with soil depth, use the value at eight inches of depth, which is less than that at the surface.

Limit the one-time application volume to an amount that will bring the soil to field moisture capacity. Limit application rates to the water-holding capacity of the top eight inches of the soil profile. The amount applied must not exceed the holding capacity of the soil at the time of application. Inspect fields for broken tiles and other possible short-circuit routes that could result in a direct discharge of manure to drainage tile and surface-drainage ditches. If rapid infiltration to subsurface drainage tile is a problem, consider light disking, shallow chisel plowing, or other tillage operations before irrigating manure and wastewater to improve the soils infiltration and holding capacity. Lower application rates and multiple passes with irrigation equipment may also be necessary.

TIMING OF APPLICATION

Crop rotation and seasonal variations affect when manure should be applied. In a corn-soybean rotation, the fall, after the crops are harvested, is the best time to apply manure. Generally, the fall has drier weather so compaction problems can be minimized. Fieldwork can also be accomplished in the fall to incorporate the manure. Sometimes manure can be applied in the spring if weather conditions and time permit. Usually, manure cannot be applied during the growing season, although some liquid systems may permit side-dress applications of manure to corn.

If wheat or oats are in the rotation, the manure can be applied in the late summer months. For wheat or oats, winter and spring applications of manure to the growing crop are not recommended. Forage crops (grasses and legumes) are capable of using more nutrients than row crops (corn, soybeans, and wheat).

A planned grasing system can substantially reduce the manure that must be handled and applied and can reduce costs and environmental hazards. Manure can be applied to hay or pasture land but smaller applications are need to preserve forage quality and to limit crop damage. It is preferable to apply manure on pastures and hayland soon after cutting or grasing before re-growth has occurred. Also, limit the application rate to avoid salt damage and/or coverage to the pasture and hayland.

APPLICATION OF MANURE ON FROZEN SOIL

Application on frozen and snow-covered soil is not recommended. However, if manure application becomes necessary on frozen or snow-covered soils, only limited quantities of manure should be applied. Frozen soil means that the soil surface is frozen so that manure cannot be injected into the soil profile.

If winter application becomes necessary, applications should be applied only if ALL the following criteria are met:

- Application rate is limited to 10 wet tons per acre for solid manure with more than 50 per cent moisture and five wet tons for manure with less than 50 per cent moisture. For liquid manure, the application rate is limited to 5,000 gallons per acre.
- Applications are to be made on land with at least 90 per cent surface residue (*e.g.*, good quality [grass] hay or pasture field, all corn grain residue remaining after harvest, all wheat residue cover remaining after harvest).
- Manure should not be applied on more than 20 contiguous acres. Contiguous areas for application are to be separated by a break of at least 200 feet. Utilize areas for winter manure application that are the farthest from streams, ditches, waterways, and surface water and use areas that present the least run-off potential.

- Increase the application setback distance to 200 feet minimum from all grassed waterways, surface drainage ditches, streams, surface inlets, and water bodies. Minimum suggested setback distances are doubled for winter application of manure to frozen or snow-covered soils. This distance may need to be further increased due to local conditions.
- Additional winter application criteria for fields with significant slopes of more than 6 per cent. Manure should be applied in alternating strips 60 to 200 feet wide generally on the contour, or in the case of contour strips on the alternating strips.

APPLICATION OF MANURE ON STEEP SLOPES

Manure should not to be applied to cropland with slopes of more than 15 per cent or to pastures/hayland with slopes of more than 20 per cent unless one of the following precautions is taken:

- Immediate incorporation or injection with operations done on the contour, UNLESS the field has 80 per cent ground cover (residue and/or canopy).
- Applications are timed during periods of lower run-off and/or rainfall.
- Lower rates can be applied by using split applications (separated by rainfall events). Apply no more than 10 wet tons/acre for solid manure, or 5,000 gallons/acre for liquid manure.
- The field is established and managed in contour strips with alternate strips in grass or legume.

Timing of manure application should also consider the potential impact on neighbours. To develop and maintain good neighbour relations, give adequate notice of the intent to land-apply manure and do not haul and spread on weekends, holidays, or important events. Good communication is key to minimizing neighbours complaints.

MANURE APPLICATION RECORD KEEPING

Keep good field records of soil and manure test results, yields achieved, and nutrients applied (time, form, rate, and method of application). Records should be kept for a period of five years or longer (metals analyses and associated application rates and locations should be maintained permanently):

- Quantity of manure produced and its appropriate analysis.
- The last three soil-test results.
- Dates, analysis, and amounts of manure that are land-applied.
- The dates and amounts of manure removed from the system due to feeding, energy production, or export from the operation.
- Manure application methods.
- Crops grown and yields (both yield goals and measured yield).
- Other tests, such as determining the nutrient content of the harvested product.
- Calibration of application equipment.
- Soil moisture and weather conditions (temperature and wind direction) at the time of application.
- Consider annual reviews to determine if changes in the nutrient budget are desirable (or needed) for the next planned crop.

SAFETY ASPECTS

Liquid-manure-handling systems can reduce labour requirements in confinement facilities but can introduce hazards due to the toxic effects of manure gases, manure run-off into streams, and offensive odors. Outdoor and open-top manure storages can also be potential drowning sites. Under certain conditions, manure gases may be fatal to both humans and livestock. Poor ventilation or ventilation failure in a tightly constructed building can threaten the health and life of animals. To protect humans, manure storage areas should first be ventilated or, where necessary, self-contained breathing equipment should be used when entering manure storage areas. Increased gas levels above manure pits in buildings can also slow the daily gain of animals.

DANGEROUS SITUATIONS

Dangerous situations resulting from manure gases are associated with four main gases that are produced as manure decomposes.

Ammonia (NH_3) is released from fresh manure/urine and during decomposition. Ammonia levels tend to be high in buildings with litter, solid floors, or scrapers because manure spread over the floor increases ammonia release. Heated floors also increase ammonia release. Ammonia is very soluble in water, so liquid-manure systems release less ammonia. High pH levels cause more ammonia to be released into the air.

Concentrations in ventilated hog buildings have been measured as high as 35 ppm (slightly irritating to eyes and nose) and in unventilated buildings at 176 ppm, which produces extreme discomfort. At 100 to 200 ppm, ammonia causes sneesing, salivation, and loss of appetite for hogs. Prolonged exposure may lead to respiratory diseases in people and animals.

Carbon dioxide (CO_2) is released through livestock respiration and manure decomposition, and by unvented heaters. Most of the gas in bubbles coming from stored manure or lagoons is CO_2. Death of animals in closed confinement buildings following a ventilation-equipment failure (such as that caused by a power failure) is due in part to excessive CO_2. Vigourous agitation of stored manure can release a slug of CO_2.

Hydrogen sulfide (H_2S) is the most toxic gas from liquid manure storage. Dangerous concentrations can be released by agitation of stored liquid manure. Concentrations reaching 200 to 300 ppm have been reported in a building a few minutes after starting to pump out a storage pit and have been as high as 800 ppm during vigourous agitation. Exposure to 200 ppm for 60 minutes will cause headaches and dizziness; 500 ppm for 30 minutes will cause severe headache, nausea, excitement, or insomnia. High concentrations of 800 to 1,000 ppm cause immediate unconsciousness and death through respiratory paralysis unless the victim is moved to fresh air, and artificial respiration is immediately applied. Even the characteristic rotten-egg smell of H_2S does not give adequate warning because the sense of smell is rapidly fatigued by H_2S, and high concentrations do not give proportionately higher odour intensity.

Methane (CH_4) is generated in the decomposition of manure under strict anaerobic (no air) conditions. It is insoluble in water and lighter than air and will accumulate in stagnant air corners in the top of enclosed pits or rooms. CH_4 is not toxic, but high concentrations can produce an asphyxiating atmosphere. Concentration in confinement housing is normally well below the lower end of the 5 per cent to 15 per cent explosive range (Table). Explosions attributed to methane have occurred around manure storage pits.

Table 7.6 Characteristics and Effects of Gases Produced in Decomposing Manure

Gas	Odour	Density	Exposure Limits	Effects
Ammonia (NH_3)	Pungent	Lighter than air	10 ppm	Irritation to eyes and nose. Asphyxiating at high levels.
Carbon Dioxide (CO_2)	None	Heavier than air	5,000 ppm	Drowsiness, headache. Can be asphyxiating.
Hydrogen Sulfide (H_2S)	Rotten-egg smell	Heavier than air	10 ppm	Toxic: Causes headache, dizziness, nausea, unconsciousness, death.
Methane (CH_4)	None	Lighter than air	1,000 ppm	Headache, asphyxiant, explosive in 5% to 15% mixture of methane with air.

FATALITIES

Fatalities may occur when people enter manure-storage structures, including covered manure pits, and are probably due to CO_2 and H_2S because these gases are heavier than air. Caution should also be taken when agitating manure as the asphyxiating effect of NH_3, CO_2, and CH_4 combined with the toxic effect of H_2S could be fatal.

Another potential risk, especially for children, is drowning in a pit, storage tank, and earthen storage basin or lagoon. Failure and breakage of slats or covers on pits and lack of protective barriers or railings around pit openings during agitation can lead to accidents. Push-off platforms or ramps (piers) can be a site for the tractor scraper and driver to tumble into an open storage structure or lagoon. Crusts on earthen storage basins can be a problem, especially for children, as they may appear capable of supporting ones weight, but they are not.

PRECAUTIONS

When designing manure structures and systems, think safety. When operating or managing manure equipment, think safety.

Consider the following major safety points when designing and operating manure equipment, structures, or systems:

- Do not enter a manure pit unless absolutely necessary and then only if:
  - The pit is ventilated beforehand.
  - You have supplied air to a mask or a self-contained breathing apparatus.
  - You are wearing a safety harness and attached rope with at least two people standing by who are capable of pulling you out.
- When agitating a manure storage, always have at least one additional person available who can go for help if you are overcome by gases.
- Properly designed and operated ventilation systems can reduce the concentration of gases within the animal zone, improving animal performance. Poorly designed or improperly adjusted ventilation air inlets may actually increase gas concentrations at the animal level.
- When possible, construct lids for manure pits or tanks and keep access covers in place. If an open ground-

level pit or tank is necessary, build a fence around it and post with Keep Out and Danger Manure Storage signs.

- Get help before attempting to rescue livestock or people that have fallen into a manure-storage structure.
- Build railings alongside all walkways or piers of open manure storage structures.
- Permanent ladders on the outside of above-ground tanks should have entry guards locked in place, or the ladder should be terminated above the reach of individuals.
- Never leave a ladder standing against an above-ground tank.
- Construct permanent ladders on the inside wall of all pits and tanks, even if covered. Use of non-corrosive material is important.
- Fence in earthen storage basins and lagoons and erect signs: Caution Manure Storage. The fence is also needed to keep livestock away from these structures. Additional precautions include a minimum of one lifesaving station equipped with a reaching pole and a ring buoy on a line.
- All push-off platforms or piers need a barrier strong enough to stop a slow-moving tractor. It should be low enough so that livestock cannot slide underneath.
- If possible, move animals before agitating manure stored in a pit underneath a building. Otherwise, if the building is mechanically ventilated, turn fans on full capacity when beginning to agitate, even in the winter, or if the building is naturally ventilated, do not agitate unless there is a brisk breeze. Watch animals closely during agitation, and turn off the pump at the first sign of trouble. The critical area of the building is where the pumped manure breaks the liquid surface in the pit.
- If manure storage is outside the livestock building, provide a water trap or other anti-back flow device to

prevent storage gases from entering, especially during agitation.

- If an animal drops over, do not try to rescue it. You might become a victim of toxic gases. Turn off the pump, and do not enter the building until gases have had a chance to escape.
- Due to the possibility of explosion and fire, dont smoke, weld, or use an open flame in confined, poorly ventilated areas where methane can accumulate. Electric motors, fixtures, and wiring near manure-storage structures should be kept in good condition.
- Keep all guards and safety shields in place on pumps, around pump hoppers, on manure spreaders, tank wagons, power units, etc.

Take time now to review your total manure management system from a safety viewpoint. Think through each step of the collection system, storage or treatment units, and the land application phase. Are there dangerous areas in construction or operation? If so, make them safe. It could save your life or the life of a loved one or employee.

EMERGENCY ACTION PLAN

Every livestock farm should have an Emergency Action Plan in place. What is an Emergency Action Plan and why have one? It is a well-thought-out, simple, basic, common-sense plan that will help those involved with an emergency to make the right decisions.

A plan is needed:

- To meet the requirements of many states for a plan.
- To keep humans and livestock safe.
- To rectify an emergency situation.
- To protect the environment.
- To teach family members and employees.
- To record for future situations (prevention, law suits, etc.).
- To ensure notification of proper authorities.

SAFETY EQUIPMENT

Locate first-aid or rescue equipment near the manure-storage area. Clearly mark a wall closet or box and store the equipment inside it. Make occasional checks to ensure the equipment is in good order and has not been removed. Post the phone number of the local fire department/rescue squad on the wall beside the box and also near the telephone.

Personal protective equipment that includes air packs and face masks, nylon lines with snap buckles, and a parachute-type body harness with D rings for attaching lines can be obtained from supply sources of industrial safety and hygiene equipment. Look in the yellow pages under safety, safety equipment, industrial safety and hygiene, or safety supplies. These supply sources can also provide information on monitoring or measuring devices used to test hazardous atmospheres. Be sure to specify the gases you are dealing with when asking for or purchasing equipment.

Familiarize yourself, your workers, and your family with the proper operation of all safety equipment. Local medical (rescue) teams can assist in this education.

IMMEDIATE FIRST-AID PROCEDURES

- Do not attempt to rescue a victim from a hazardous gas situation unless you are protected with a supplied air-breathing apparatus.
- Have someone telephone for an emergency medical (rescue) squad, informing them there is a victim of toxic (manure) gas asphyxiation.
- If the victim is free from the immediate area of danger and there is no personal threat to your life, take the following steps:
  - With the victim on his or her back, check for breathing, then give four quick mouth-to-mouth breaths and check for a pulse.
  - If there is a pulse, continue mouth-to-mouth breathing every five seconds (12 per minute).
  - If there is no pulse, start CPR (cardiopulmonary resuscitation) immediately. When the emergency squad arrives, the victim should receive a high

concentration of oxygen at the scene and in transport.

If members of your family have not taken CPR and first-aid training, enroll them in a course at your earliest opportunity. Periodic refresher courses in CPR are recommended.

VICTIMS OF DROWNING

- Rescue the person from the drowning situation using standard water-rescue technique.
- If the victim is unconscious or not breathing, use standard CPR procedures.
- Have someone telephone for an emergency medical (rescue) squad, informing them there is a victim of drowning.

8

Manure Handling

INTRODUCTION

When properly managed, manure nutrients can be a valuable resource for the farm; however, failure to manage these nutrients wisely may hurt farm income, land, water, and air resources. Presented here is an overview of the market and non-market costs and benefits that producers should address before investing in a manure-handling system. Estimates of the market costs and benefits are provided for representative operations.

Often, manure storage is necessary to efficiently utilize available nutrients for growing crops and to minimize adverse environmental impacts. Yet, storage is only one component of a manure-handling system. Considered here are the costs of owning and operating a manure-handling system. A manure-handling system is defined as the structures, equipment and labour required to handle and/or store manure for an extended period of time. The benefits of a manure-handling system are realized when manure nutrients are used as a replacement for commercial fertilizers. Manure, depending upon the animal, contains 70 to 80 per cent of the nitrogen, 60 to 85 per cent of the phosphorus, and 80 to 90 per cent of the potassium fed. Recycling these nutrients through growing crops can benefit the farm operation and the environment.

OFF-SITE IMPACTS

Properly managed feedlots, manure stacks, and manure spreading can minimize run-off and the magnitude of other off-site impacts. Nutrient rich waters promote excessive algae and aquatic plant growth which can reduce wildlife habitat, recreational activities, and can increase downstream water-treatment costs. In addition, bacteria and other pathogens may enter surface waters with run-off, causing health concerns for end users.

The cost for water treatment alone can be staggering. For example, a water filtration plant capable of minimizing the potential contamination of Giardia cysts and viruses in the source waters for New York City was estimated to cost between $3 and $8 billion to build and an additional $300 million to operate each year.

Over application of manure nutrients is costly for animal producers. Excess nutrients beyond the crops need provides no additional yield response, and increases the risk these nutrients will move off-site. Manure nutrients should be applied where they can be fully utilized by growing crops, increasing yields and reducing potential risks to the environment. The value of manure, as a nutrient resource, is only realized when manure is substituted for fertilizer. To do so, can increase farm profit.

Manure handling systems are unique to each operation and the individual management style. There are many factors to consider before selecting a system. Is there enough equipment and labour available to operate the system at critical times of the year? How well does the system control odors? Can this operation best handle manure in liquid or solid form? What is the initial capital requirement? How will changes to the current manure-handling practice impact the demand for labour and equipment, and ultimately farm profits?

CHARACTERISTICS OF A MANURE-HANDLING SYSTEM

Four general characteristics define a manure-handling system. These are structural, equipment, nutrient, and labour. Three of these characteristics structural, equipment, and labour define the costs of owning and operating the system. Nutrient characteristics define the benefit of manure when utilized as a substitute for purchased fertilizer.

Table 8.1 Characteristics of a Manure-Handling System.

Characteristic	Attribute
Structural	• Type of structure. • Design size (volume). • Cost of construction. • Cost of secondary structures. • Useful life. • Interest rate. • Insurance.
Equipment	• Type of equipment. • Size of equipment. • Cost of equipment. • Hours of use. • Cost to own and operate. • Hauling distance. • Safety. • Custom applicators.
Labor	• Hours required. • Cost per hour. • Peak demand. • Availability.
Nutrient	• Concentration. • Crop rotation. • Land available and soil nutrient levels.
Other considerations	• Odor management. • Hauling distance. • Cost of current system. • Management requirements. • Future needs. • Manure contracts. • Type of bedding used. • Good neighbour issues.

STRUCTURAL CHARACTERISTICS

Each system begins by sizing the manure storage structure. Not only do the number and type of animals determine the volume requirements, but also the total desired or needed storage period, the inclusion or exclusion of feedlot run-off, milking centre wastewater, silage leachate, rainfall, availability of land, as well as other factors.

Your local Natural Resource Conservation Service can provide guidelines to accurately size a manure storage structure to meet current needs as well as planning for the future. In some cases, push-off ramps, reception pits, liners, and other secondary structures must be built to make the system operational. These additional structures add to the initial cost of the manure storage structure and impact the total cost of owning and operating the system.

EQUIPMENT CHARACTERISTICS

The storage structure is only one aspect of the manure-handling and storage system. Each system requires equipment to move manure into and out of the holding structure. It is necessary to include the cost of owning and operating this equipment as a cost of the manure-handling system. Ownership and operating costs for the equipment include depreciation, interest, insurance, housing, and taxes as well as maintenance, repair, fuel, oil, and labour. The sum of these costs, on an annual basis, is the annual cost of owning and operating the manure-handling system.

Each system requires equipment to transport manure from the storage structure to the field for application and nutrient utilisation. Some systems require a substantial investment in specialized equipment while others may more fully utilize existing equipment. An important question to ask Is there sufficient equipment available to handle manure in a timely manner? For example, to move 1.4 million gallons of manure from a holding pond with a 3,000-gallon tanker will require more than 450 loads.

Can your operation meet this kind of demand on labour and equipment when demand on labour and equipment is already high? For example, manure hauling prior to planting and/or during harvest to fully utilize available nutrients. Alternatively, custom applicators specialising in manure application are available for hire. However, several important questions must be addressed. First, can a quality applicator be hired when the farm needs to apply manure nutrients? Will manure nutrients be applied when and where they are needed and in an environmentally responsible manner? Is it cost effective?

LABOUR CHARACTERISTICS

Labour requirements must be understood prior to investing in a system. Storing manure for extended periods can provide many advantages, but it also presents many challenges. For many operations, manure is frequently collected, and transferred into storage. This routine continues for months until the storage structure becomes full, at which point, dedication of labour and equipment is required to empty the holding structure.

Expanding upon the previous example, hauling two loads of manure per hour will require over 230 hours per year to haul 1.4 million gallons of manure. That is more than four weeks of continuous hauling each year. Furthermore, these labour requirements may coincide with spring planting, summer forage production, fall harvest, and fit within a narrow window of suitable soil moisture. Can your operation function under these constraints? Will additional labour be required and if so, is it available?

NUTRIENT CHARACTERISTICS

Contained within the manure holding structure is a reserve of nutrients that can reduce the need for purchased fertilizer. A laboratory analysis may be used to determine the nutrient content of manure in the holding structure. Local Extension offices have guidelines for collecting and shipping manure samples for nutrient analysis. Alternatively, guidelines for average manure nutrients can be obtained from this publication. Using this information, the total quantity and value of each nutrient can be determined for the volume of manure produced.

To maximize the value of manure, it should be applied at rates that meet the nutrient requirements of growing crops, assuming other factors such as a limiting nutrient, slope, leaching, and run-off potential are not more restrictive. Generally, the limiting nutrient is phosphorus, but it may be nitrogen or potassium in some situations. Nutrient utilisation plans should be developed and followed to maximize the benefits of manure and minimize the potential for environmental damage.

CONSIDERATIONS

ODOURS

Manure, especially odours associated with manure, readily move off-site, and in some situations become a nuisance to those downwind. These impacts are real and can negatively impact the farms long-term viability. This impact can be measured as a change in perceptions of how well the farm is managed, quantified as legal fees accumulate defending civil action suits, or as a change in the value of neighbouring properties. Regardless, the producers may pay awards from a civil action suit and incur the costs associated with implementing odour-reduction technology. Odour-reduction technology can be costly, depending upon the extent of odour control desired. Generally, it becomes more costly to remove increasingly more and more odour.

HAULING DISTANCE

Hauling distance is influenced by factors such as land availability, crop rotation and nutrient need, current soil nutrient levels, slope, and the potential for manure entering water resources. In addition, distance from neighbours and public-use facilities should be considered. These factors should be assessed to determine which fields are used for manure application, which will determine the distance manure is hauled.

Hauling distance may be a significant factor influencing the manure-handling system decision. As animal density per acre of land increases, manure must be moved greater distances if soil nutrient levels are to remain in balance. Generally, liquid manure can be handled efficiently when moved relatively short distances. However, solid manure has a higher nutrient density and can be hauled greater distances more economically than dilute liquids.

MANURE-HANDLING SYSTEMS

Outlined here is a daily hauling system that handles manure

as a semi-solid. This system is followed by three alternative manure-handing systems, which differ by the volume of manure and wastewater stored and the method used for manure application. Two of the liquid systems use an earthen holding pond to store animal manure and all wastewater sources. These two systems differ primarily by the total capacity of the storage structure desired. The fourth system handles manure as a semi-solid and diverts wastewater from other sources into a settling basin with a vegetative filter area for treatment. *This analysis includes the cost of the secondary structures needed to make each system work and is sized for 100 lactating dairy cows weighing 1,400 lb each, on average.*

Daily Haul

Often, a daily haul system will have little or no manure storage capacity beyond what accumulates in the barn and/or in the spreader. Handling manure from this type of confinement system requires a tractor, box spreader, and loader. Manure is scraped directly into the box spreader and transported to the field for spreading daily or very frequently. The total cost of owning and operating this type of system for 100 lactating dairy cows is about $18,000 per year which includes a vegetative filter area to treat feedlot run-off, silage leachate, and milking centre wastewater.

Table 8.2 Estimated Cost for Two Daily Haul Systems

	Daily Haul (365 Day)	Daily Haul (180 Days)
Tons of manure hauled	2,700	1,350
Total cost	$18,000	$15,800
Nutrient value	$12,100	$12,100
Net cost	$5,900	$3,700
Cost per cow per year	$59	$37

One hundred lactating dairy cows generate about 2,700 tons of manure (including bedding) each year. The nutrient value of this manure is estimated to be about $12,100 when valued at commercial fertilizer rates. In 2001 Ohio farmers paid $0.29/lb of nitrogen, $0.25/lb of phosphorus, and $0.14/lb of potassium. The net cost (cost of owning and operating equipment plus the cost of owning and operating settling basin less the value of the manure nutrients) for this type of manure handling is expected to be about $6,000 per year ($59 per cow per year).

Often dairy operations of this size will keep cows on pasture for six months of the year. This practice reduces the annual cost of manure handling. For these operations, about 1,350 tons of manure would be hauled during periods when animals are confined (six months). During the time animals are on pasture, it is assumed that all manure generated during this period is distributed on the pasture, and the nutrients are utilized by the growing crop. Any supplemental fertilization of the pasture accounts for the addition of the manure nutrients. This system is expected to have an annual cost of owning and operating of about $3,700 per year ($37 per cow per year).

Manure and Wastewater Storage

Alternatively, animal manure can be stored for an extended period of time and applied when growing crops can more fully utilize available nutrients. Three systems are presented that utilize varying manure storage strategies.

Table 8.3 Manure Handling and Storage System Overview

365-Day Liquid-Manure System (1,400,000 gal)	**180-Day Liquid-Manure System (700,000 gal)**	**90-Day Solid-Manure System (675 ton)**	**365-Day Daily Haul (2,700 ton)**
Designed for: • Animal manure • Milking centre wastewater • Feedlot runoff • Silage leachate • Rainwater	Designed for: • Animal manure • Milking centre wastewater • Feedlot runoff • Silage leachate • Rainwater	Designed for: • Animal manure Holding pond: • Feedlot runoff • Milking centre wastewater • Silage leachate • Rainwater	No storage beyond barn accumulation and spreader capacity Settling basin + filter area: • Milking centre wastewater • Silage leachate • Feedlot runoff

Two liquid manure-handling systems store all sources of manure and wastewater in an earthen holding structure. These two systems differ by the number of days animals are confined which affects the total number of days of storage needed during the year. One liquid system is designed for a total confinement facility desiring 365 days of storage for all animal manure and sources of wastewater (feedlot run-off, silage leachate, and milking centre wastewater). The second liquid-manure system is designed for a pasture-based dairy which confines animals for about 90 days of the year.

The final system handles manure as a solid, semi-solid, and excludes all sources of water. The covered holding structure excludes rainwater. Feedlot run-off, milking centre wastewater, and silage leachate are diverted into a holding pond which is periodically land applied. The cost of these secondary structures are included in this analysis.

NUTRIENT BENEFITS

Recycling excreted nutrients is one benefit of manure that is easily quantified. A simple manure analysis or estimate of available nutrients can be used to value manure using current market prices of the nutrients it will replace. In Table 8.4 the expected quantities of each nutrientnitrogen, phosphorus, and potassiumcontained in each manure storage structure (one-time capacity).

The total value of these nutrients are based upon the average price paid by Ohio farmers for commercial fertilizer: $0.29, $0.25, and $0.14 per pound of nitrogen, phosphorus, and potassium, respectively. Animal manure nutrients can vary considerably and are dependent upon the animal and the feeding programme. Laboratory testing of animal manure is recommended to better quantify available nutrients.

The nutrient benefits of manure nutrients are only realized when they are used as a substitute for purchased fertilizer. In many situations, excess nutrients have accumulated in the soil from years of over application. Nutrients beyond what are required for the growing crop will provide no additional yield. These excess nutrients should be considered an additional cost of production.

That is, these nutrients could be better utilized where a crop response would be achieved by replacing additional purchased nutrients. Here it is assumed that manure nutrients are fully utilized, and the value of this nutrient resource reduces the cost of owning and operating the manure-handling system.

If manure nutrients are applied on soils already saturated with nutrients, the nutrient benefit will not be realized. Thus, the cost of owning and operating the manure-handling system increases.

Table 8.4 Summary of Nutrient Benefits by System*

Nutrient	365-Day Liquid System	180-Day Liquid System	90-Day Solid System	365-Day Daily Haul
Total Nitrogen (lb)**	30,300	15,150	7,575	30,300
Total P_2O_5 (lb)	15,200	7,600	3,800	15,200
Total K_2O (lb)	17,200	8,600	4,300	17,200
Total value	$12,100	$6,050	$3,025	$12,100

Note: * Assumes a one-time capacity or annual value for daily haul.

** Assumes 50% of total nitrogen is organic, and one-third of organic nitrogen is available in the year it is applied.

Equipment Characteristics

Manure nutrient utilisation requires that manure be land applied at critical times of the year. Ideally, this is when a growing crop is available to utilize available nutrients. This, in turn, requires that equipment be available for spreading. Generally, manure is transported to the field by tractor-drawn spreaders, but manure can be pumped directly by means of irrigation equipment to a drag-line system. Tractor-drawn transport generally takes less equipment than does the drag-line. As more equipment is required, the annual cost of owning and operating the equipment also increases.

Table 8.5 Equipment Requirements and Land Application Options

Liquid Manure (broadcast)	Semi-Solid Manure (broadcast)	Liquid Manure (injection)
• Liquid tanker • Tractor 1 • Tractor 2 • Utility tractor • Chopper pump	• Box spreader • Tractor 1 • Skid loader	• Drag-line • Tractor 1 • Tractor 2 • Utility tractor • Chopper pump • Toolbar • Irrigation equipment

COMPARISON OF MANURE HANDLING SYSTEMS

The bottom line for most decisions is what it will cost. Table summarizes the costs and benefits of each system outlined, using different storage capacities and land-application practices for a 100-cow dairy. Outlined are the annual costs associated with owning and operating the manure-holding structure, any secondary structures necessary to make the system operational, and equipment necessary for land application. A range of values is given for those systems that are designed for less than one year storage; these values are based on the one-time capacity and annual use of the system. In other words, some operations may only store manure to satisfy the one-time capacity each year while others may use the system for year round confinement. For example, a solid manure system sized for 90-day storage is expected to cost about $19,000 per year, while this same system used for 365 days is expected to cost about $22,500 per year. Basically, this reflects the cost of equipment and labour needed to move the manure out of storage three additional times each year.

For each system, equipment has been identified (Table), and the cost of owning and operating this compliment has been estimated. Again, a range of values is presented and represents the estimated cost of owning and operating the equipment for the design capacity and for 365 days of storage. For example, the yearly cost of the equipment necessary to make the 180-day liquid-manure storage systems operational is expected to be between $20,500, if the system is filled only once per year, and $25,500, if it is filled and emptied twice per year.

Each manure-storage structure contains some quantity of manure nutrients. The value of these nutrients is shown and is calculated based on estimated nutrient content for the one-time volume of manure in storage. Manure nutrients were valued as commercial fertilizer and reduce the cost of owning and operating each system (system maintenance + annual cost of structure + application cost-nutrient value/ 100 cows = per-cow cost of owning and operating the system).

Shown is a range of nutrient values reflecting the one-time storage capacity of the structure through full utilisation, *i.e.*, store manure 365 days a year. The value of manure nutrients assumes these nutrients are fully utilized by the growing crop. If manure nutrients are applied in excess of the crop needs and there is no benefit to storing these nutrients in the soil profile, the value of these nutrients is greatly reduced. In some situations, manure applied where soil nutrients are in excess will increase the potential that these nutrients will leach, move off-site, and become an environmental hazard.

Table 8.6 System Summary

	365-Day Liquid System	180-Day Liquid System	90-Day Solid Manure	365-Day Daily Haul
One-Time Capacity[1]	1.4 M gal	700K gal	675 ton 2,700 ton	
System Maintenance[2]	$500	$275	$817	$100
Annual Cost of Structure[3]	$3,200	$1,900	$6,300	$1,150
Application Costs/Storage Capacity				
Tanker/spreader[4]	$27,000	$20,500-$25,500	$11,900-$15,400	$16,700
Drag-line[5]	$28,000	$22,400-$24,618	NA	NA
Custom applicator[6]	$8,400	$4,200-$8,400	$1,300-$5,200	NA
Nutrient Value/Storage Capacity				
All nutrients (N,P,K)[7]	$12,100	$6,050-$12,100	$3,025-$12,100	$12,100
Cost to Own and Operate Storage and Handling System per Cow/Storage Period				
Tanker/spreader[8]	$186	$156-$166	$104-125	$59
Drag-line[9]	$196	$125	NA	NA
Custom applicator[10]	$0	($15) - $3	$2-$54	NA

Notes: 1. Maximum one-time design capacity of storage structure.

2. Annual estimated cost to maintain structure (2 per cent of total cost).

3. Annual ownership cost includes interest, depreciation, and insurance. Includes setting basin and vegetative filter area required for milking centre wastewater, feedlot run-off, and silage leachate; system includes liquid holding pond for milking centre wastewater, feedlot run-off, and silage leachate (46,000 gal/90 day).

4. Assumes a 5,000 gallon tankers is used; equipment compliment identified in table 24. Each load requires 30 min. to load, travel to field, unload, and return to storage structure.
5. Drag-line uses irrigation equipment and continues application of manure.
6. Custom applicator is available and provides all equipment neccassary for land application.
7. Manure nutrients are valued equal to commercial fertilizer and valued at $0.29, $0.25 and $0.14 per pound of nitrogen, phosphorus, and potassium, respectively. Value for animal manure nutrients based upon one-time capacity and 365-day storage.
8. Estimated cost of using tractor-drawn 5,000-gallon liquid tanker or 12-ton box spreader.
9. Estimated cost of using a drag-line system to apply liquid manure.
10. Based upon $6/1,000 gal or $1.50/ton of manure applied in an environmental sound manner.

The liquid-manure system stores all sources of wastewater, run-off, silage leachate, and rainfall in an earthen holding pond. One system has storage capacity for 365 days and is expected to cost upwards of $200 per cow per year, depending on the land application option used. Conversely, the liquid system that has 180 days of storage is expected to cost upwards of $166 per cow per year.

The semi-solid manure-handling system excludes all additional sources of water, including rainwater. However, this system has a high capital-investment requirement because of the building materials used, increased water exclusion requirement (roof), the need for a secondary wastewater treatment structure, and associated handling equipment. This system stores manure for 90 days and has an expected cost of about $125 per cow per year, depending on land-application options and the extent the structure is utilized.

INSECT AND PEST CONTROL

Managing manure properly with good sanitation is the best way to control flies on livestock farms. The fly life-cycle takes about two weeks, one for the larvae to develop and one for the larvae to pupate prior to emerging as an adult fly. Manure is a favourite place for flies to lay their eggs, but wet feed and seepage from silos also are prime areas for fly breeding. Preventing water leaks and seepage from outside sources into the animal housing, feed distribution, and feed storage areas can help to minimize fly breeding. Barnyards should be well drained, and vegetative growth around the facilities should be kept low to minimize areas where flies might breed.

Manure should be removed from animal quarters frequently and stored in facilities that will minimize fly breeding. Many dairy farms use free-stall housing and avoid bedded manure packs, thus less manure remains in the animal housing area for infestation by flies. Also, many dairy farms have changed to inorganic bedding (*e.g.*, sand) in free stalls, which is less desirable for fly breeding than organic bedding. Most swine and poultry operations are enclosed, and manure does not build up in the housing area for swine.

The use of lagoons and pits for manure storage prevents flies from laying eggs in the manure, because there is an inadequate amount or type of biomass to provide ova position stimulant (stimulant that must be present for flies to lay eggs). For stacked manure, moisture should be less than 30 per cent to discourage fly breeding. Coverage of this storage area will limit moisture from precipitation, reducing the risk of run-off and fly infestation.

Fly larvae can still develop in manure spread on the field, but this can be minimized by spreading the manure when conditions are not wet and by thinly spreading the manure to reduce drying time. For totally enclosed animal housing and handling facilities, the structure must be designed to limit entry of flies either by providing airtight facilities or screen doors and windows where appropriate.

An Integrated Pest Management (IPM) programme needs to be implemented on every farm. The IPM can consist of a wide array of practices to monitor and control pests. The use of biological and chemical controls needs to be considered in the IPM programme. Products are available to control flies on the animals, and pesticides are available for use in the areas of the facility not occupied by the animals.

ECONOMIC INJURY LEVEL

The threshold density for determining when to control flies depends on the area where the control measures will be taken. In general, the threshold at homes is very low, and control actions are taken with few flies. The threshold density of the house fly at waste-management sites may be 150 flies per fly paper per 30 minutes.

House flies can be monitored with baited traps, sticky ribbons, or spot cards on livestock facilities. Spot cards are three-inch by five-inch white index cards attached to a fly resting surface. A minimum of five cards should be placed in each animal facility and left in place for seven days. A count of 100 or more fecal or vomit spots per card per week indicates a high level of fly activity.

PESTICIDE PROGRAMME

For successful fly control, organize a control programme that best fits your farm. A single pesticidal product rarely gives the most effective and economical control. It is normally best to use a combination of pesticide applications, such as residual wall sprays, space or aerosol sprays, baits, and larvicides, during the fly season. Because fly resistance is always a possibility, it is best to rotate different chemical-family insecticides, especially when one group begins to lose effectiveness. Consider alternating synthetic pyrethroids with organophosphates. Do not wait for heavy fly populations. It is much easier and less expensive to prevent heavy fly buildup than to control heavy fly populations after buildup. As fly populations begin to build up, take time to treat and treat regularly.

FEED ADDITIVES

Oral larvicides or insecticides given through the feed prevent the development of flies in manure. Certain states do not recommend the use of oral larvicides or insecticides given through the feed. Oral larvicides are usually fed from May through September. Animals must consume the recommended dosage for the feed additive to be effective. They are not effective against adult flies. Oral larvicides should be used in conjunction with good manure sanitation. A supplemental fly-control programme is needed where flies breed in manure from untreated animals or other organic sources. Feed additives often are not the answer to fly control unless used extensively. All feces must be treated within an area to effectively reduce fly populations. The required treatment area must be several miles across because flies can move readily from herd to herd over an area of several miles within one or two days. This treatment is usually more effective in controlling horn flies and is not very effective against face flies. Feed additives do not control housefly and stable-fly larvae that develop in sites other than fresh manure. Follow label directions and precautions when using oral larvicides and insecticides in the feed.

MANURE TREATMENTS

Manure treatment (larviciding), applied directly to the manure surface to control fly maggots, is discouraged because beneficial arthropods associated with manure can be killed. Also, adding extra moisture to the manure can result in additional fly breeding with increased fly resistance to insecticides. Effort should be made to keep all manure as dry as possible, less than 30 per cent moisture, to greatly reduce or halt fly breeding. However, if manure cannot be kept dry or removed on a weekly basis, it is possible to use manure sprays.

Use a hoe or a trowel to sample the larvae present in manure before treatment. Hot spots with high larvae and egg counts can be spot-treated. Apply treatment sprays to wet the manure surface but do not soak. Repeat applications as necessary but not more often than once every seven days. Avoid widespread use of manure sprays, but treating the edges of a covered manure stack may be helpful. Do not apply where animals or birds can come in contact with treated manure. Follow mixing and application directions before use. Do not apply treated manure to crops not approved on the insecticide label.

BIOLOGICAL CONTROL

Biological control is the reduction or mitigation of pests and pest effects through the use of natural enemies. Naturally occurring parasites (wasps) and predators (beetles and mites) in dry manure accumulations undisturbed over long periods of time attack and kill fly larvae and pupa stages. To encourage the establishment of natural enemies, farm operators should avoid excessive use of residual insecticides, especially synthetic pyrethroids. Fly parasites are tiny wasps that kill fly pupae. They attack only fly pupae in manure and are so small (similar in size to gnats) that they go unnoticed by humans and livestock. Farmers can make frequent releases of small numbers of these beneficial wasps to augment their existing populations of beneficial insects. The wasp females seek out fly pupae, kill them, and then lay eggs within the dead pupae. These eggs hatch and mature into a new generation of beneficial parasitic wasps.

Fly parasites are useful for the control of house flies, stable flies, blowflies, and many other fly species. They cannot sting or bite humans or animals. Advantages of fly parasites are ease of application and reduced need for chemical pesticides. Using fly parasites also prevents buildup of resistance to chemical pesticides, prevents immature flies from maturing to adult flies, and is cost-effective. With application, there is no equipment, no mixing, and no feed additives. Simply sprinkle them out of the bag onto the manure or staple the opened bag to posts or rafters near areas where fly breeding is a problem.

Although fly parasites are an integral part of a good Integrated Pest Management (IPM) programme, insecticides will still play a role in your control programme. Insecticide use should be restrained. If biological control agents are to significantly contribute to fly-control programmes, they must be integrated with chemical control, manure management, and moisture control to best enhance the beneficial populations. If you have a serious adult fly problem now, it is recommended that you use natural pyrethrins to get the adult population under control before introducing fly parasites. Permethrin is highly toxic to parasites and should be used with caution.

Larvicide use should also be limited, because most larvicides will kill beneficial insects as well. However, if you have a hot spot of heavy fly larvae, larvicides can be used without inflicting much damage on the overall beneficial insect population. Insect

Growth Regulator (IGR), such as cyromazine (Larvadex) approved for poultry operations, does not affect beneficial insects. It only kills the fly larvae. This is the only larvicide that does not harm beneficial insects and can safely be applied to the breeding site without fear of destroying the beneficial insect populations. Sticky paper, tapes, or ribbons and bait traps will help reduce the adult fly population without hurting the natural enemies. Weekly removal and spreading of manure disrupts the fly life-cycle and prevents new adults from emerging in and around the barn. Removing the manure also helps the parasitic wasps, which find fly pupae more easily if the depth of the manure is relatively shallow. Leaving some surface manure behind when you clean out will keep the new generation of wasps in the barn.

Flies have the ability to produce more eggs, produce a new generation in a much shorter period of time, and travel much greater distances than fly parasites. Consequently, it is best to release small amounts of fly parasites throughout the fly season rather than just one large release. Make weekly releases of 250 wasps per animal from mid to late May to August or September. Some farmers practice the release of 200 parasites per milking cow or 1,000 parasites per calf. Commercial farms that generate large quantities of manure should import fresh parasites weekly. For small farms, choose a biweekly, triweekly, or monthly schedule. Many companies who sell parasites advertise their products in farm magazines but not all of them sell the right species adapted for the Ohio climate. Dairy farmers should purchase Muscidifurax raptor and avoid Nasonia vitripennis.

Existing data indicates that in the Midwest the recommended species are as follows:

Fly Parasite Species	Flies Attacked
Muscidifurax zaraptor	**House fly pupae preferred. Also attacks stable flies.**
Comments: *Muscidifurax zaraptor* stays nearer the surface where house fly pupae are more commonly found. Populations peak in summer, often July and August when the fly population peaks. This species is often the dominant parasitoid species in Midwest feedlots. Considered best against house fly pupae. Early season spring releases show promise. *M. zaraptor* moves out evenly from release sites, killing off concentrated house fly populations within 50 feet of release sites.	

(Contd...)

Muscidifurax raptor	House and stable fly pupae
Comments: An outdoor species that also works indoors. M. raptor prefers dry, dark habitats and is active almost year-round, preferring cool temperatures and readily reproducing on late-season freeze-killed fly pupae. It has the potential to parasitize 20 fly pupae per day for one to four weeks. Early-season inundative releases have been helpful against house flies. M. raptor populations increase in late September and October when temperatures drop.	
Spalangia nigroaena	**Stable fly pupae preferred. Also attacks house fly, horn fly, little house fly, dump fly, false stable fly, etc.**
Comments: Works well against both stable flies and house flies. S. nigroaenea digs deep into manure where stable fly pupae are found. Parasite release costs are usually offset by reduction in insecticide treatments. In research trials, dairy farmers using fly parasites have made as much as 80% fewer insecticide treatments with 50% lower fly populations than with conventional insecticide control. There is still much to learn on using fly parasites most effectively in fly management programs.	

Mosquito Control

Water management that prevents mosquito breeding is essential for effective control. Eggs do not hatch unless they are in water. Locate standing water on premises and eliminate it if possible. Drain or fill stagnant water pools, puddles, ditches, or swampy areas around the facility. Tires, in particular, require special mention because they are ideal breeding places for vector mosquitoes. Stagnant ponds, which are highly septic, and waste lagoons also can be breeding areas for a large number of mosquitoes. Mosquito larvae live around the edges of ponds and waste lagoons. A waste lagoon with a heavy crust will shelter fewer mosquitoes than a waste lagoon with floating scum and floating debris. Excessive amounts of emergent aquatic vegetation will also shelter mosquitoes.

Follow these steps to reduce mosquito breeding areas:

- Remove tin cans, old tires, buckets, glass jars, and other water-holding containers.
- Clean out roof gutters so that water does not accumulate. Examine flat roofs after rains to make certain that no water remains more than one week.
- Drain or fill stagnant water pools, puddles, and ditches or swampy areas around the farm.
- Place tight covers over cisterns, cesspools, septic tanks, fire barrels, rain barrels, and tubs where water is stored. Drain tarps and silage covers where water may collect.

- Drain tree holes and fill with Treekote and mortar.
- Keep the grass mowed around ponds and lagoons and other bodies of water, taking care to keep clippings out of the water. Maintain farm ponds and waste lagoons according to good management practices.
- Stock ponds and reservoirs with mosquito-eating fish, such as green sunfish, bluegills, guppies, or any surface-feeding minnow.
- Keep drainage ditches on property clean and flowing.

Control of Rattailed Maggotss

Frequently during the warm summer months, rattailed maggots are reported as a nuisance. These creatures are not a problem as long as they remain in the liquid manure pit; however, they are known to move out of the pit or lagoon in large numbers, contaminating livestock feed, accumulating in electrical boxes and causing short circuits, and congregating in stacks of egg cartons and other unwanted places. The maggots migrate to a drier place for pupation.

Rattailed maggots, known as the larval or immature stage of syrphid flies, are about 1-1/4 inches long. The body portion is about three-fourths of an inch long, and the tail portion (breathing tube) one-half inch long. These maggots are white-coloured with the body portion an elongated, oval, cylindrical shape, which is wrinkled and semitransparent, protracting into a long breathing tube (tail).

These larvae of the Syrphid fly live in highly polluted water, such as livestock lagoons, abandoned fish pools, foul pools, and streams associated with barnyards, etc. Maggots are able to live in the water, if sufficient solids are present as food. The adult flies resemble honey bees in appearance and are often seen hovering near the ground in the barnyard. These flies do not bite or sting humans and are considered beneficial because they kill aphids.

CONTROL MEASURES OF RAT-TAILED MAGGOTS

Non-chemical treatment. Since, this maggot breeds and feeds in highly polluted waters, efforts must be made to keep the lagoon in the optimum condition, promoting a more nearly ideal anaerobic condition. Never allow accumulations of manure above the water line, either floating or sticking to the sides, because these conditions enhance fly development. Keep the banks steep and weeds under control.

Use loose soil and construct a soil barrier between the milk house and the rat-tailed maggot source. As maggots migrate to the soil barrier, they will dig into it to pupate rather than move into the milk house. Try to agitate the pit contents frequently during the spring and summer by pumping the pits routinely (at least once a week) to disrupt maggot development. Always maintain a waterline above the manure solids and clean out the pit contents on a routine basis. Chemical treatment. Unfortunately, there are no good pesticide control measures. There has been some success by layering either Ravap or Larvadex larvicide on the liquid and manure surface. Read the label for application instructions and safety guidelines. For best results, do not agitate the pit contents after application. The pesticides are typically mixed with fuel oil, which clogs the long breathing tube of the rat-tailed maggot, similar to oils applied to the surface of stagnant, non-moving water to kill mosquito larvae.

Control of Rodents

Control of rodents around livestock structures is best accomplished by minimizing their access to a food supply. Farmers control rodents by proper storage of feed, proper disposal of spoiled feed, and limiting areas attractive as living quarters for rodents. The presence of rodents in enclosed livestock facilities can be minimized by proper design of structures and use of proper methods to eliminate rodents that do enter the facilities. Farmers must control rodents to minimize costs caused by feed loss, damage to livestock and feed structures, and spread of disease carried by rodents. Rats can get through a 1/2-inch hole, and mice only need 1/4 inch. Rats drink water three times a day and feed nocturnally twice a day.

Construction and Design

Rodent-proofing must include protective devices on pipes,

electrical cables and conduits, drains, and other equipment where rodents travel. In addition to preventing access to buildings along these routes, attention must be given to reducing shelter and food and water sources that rats and mice use. Both rats and mice use drainage pipes or sewage systems as routes to enter buildings. Equip floor drains with metal grates fastened securely in place. Use grate openings that are 1/4 inch across or less.

Manure management systems in livestock facilities may be of a type where manure water is periodically drained from the building to a lagoon or other storage area. Extend discharge pipes far enough over the bank or into the lagoon to prevent rodents from jumping or crawling into the open end. Install rodent shields or use a downward-turned elbow to prevent rodents from gaining access.

A floating metal cover at the open end of the discharge pipe, with a hinge at its upper edge, can also be effective. The hinge must operate easily so water or manure will open the cover, but the cover must fall back into the closed position when the flow stops. These covers sometimes freeze shut, so they must be checked regularly. Always cap pump-out ports for manure storage pits when they are not in use. When left open, they allow easy entry to rodents.

9

Fertilizer Consumption by Crop

CROPS

NITROGEN

The actual (or most probable) rates of nitrogen for crops grown in regions of Poland are presented in Table. The rates of nitrogen are the highest for sugar and fodder beets (in spite of manure application), maize, rapeseed and wheat. High rates of nitrogen are also applied on vegetables and triticale. The lowest rates are applied on rye, oats, pulses and fodder crops. The low rate for grassland is to a certain extent misleading because there are no separate coefficients of preference for meadows and pastures. Part of the area of pastures is, moreover, not fertilized. However, due to the alternative utilisation of most grassland in Poland (for both hay and grasing) it seems practical to calculate the average rate of nitrogen for the total grassland area.

Table 9.1 Actual Rates of Nitrogen Applied to Crops in the Regions of Poland

Region or Province	Grassland	Wheat	Grain Maize	Potatoes	Sugar Beet
1	2	3	4	5	6
Dls	29	49	62	36	91
Kuj	59	98	124	75	182
Lub	34	56	71	41	105

(Contd...)

1	2	3	4	5	6
Lus	53	88	112	65	164
Lod	46	77	98	57	145
Mal	30	51	64	37	95
Maz	35	58	74	43	108
Opl	46	77	97	56	143
Pdk	18	31	39	22	57
Pod	39	66	83	48	123
Pom	50	83	105	61	155
Sls	32	53	68	39	100
Swi	28	46	59	34	87
Wrm	43	71	90	52	133
Wlp	56	93	118	68	173
Zpm	54	89	113	66	167
Poland	39	65	82	47	121

PHOSPHORUS

Present phosphorus rates are presented in Table 9.2. These rates are the highest for sugar and fodder beet, maize and rapeseed. Rates of phosphorus per hectare of agricultural land are higher in Opl and Pom regions than the average for Poland, however in Pom region the share of set-aside (unfertilized) land is three times higher in comparison to Opl region. Therefore the rates of phosphorus for the individual crops in Pom region far exceed those in Opl region.

Table 9.2 Actual Rates of Phosphorus Applied to Crops in the Regions of Poland

Region or Province	Rapeseed	Wheat	Grain Maize	Potatoes	Sugar Beet
1	2	3	4	5	6
Dls	32	22	28	16	41
Kuj	31	21	27	16	40
Lub	37	25	32	18	47
Lus	42	28	36	21	53
Lod	26	18	223	13	34
Mal	41	28	35	20	52
Maz	43	29	37	21	55
Opl	37	25	32	19	47

1	2	3	4	5	6
Pdk	24	16	21	12	31
Pod	38	26	33	19	49
Pom	61	41	52	30	77
Sls	24	16	21	12	31
Swi	28	19	24	14	36
Wrm	29	20	25	14	37
Wlp	35	24	30	18	45
Zpm	33	23	29	17	43
Poland	33	23	29	17	43

POTASSIUM

The rates of potassium application are presented in Table. They are highest for sugar beet, maize and rapeseed and lowest for rye, pulses and fodder crops. Care is taken with potassium fertilization in western and northern Poland but it is neglected in the middle and eastern parts of the country.

Table 9.3 Present Rates of Potash Applied to Crops in the Regions of Poland

Region or Province	Rapeseed	Wheat	Grain Maize	Potatoes	Sugar Beet
Dls	38	26	33	19	49
Kuj	42	29	36	21	53
Lub	43	29	37	21	55
Lus	45	31	39	22	57
Lod	31	21	26	15	39
Mal	43	29	37	222	55
Maz	52	36	45	26	66
Opl	60	41	52	30	77
Pdk	26	18	23	13	33
Pod	41	28	35	20	52
Pom	78	53	67	39	99
Sls	35	24	30	17	44
Swi	25	17	22	13	32
Wrm	38	26	33	19	49
Wlp	48	33	42	24	62
Zpm	55	38	48	28	71
Poland	42	29	36	21	53

NUTRIENT

INTRODUCTION

The balances are calculated as soil surface nutrient balances according to the method prepared in Poland in the context of the MAINTAINE research project supported by EC. This method is in general agreement with the official OECD methodology. The original method or model called MACROBIL was aimed at balancing nutrients at the farm level. It has been adapted slightly for the purposes of this report where regions and the whole of Poland are regarded as the equivalents of the big farms. The model was fed with the following data: area and yield of the crops, number of animals of different kinds and ages (calves, cattle, sows, fattening pigs and so on), consumption of mineral fertilizers and balance coefficients for phosphorus and potassium.

In the nitrogen balance, on the input side the nutrients in fertilizers, manure, and crop by-products incorporated into the soil, biological N fixation and N atmospheric deposit are identified. The same items, apart from biological fixation and atmospheric deposition, are given for phosphorus and potassium. The right side of the balance consists of the nutrients removed with the total yield of the crop. For the sake of interpretation of the final balance, the input of nitrogen is expressed in units of so-called acting N as well as total N. Acting nitrogen is the amount of N from the given source (*e.g.* manure, crop residues, biological fixation) showing the same effect as the corresponding amount of nitrogen in mineral fertilizers. The amount of acting nitrogen is calculated according to the formula:

*Acting Nitrogen = Total Nitrogen * Nitrogen Equivalent*

The nitrogen equivalents are derived from the result of field experiments and relate the efficiency of N from a given source to the efficiency of N in mineral fertilizers taken for 1. Nitrogen equivalents are less than one for some sources, such as cereal and rape straw, and may even be negative (nitrogen immobilisation). Nitrogen equivalent for fertilizers equals one (by definition).

The amounts of removed phosphorus and potassium also are corrected by balance equivalents. The balance equivalent is the ratio between the phosphorus and potassium uptake at the actual (or planned) yield and the optimal rate of these elements. These equivalents were calculated on the basis of long term field experiments with increasing rates of phosphorus and potassium fertilizers. For calculations at the regional level these equivalents were modified and correspond to the soil fertility status.

Table 9.4 Nitrogen Balance, kg N/ha of Agricultural Land

Region or Province	Input N Total	N Acting	Removal* N Total	N Total	Balance N Acting
Dls	73.3	53.8	71.7	2.0	-18.0
Kuj	139.0	112.3	74.0	65.1	38.3
Lub	86.2	67.1	62.2	24.0	4.9
Lus	81.8	67.8	45.0	36.8	22.9
Lod	100.7	79.3	56.6	44.2	22.7
Mal	92.8	69.5	69.7	23.1	-0.2
Maz	86.6	65.2	55.6	31.0	9.6
Opl	123.2	93.1	94.6	28.5	-1.5
Pdk	72.8	52.6	59.5	13.3	-6.9
Pod	100.1	75.9	62.1	39.0	13.9
Pom	103.9	84.5	60.7	43.2	23.8
Sls	82.1	62.9	60.0	22.1	2.9
Swi	85.3	65.9	53.5	31.7	12.4
Wrm	86.7	69.7	59.3	27.4	10.4
Wlp	135.9	105.2	77.1	58.8	28.1
Zpm	95.0	79.8	55.0	40.0	24.9
Poland	97.6	75.7	63.5	34.2	12.2

Note: * The amounts of nutrients removed with the crop products.

The input of total nitrogen in the whole of Poland and in all individual regions is higher than nitrogen removal, giving a positive nitrogen balance or N surplus. Nevertheless only in a few regions, (Kuj, Lod, Pom, Wlp and Zpm), are the surpluses of nitrogen slightly in excess of 40 kg N per ha of agricultural land, which is considered to be acceptable in most countries of the European Union. The balance of acting nitrogen is in the whole country still positive but in several regions (Dln, Mal, Opl, Pdk) deficiencies of this element are recorded.

The input of phosphorus in Poland and in most regions except Dln and Sls is higher than the P removed by the crop and there is an apparent P surplus. Nevertheless the output of phosphorus should be slightly higher (the balance coefficient for Poland is 1.12) than removal and hence, the phosphorus input and output are practically in balance. In six regions (Dln, Lod, Pdk, Sls, Wrm and Zpm) the phosphorus balance, taking account of the soil fertility, is negative.

Table 9.5 Phosphorus Balance, kg P_2O_5/ha of Agricultural Land

Region or Province	Input	Removal*	Output**	Balance
Dls	26.0	29.1	30.2	-4.2
Kuj	37.5	30.2	30.2	7.4
Lub	29.9	24.4	29.0	0.9
Lus	23.9	18.4	18.8	5.2
Lod	26.6	22.1	27.1	-0.6
Mal	32.9	24.5	30.8	2.1
Maz	32.1	21.3	24.0	8.1
Opl	40.3	39.3	37.4	2.9
Pdk	23.9	21.3	26.5	-2.6
Pod	33.5	23.0	30.1	3.3
Pom	42.5	24.2	24.7	17.9
Sls	22.8	22.8	26.9	-4.1
Swi	27.1	20.2	26.6	0.5
Wrm	22.7	22.1	25.4	-2.7
Wlp	43.3	31.6	31.0	12.3
Zpm	24.1	22.8	27.1	-3.0
Poland	30.9	24.8	27.8	3.2

Notes: * The amounts of nutrients removed with the crop products.

** Output = removal multiplied by the balance equivalent.

Potassium input in the country as a whole and in practically all regions except Dln exceeds removal but due to the poor potassium status of most soils, the output of this element should in any case be higher than the mere removal (the balance coefficient for Poland is 1.30). In consequence the potassium balance calculated as the difference of input and output for the country as a whole is negative and in some regions potassium deficiencies exceed 10 kg K_2O per ha of agricultural land. It may be surprising that, with the low consumption of nutrients in fertilizers and manure, the nutrient balances show surpluses or comparatively low deficiencies. This can be explained by the low or even very low crop yields recorded in the country and consequently the low nutrient removal with the harvested crop products.

Table 9.6 Potash Balance, kg K_2O/ha of Agricultural Land

Region or Province	Input	Removal*	Output**	Balance
Dls	53.6	60.5	65.3	-11.7
Kuj	85.3	66.8	75.5	9.8
Lub	64.5	51.2	65.6	-1.0
Lus	41.8	36.6	53.1	-11.3
Lod	63.5	51.4	77.0	-13.6
Mal	74.2	57.2	65.8	8.4
Maz	71.8	47.3	72.3	-0.5
Opl	94.4	80.9	94.6	-0.2
Pdk	57.4	60.5	63.7	-6.2
Pod	79.5	50.1	73.7	5.8
Pom	79.0	51.5	63.9	15.1
Sls	54.8	49.5	58.9	-4.1
Swi	59.1	44.2	58.3	0.8
Wrm	52.0	48.8	58.6	-6.5
Wlp	95.0	68.5	97.2	-2.2
Zpm	54.1	45.8	60.9	-6.8
Poland	68.7	54.1	70.3	-1.6

Notes: * The amounts of nutrients removed with the crop products.
** Output = removal multiplied by the balance equivalent.

The productivity of agriculture differs considerably among the regions in Poland. In this context, it is interesting that the nutrients removed per unit of yield are practically the same in all regions, which proves that there is a very close relation between the crop yields and the amount of nutrients at the disposal of the crop. Reversing this relationship, one can conclude that further growth of crop production depends considerably on the increased consumption of fertilizers and manure. The crop yields converted into cereal units and the uptake of nutrients per cereal unit are presented in Tables.

Table 9.7 Crop Yields and Nutrients Uptake Per Yield Unit in Regions of Poland

Region	Crop yields converted into cereal units/ha*		Nutrients uptake per cereal unit kg per unit		
	Agricultural land	Arable land	N	P_2O_5	K_2O
Dln	30.4	34.8	2.36	0.96	1.99
Kuj	32.2	33.8	2.30	0.94	2.07
Lub	27.6	29.7	2.25	0.89	1.86
Lus	19.7	22.7	2.28	0.93	1.86
Lod	25.0	25.4	2.27	0.88	2.06
Mal	26.6	28.2	2.62	0.92	2.15
Maz	24.4	24.8	2.28	0.87	1.94
Opl	39.9	43.3	2.37	0.98	2.03
Pdk	23.3	24.9	2.56	0.92	2.17
Pod	23.0	11.1	2.70	1.00	2.18
Pom	25.1	27.2	2.42	0.96	2.05
Sls	24.3	25.7	2.47	0.94	2.04
Swi	23.3	24.5	2.30	0.87	1.90
Wrm	22.2	23.3	2.67	1.00	2.20
Wlp	33.0	35,3	2.34	0.96	2.08
Zpm	23.4	26.5	2.35	0.97	1.96
Poland	26.5	28.5	2.40	0.94	2.04

Note: * Cereal units as given in table below.

Table 9.8 Equivalents of Crop Yields in Cereal Units.

Crop, Product and Yield in kg	Cereal Units
Cereals, grain, 100 kg	1
Pulses, grain, 100 kg	1.20
Rape, seeds, 100 kg	2.00

Potato, sugar beets, tubers or roots 100 kg	0.25
Fodder beets, roots, 100 kg	0.12
Fodder crops, green matter 100 kg	0.10 to 0.14
Meadows and grasses, hay, 100 kg	0.40 to 0.50
Vegetables, fresh matter 100 kg	0.20

PRICES OF MINERAL FERTILIZERS

Until 1990 the sale or rather the distribution of fertilizers was organized uniformly and the retail prices were lower than the production costs (the ratio of prices to production costs was 0.51, 0.17 and 0.43 for nitrogen, phosphorus and potassium fertilizers respectively). In a transformed economy, the market determines the prices of fertilizers. In the years 1989 to 1993 the prices of nitrogen fertilizers (N) increased 30 times, phosphorus (P_2O_5) 36 times and potassium (K_2O) 44 times. In the years 1993 to 1997 the prices of fertilizers increased at the rate comparable to the rate of inflation.

In the years 1998 to 2001 the price trend flattened out and the price increases were below the inflation rate (with the exception of 2001). This means that mineral fertilizers have become relatively cheaper.

This can be explained by the surplus of fertilizers from domestic production and the strong competition for the market between the fertilizer plants. Another reason is the substantial, although only partly controlled, import of cheap fertilizers from eastern European countries. The prices of fertilizers are almost the same in all regions as a consequence of the policy of the fertilizer producers.

Table 9.9 Prices of Basic Fertilizers

Fertilizer & % Nutrients	Prices PLN*/kg Nutrient (N, P_2O_5, K_2O)			
	1998	1999	2000	2001
Calcium amm. nitrate 28%	1.51	1.50	1.66	1.96
Ammonium nitrate 34%	1.28	1.21	1.39	1.61
Urea 46 %	1.16	1.16	1.30	1.51
Single superphosphate 18%	1.72	1.97	1.98	2.19
Triple superphosphate 46%	1.81	1.85	1.96	2.08

(Contd...)

NP fertilizer 18-46	1.50	1.59	1.62	1.65
NPK fertilizer 8-24-24	1.37	1.48	1.61	1.70
Potassium chloride 57%	0.80	0.93	1.02	1.04
Yearly rate of increase**	8%	5%	8%	9%
Yearly rate of inflation**	8.5%	9.8%	8.6%	3.6%

Notes: * 100 PLN = 24.6 euros in June 2002

** In relation to the previous year.

During the same period, the prices of agricultural products also increased but until 1994 at a slower pace than the prices of fertilizers. In the years 1994 to 1997, the rate of increase of the prices of wheat was slightly higher than the rate of increase of the fertilizer price.

In consequence, the fertilizer/grain price ratio widened at the beginning of the 1990s and narrowed slowly in the second half of this decade. During the years 1998 to 2001 the index of the grain and fertilizer price relationship opened again and the farmer had to sell about 3 kg of wheat grain to buy 1 kg N, about 4 kg of wheat grain to buy 1 kg P_2O_5 and almost 2 kg of grain to buy 1 kg K_2O.

Table 9.10 Price of 1 kg Nutrient Expressed in kg of Winter Wheat Grain

Fertilizer & % Nutrients	Price Ratio			
	1998	1999	2000	2001
Calcium amm. nitrate 28%	3.2	3.6	2.8	3.6
Ammonium nitrate 34%	2.7	3.0	2.5	3.0
Urea 46%	2.5	2.7	2.3	2.8
Single superphosphate 18%	3.3	4.2	3.6	3.9
Triple superphosphate 46%	3.7	4.3	3.6	3.9
NP fertilizer 18-46	3.1	3.6	3.0	3.1
NPK fertilizer 8-24-24	2.9	3.3	2.9	3.2
Potassium chloride 57%	1.6	2.0	1.8	2.0

In view of the fact that the profitability of nitrogen fertilizers is 3 to 4 times higher than that of phosphorus and potassium, it is obvious why the consumption of phosphorus and potassium dropped more dramatically compared with the consumption of nitrogen fertilizers.

The only fertilizer product still subsidized by the State is lime, but the share of the subsidy in the total cost of production and distribution of limestone and dolomitic limestone shows a decreasing trend.

Table 9.11 Subsidisation of Calcium and Magnesium Amendments

Item	Subsidies		
	1997	1999	2001
Total subsidy in PLN*106	192	64	64
Subsidy change, %	10.8	-35	-1.1
Yearly rate of inflation, %	13	9.8	3.6
Subsidy as % of the cost	44	25	25

At the end of the central planning period, the subsidy accounted for more than 70 per cent of the total cost of liming and in 1993 it still amounted to 66 per cent. In 1997 this share was cut down to 44 per cent and in 1999/2001 to a mere 25 per cent of the total cost of liming. This is a crucial problem for Polish agriculture since, high acidity is one of the most limiting factors of soil fertility and crop yields in the country.

PROFITABILITY OF FERTILIZER USE

The data from the former 49 provinces were used to create models for relating yield and fertilizer consumption. Two models, one simplified and the other a full model were developed. The following crop prices were used to estimate profitability.

Table 9.12 Prices of Plant Products

Product	Price, PLN, Per Tonne				
	1998	1999	2000	2001	Average
Wheat, grain	478	430	497	511	479
Rye, grain	332	294	380	364	342
Sugar beet	89	98	101	112	100
Rapeseed, seeds	895	644	806	830	793

The prices of plant products given in this table are averages for the whole country. They show large fluctuations between years and regions. With the exception of a few products *i.e.* sugar beet, rapeseed grain, high quality wheat grain and some special products (tobacco, hemp), demand is too low in comparison with production. In 1998 the prices of most crops decreased dramatically and farmers could hardly cover their costs. The average price of 1 kg NPK ($N+P_2O_5+K_2O$) for the years 1999 to 2001 was 1.41 PLN, and the average price of 1 kg of wheat grain (taken to be equivalent to the value of 1 kg of grain unit) was 0.48 PLN. The profitability of mineral fertilization of grain in Poland is therefore fairly high and can be roughly estimated at 3.1 PLN yield value per 1 PLN spent on fertilizers. The more complete model gave a somewhat lower response than the simplified model but it was still substantial at 2.4 PLN yield value per 1 PLN spent on fertilizers.

Similar calculations have been performed for certain other crops. The simplified model gave an average mineral fertilizer efficiency of 30 tonnes potatoes and 50 tonnes of sugar beet per kg NPK.

Table 9.13 Profitability of Mineral Fertilization for Selected Crops

Crop	Yield Increase Per 1 kg NPK	Value of Yield Increase PLN	Cost of Fertilizers PLN/kg NPK	Cost/Value Ratio
Wheat	9.84	4.71	1.41	3.3
Barley	7.77	4.19	1.41	3.0
Triticale	7.27	3.42	1.41	2.4
Rapeseed	6.61	5.24	1.41	3.7
Potato	30.32	3.64	1.41	2.6
Sugar beet	50.27	5.03	1.41	3.6

MAKING SUPERIOR COMPOST

The potency of composts can vary greatly. Most municipal solid waste compost has a high carbon to nitrogen ratio and when tilled into soil temporarily provokes the opposite of a good growth response until soil animals and microorganisms consume most of the undigested paper. But if low-grade compost is used as a surface mulch on ornamentals, the results are usually quite satisfactory even if unspectacular. If the aim of your own composting is to conveniently dispose of yard waste and kitchen garbage, the information in the first half of the book is all you need to know. If you need compost to make something that dependably GROWS plants like it was fertilizer.

HISTORY

Before the twentieth century, the fertilizers market gardeners used were potent manures and composts. The vegetable gardens of country folk also received the best manures and composts available while the field crops got the rest. So I've learned a great deal from old farming and market gardening literature about using animal manures. In previous centuries, farmers classified manures by type and purity. There was 'long' and 'short' manure, and then, there was the supreme plant growth stimulant, chicken manure.

Chicken manure was always highly prized but usually in short supply because preindustrial fowl weren't caged in factories or permanently locked in hen houses and fed scientifically formulated mixes. The chicken breed of that era was usually some type of bantam, half-wild, broody, protective of chicks, and capable of foraging. A typical pre-1900 small-scale chicken management system was to allow the flock free access to hunt their own meals in the barnyard and orchard, luring them into the coop at dusk with a bit of grain where they were protected from predators while sleeping helplessly. Some manure was collected from the hen house but most of it was dropped where it could not be gathered. The daily egg hunt was worth it because, before the era of pesticides, having chickens range through the orchard greatly reduced problems with insects in fruit.

The high potency of chicken manure derives from the chickens' low C/N diet: worms, insects, tender shoots of new grass, and other proteinaceous young greens and seeds. Twentieth-century chickens 'living' in egg and meat factories must still be fed low C/N foods, primarily grains, and their manure is still potent. But anyone who has savored real free-range eggs with deep orange yokes from chickens on a proper diet cannot be happy with what passes for 'eggs' these days. Fertilizing with pure chicken manure is not very different than using ground cereal grains or seed meals. It is so concentrated that it might burn plant leaves like chemical fertilizer does and must be applied sparingly to soil. It provokes a marked and vigourous growth response. Two or three gallons of dry, pure fresh chicken manure are sufficient nutrition to GROW about 100 square feet of vegetables in raised beds to the maximum.

Exclusively incorporating pure chicken manure into a vegetable garden also results in rapid humus loss, just as though chemical fertilizers were used. Any fertilizing substance with a C/N below that of stabilized humus, be it a chemical or a natural substance, accelerates the decline in soil organic matter. That is because nitrate nitrogen, the key to constructing all protein, is usually the main factor limiting the population of soil microorganisms. When the nitrate level of soil is significantly increased, microbe populations increase proportionately and proceeds to eat organic matter at an accelerated rate.

That is why small amounts of chemical fertilizer applied to soil that still contains a reasonable amount of humus has such a powerful effect. Not only does the fertilizer itself stimulate the growth of plants, but fertilizer increases the microbial population. More microbes accelerate the breakdown of humus and even more plant nutrients are released as organic matter decays. And that is why holistic farmers and gardeners mistakenly criticize chemical fertilizers as being directly destructive of soil microbes. Actually, all fertilizers, chemical or organic, *indirectly* harm soil life, first increasing their populations to unsustainable levels that drop off markedly once enough organic matter has been eaten. Unless, of course, the organic matter is replaced.

Chicken manure compost is another matter. Mix the pure manure with straw, sawdust, or other bedding, compost it and, depending on the amount and quantity of bedding used and the time allowed for decomposition to occur, the resultant C/N will be around 12:1 or above. Any ripened compost around 12:1 still will GROW plants beautifully. Performance drops off as the C/N increases.

Since, chicken manure was scarce, most pre-twentieth century market gardeners depended on seemingly unlimited supplies of "short manure," generally from horses. The difference between the 'long' and the 'short' manure was bedding. Long manure contained straw from the stall while short manure was pure street sweepings without adulterants. Hopefully, the straw portion of long manure had absorbed a quantity of urine.

People of that era knew the fine points of hay quality as well as people today know their gasoline. Horses expected to do a day's work were fed on grass or grass/clover mixes that had been cut and dried while they still had a high protein content. Leafy hay was highly prized while hay that upon close inspection revealed lots of stems and seed heads would be rejected by a smart buyer. The working horse's diet was supplemented with a daily ration of grain. Consequently, uncomposted fresh short manure probably started out with a C/N around 15:1. However, don't count on anything that good from horses these days. Most horses aren't worked daily so their fodder is often poor. Judging from the stemmy, cut-too-late grass hay our local horses have to try to survive on, if I could find bedding-free horse manure it would probably have a C/N more like 20:1. Manure from physically fit thoroughbred race horses is probably excellent.

Using fresh horse manure in soil gave many vegetables a harsh flavour so it was first composted by mixing in some soil (a good idea because otherwise a great deal of ammonia would escape the heap). Market gardeners raising highly demanding crops like cauliflower and celery amended composted short manure by the inches-thick layer. Lesser nutrient-demanding crops like snap beans, lettuce, and roots followed these intensively fertilized vegetables without further compost.

Long manures containing lots of straw were considered useful only for field crops or root vegetables. Wise farmers conserved the nitrogen and promptly composted long manures. After heating and turning the resulting C/N would probably be in a little below 20:1. After tilling it in, a short period of time was allowed while the soil digested this compost before sowing seeds. Lazy farmers spread raw manure load by load as it came from the barn and tilled it in once the entire field was covered. This easy method allows much nitrogen to escape as ammonia while the manure dries in the sun. Commercial vegetable growers had little use for long manure. One point of this brief history lesson is GIGO: garbage in, garbage out. The finished compost tends to have a C/N that is related to the ingredients that built the heap. Growers of vegetables will wisely take note.

Anyone interested in learning more about preindustrial market gardening might ask their librarian to seek out a book called *French Gardening* by Thomas Smith, published in London about 1905. This fascinating little book was written to encourage British market gardeners to imitate the Parisian marciér, who skillfully earned top returns growing out-of-season produce on intensive, double-dug raised beds, often under glass hot or cold frames. Our trendy American Biodynamic French Intensive gurus obtained their inspiration from England through this tradition.

HEAP

The easiest and most sure-fire improver of compost quality is time. Making a heap with predominantly low C/N materials inevitably results in potent compost if nitrate loss is kept to a minimum. But the C/N of almost any compost heap, even one starting with a high C/N will eventually lower itself. The key word here is*eventually*. The most dramatic decomposition occurs during the first few turns when the heap is hot. Many people, including writers of garden books, mistakenly think that the composting ends when the pile cools and the material no longer resembles what made up the heap. This is not true. As long as a compost heap is kept moist and is turned occasionally, it will continue to decompose. 'Curing' or 'ripening' are terms used to describe what occurs once heating is over.

A different ecology of microorganisms predominates while a heap is ripening. If the heap contains 5 to 10 per cent soil, is kept moist, is turned occasionally so it stays aerobic, and has a complete mineral balance, considerable bacterial nitrogen fixation may occur.

Most gardeners are familiar with the microbes that nodulate the roots of legumes. Called rhizobia, these bacteria are capable of fixing large quantities of nitrate nitrogen in a short amount of time. Rhizobia tend to be inactive during hot weather because the soil itself is supplying nitrates from the breakdown of organic matter. Summer legume crops, like cowpeas and snap beans, tend to be net consumers of nitrates, not makers of more nitrates than they can use. Consider this when you read in carelessly researched garden books and articles about the advantages of interplanting legumes with other crops because they supposedly generate nitrates that 'help' their companions.

But during spring or fall when lowered soil temperatures retard decomposition, rhizobia can manufacture from 80 to 200 pounds of nitrates per acre. Peas, clovers, alfalfa, vetches, and fava beans can all make significant contributions of nitrate nitrogen and smart farmers prefer to grow their nitrogen by green manuring legumes. Wise farmers also know that this nitrate, though produced in root nodules, is used by legumes to grow leaf and stem. So the entire legume must be tilled in if any net nitrogen gain is to be realized. This wise practice simultaneously increases organic matter.

Rhizobia are not capable of being active in compost piles, but another class of microbes is. Called azobacteria, these free-living soil dwellers also make nitrate nitrogen. Their contribution is not potentially as great as rhizobia, but no special provision must be made to encourage azobacteria other than maintaining a decent level of humus for them to eat, a balanced mineral supply that includes adequate calcium, and a soil pH between 5.75 and 7.25. A high-yielding crop of wheat needs 60-80 pounds of nitrates per acre. Corn and most vegetables can use twice that amount. Azobacteria can make enough for wheat, though an average nitrate contribution under good soil conditions might be more like 30-50 pounds per year.

Once a compost heap has cooled, azobacteria will proliferate and begin to manufacture significant amounts of nitrates, steadily lowering the C/N. And carbon never stops being digested, further dropping the C/N. The rapid phase of composting may be over in a few months, but ripening can be allowed to go on for many more months if necessary. Feeding unripened compost to worms is perhaps the quickest way to lower C/N and make a potent soil amendment. Once the high heat of decomposition has passed and the heap is cooling, it is commonly invaded by redworms, the same species used for vermicomposting kitchen garbage. These worms would not be able to eat the high C/N material that went into a heap, but after heating, the average C/N has probably dropped enough to be suitable for them.

The municipal composting operation at Fallbrook, California makes clever use of this method to produce a smaller amount of high-grade product out of a larger quantity of low-grade ingredients. Mixtures of sewage sludge and municipal solid waste are first composted and after cooling, the half-done high C/N compost is shallowly spread out over crude worm beds and kept moist.

More crude compost is added as the worms consume the waste, much like a household worm box. The worm beds gradually rise. The lower portion of these mounds is pure castings while the worm activity stays closer to the surface where food is available. When the beds have grown to about three feet tall, the surface few inches containing worms and undigested food are scraped off and used to form new vermicomposting beds. The castings below are considered finished compost. By laboratory analysis, the castings contain three or four times as much nitrogen as the crude compost being fed to the worms.

The marketplace gives an excellent indicator of the difference between their crude compost and the worm casts. Even though Fallbrook is surrounded by large acreages devoted to citrus orchards and row crop vegetables, the municipality has a difficult time disposing of the crude product. But their vermicompost is in strong demand.

Method

Nineteenth-century farmers and market gardeners had much practical knowledge about using manures and making composts that worked like fertilizers, but little was known about the actual microbial process of composting until our century. As information became available about compost ecology, one brilliant individual, Sir Albert Howard, incorporated the new science of soil microbiology into his composting and by patient experiment learned how to make superior compost

During the 1920s, Albert Howard was in charge of a government research farm at Indore, India. At heart a Peace Corps volunteer, he made Indore operate like a very representative Indian farm, growing all the main staples of the local agriculture: cotton, sugar cane, and cereals. The farm was powered by the same work oxen used by the surrounding farmers. It would have been easy for Howard to demonstrate better yields through high technology by buying chemical fertilizers or using seed meal wastes from oil extraction, using tractors, and growing new, high-yielding varieties that could make use of more intense soil nutrition. But these inputs were not affordable to the average Indian farmer and Howard's purpose was to offer genuine help to his neighbours by demonstrating methods they *could* easily afford and use.

In the beginning of his work at Indore, Howard observed that the district's soils were basically fertile but low in organic matter and nitrogen. This deficiency seemed to be due to traditionally wasteful practices concerning manures and agricultural residues. So Howard began developing methods to compost the waste products of agriculture, making enough high-quality fertilizer to supply the entire farm. Soon, Indore research farm was enjoying record yields without having insect or disease problems, and without buying fertilizer or commercial seed. More significantly, the work animals, fed exclusively on fodder from Indore's humus-rich soil, become invulnerable to cattle diseases. Their shining health and fine condition became the envy of the district.

Most significant, Howard contended that his method not only conserved the nitrogen in cattle manure and crop waste, not only conserved the organic matter the land produced, but also raised the processes of the entire operation to an ecological climax of maximized health and production. Conserving the manure and composting the crop waste allowed him to increase the soil's organic matter which increased the soil's release of nutrients from rock particles that further increased the production of biomass which allowed him to make even more compost and so on. What I have just described is not surprising, it is merely a variation on good farming that some humans have known about for millennia. What was truly revolutionary was Howard's contention about increasing net nitrates. With gentle understatement, Howard asserted that his compost was genuinely superior to anything ever known before. Indore compost had these advantages: no nitrogen or organic matter was lost from the farm through mishandling of agricultural wastes; the humus level of the farm's soils increased to a maximum sustainable level; and, *the amount of nitrate nitrogen in the finished compost was higher than the total amount of nitrogen contained in the materials that formed the heap.* Indore compost resulted in a net gain of nitrate nitrogen. The compost factory was also a biological nitrate factory.

The widely read book brought him invitations to visit plantations throughout the British Empire. It prompted farmers world-wide to make compost by the Indore method. Travel, contacts, and new awareness of the problems of European agriculture were responsible for Howard's decision to create an organic farming and gardening movement.

Howard repeatedly warned in *The Waste Products of Agriculture* that if the underlying fundamentals of his process were altered, superior results would not occur. That was his viewpoint in 1931. However, humans being what we are, it does not seem possible for good technology to be broadcast without each user trying to improve and adapt it to their own situation and understanding. By 1940, the term 'lndore compost' had become a generic term for any kind of compost made in a heap without the use of chemicals, much as 'Rototiller' has come to mean any motor-driven rotarytiller.

Howard's 1931 concerns were correct—almost all alterations of the original Indore system lessened its value—but Howard of 1941 did not resist this dilutive trend because in an era of chemical farming any compost was better than no compost, any return of humus better than none.

Still, I think it is useful to go back to the Indore research farm of the 1920s and to study closely how Albert Howard once made the world's finest compost, and to encounter this great man's thoughts before he became a crusading ideologue, dead set against any use of agricultural chemicals. A great many valuable lessons are still contained in *The Waste Products of Agriculture.* Unfortunately, even though many organic gardeners are familiar with the later works of Sir Albert Howard the reformer, Albert Howard the scientist and researcher, who wrote this book, is virtually unknown today.

At Indore, all available vegetable material was composted, including manure and bedding straw from the cattle shed, unconsumed crop residues, fallen leaves and other forest wastes, weeds, and green manures grown specifically for compost making. All of the urine from the cattle shed-in the form of urine earth—and all wood ashes from any source on the farm were also included. Being in the tropics, compost making went on year-round. Of the result, Howard stated that.

"The product is a finely divided leafmould, of high nitrifying power, ready for immediate use [without temporarily inhibiting plant growth]. The fine state of division enables the compost to be rapidly incorporated and to exert its maximum influence on a very large area of the internal surface of the soil."

Howard stressed that for the Indore method to work reliably the carbon to nitrogen ratio of the material going into the heap must always be in the same range. Every time a heap was built the same assortment of crop wastes were mixed with the same quantities of fresh manure and urine earth. As with my bread-baking analogy, Howard insured repeatability of ingredients. Any hard, woody materials—Howard called them 'refractory'—must be thoroughly broken up before composting, otherwise the fermentation would not be vigourous, rapid, and uniform throughout the process. This mechanical softening up was cleverly accomplished without power equipment by spreading tough crop wastes like cereal straw or pigeon pea and cotton stalks out over the farm roads, allowing cartwheels, the oxens' hooves, and foot traffic to break them up.

Decomposition must be rapid and aerobic, but not too aerobic. And not too hot. Quite intentionally, Indore compost piles were not allowed to reach the highest temperatures that are possible. During the first heating cycle, peak temperatures were about 140°. After two weeks, when the first turn was made, temperatures had dropped to about 125°, and gradually declined from there. Howard cleverly restricted the air supply and thermal mass so as to "bank the fires" of decomposition. This moderation was his key to preventing loss of nitrogen. Provisions were made to water the heaps as necessary, to turn them several times, and to use a novel system of mass inoculation with the proper fungi and bacteria. I'll shortly discuss each of these subjects in detail.

Howard was pleased that there was no need to accept nitrogen loss at any stage and that the reverse should happen. Once the C/N had dropped sufficiently, the material was promptly incorporated into the soil where nitrate nitrogen will be best preserved. But the soil is not capable of doing two jobs at once. It can't digest crude organic matter and simultaneously nitrify humus. So compost must be finished and completely ripe when it was tilled in so that:

"... there must be no serious competition between the last stages of decay of the compost and the work of the soil in growing the crop. This is accomplished by carrying the manufacture of humus up to the point when nitrification is about to begin. In this way the Chinese principle of dividing the growing of a crop into two separate processes —(1) the preparation of the food materials outside the field, and (2) the actual growing of the crop-can be introduced into general agricultural practice."

And because he actually lived on a farm, Howard especially emphasized that composting must be sanitary and odorless and that flies must not be allowed to breed in the compost or around the work cattle. Country life can be quite idyllic—without flies.

Compost Factory

At Indore, Howard built a covered, open-sided, compost-making factory that sheltered shallow pits, each 30 feet long by

14 feet wide by 2 feet deep with sloping sides. The pits were sufficiently spaced to allow loaded carts to have access to all sides of any of them and a system of pipes brought water near every one. The materials to be composted were all stored adjacent to the factory. Howard's work oxen were conveniently housed in the next building.

SOIL AND URINE

Howard had been raised on an English farm and from childhood he had learned the ways of work animals and how to make them comfortable. So, for the ease of their feet, the cattle shed and its attached, roofed loafing pen had earth floors. All soil removed from the silage pits, dusty sweepings from the threshing floors, and silt from the irrigation ditches were stored near the cattle shed and used to absorb urine from the work cattle. This soil was spread about six inches deep in the cattle stalls and loafing pen. About three times a year it was scraped up and replaced with fresh soil, the urine-saturated earth then was dried and stored in a special covered enclosure to be used for making compost.

The presence of this soil in the heap was essential. First, the black soil of Indore was well-supplied with calcium, magnesium, and other plant nutrients. These basic elements prevented the heaps from becoming overly acid. Additionally, the clay in the soil was uniquely incorporated into the heap so that it coated everything. Clay has a strong ability to absorb ammonia, preventing nitrogen loss. A clay coating also holds moisture. Without soil, "an even and vigourous mycelial growth is never quickly obtained." Howard said "the fungi are the storm troops of the composting process, and must be furnished with all the armament they need."

CROP WASTES

Crop wastes were protected from moisture, stored dry under cover near the compost factory. Green materials were first withered in the sun for a few days before storage. Refractory materials were spread on the farm's roads and crushed by foot traffic and cart wheels before stacking. All these forms of vegetation were thinly layered as they were received so that the dry storage stacks became thoroughly mixed. Care was taken to preserve the mixing by cutting vertical slices out of the stacks when vegetation was taken to the compost pits.

Howard said the average C/N of this mixed vegetation was about 33:1. Every compost heap made year-round was built with this complex assortment of vegetation having the same properties and the same C/N. Special preliminary treatment was given to hard, woody materials like sugarcane, millet stumps, wood shavings and waste paper. These were first dumped into an empty compost pit, mixed with a little soil, and kept moist until they softened. Or they might be soaked in water for a few days and then added to the bedding under the work cattle. Great care was taken when handling the cattle's bedding to insure that no flies would breed in it.

MANURE

Though crop wastes and urine-earth could be stored dry for later use, manure, the key ingredient of Indore compost, had to be used fresh. Fresh cow dung contains bacteria from the cow's rumen that is essential to the rapid decomposition of cellulose and other dry vegetation. Without their abundant presence composting would not begin as rapidly nor proceed as surely.

CHARGING THE COMPOST PITS

Every effort was made to fill a pit to the brim within one week. If there wasn't enough material to fill an entire pit within one week, then a portion of one pit would be filled to the top. To preserve good aeration, every effort was made to avoid stepping on the material while filling the pit. As mixtures of manure and bedding were brought out from the cattle shed they were thinly layered atop thin layers of mixed vegetation brought in from the dried reserves heaped up adjacent to the compost factory. Each layer was thoroughly wet down with a clay slurry made of three ingredients: water, urine-earth, and actively decomposing material from an adjacent compost pit that had been filled about two weeks earlier. This insured that every particle within the heap was moist and was coated with nitrogen-rich soil and the microorganisms of decomposition. Today, we would call this practice "mass inoculation."

Pits *vs.* Heaps

India has two primary seasons. Most of the year is hot and dry while the monsoon rains come from dune through September. During the monsoon, so much water falls so continuously that the earth becomes completely saturated. Even though the pits were under a roof, they would fill with water during this period. So in the monsoon, compost was made in low heaps atop the ground. Compared to the huge pits, their dimensions were smaller than you would expect: 7 × 7 feet at the top, 8 × 8 feet at the base and no more than 2 feet high. When the rains started, any compost being completed in pits was transferred to above-ground heaps when it was turned.

Howard was accomplishing several things by using shallow pits or low but very broad heaps. One, thermal masses were reduced so temperatures could not reach the ultimate extremes possible while composting. The pits were better than heaps because air flow was further reduced, slowing down the fermentation, while their shallowness still permitted sufficient aeration. There were enough covered pits to start a new heap every week.

Table 9.14 Temperature Range in Normal Pit

Age in Days	Temperature in °C
3	63
4	60
6	58
11	55
12	53
13	49
14	49
	First Turn
18	49
20	51
22	48
24	47
29	46

(Contd...)

	Second Turn
37	49
38	45
40	40
43	39
57	39
	Third Turn
61	41
66	39
76	38
82	36
90	33

Table 9.15 Period in Days for each Fall of 5i C

Temperature Range	No. of Days
65°-60°	4
60°-55°	7
55°-50°	1
50°-45°	25
45°-40°	2
40°-35°	44
35°-30°	14
Total	**97 days**

Turning

Turning the compost was done three times: To insure uniform decomposition, to restore moisture and air, and to supply massive quantities of those types of microbes needed to take the composting process to its next stage.

The first turn was at about sixteen days. A second mass inoculation equivalent to a few wheelbarrows full of 30 day old composting material was taken from an adjacent pit and spread thinly over the surface of the pit being turned. Then, one half of the pit was dug out with a manure fork and placed atop the first half.

A small quantity of water was added, if needed to maintain moisture. Now the compost occupied half the pit, a space about 15 × 14 and was about three feet high, rising out of the earth about one foot. During the monsoons when heaps were used, the above-ground piles were also mass inoculated and then turned so as to completely mix the material, and as we do today, placing the outside material in the core and *vice-versa*.

One month after starting, or about two weeks after the first turn, the pit or heap would be turned again. More water would be added. This time the entire mass would be forked from one half the pit to the other and every effort would be made to fluff up the material while thoroughly mixing it. And a few loads of material were removed to inoculate a 15-day-old pit.

Another month would pass, or about two months after starting, and for the third time the compost would be turned and then allowed to ripen. This time the material is brought out of the pit and piled atop the earth so as to increase aeration. At this late stage there would be no danger of encouraging high temperatures but the increased oxygen facilitated nitrogen fixation.

The contents of several pits might be combined to form a heap no larger than 10 × 10 at the base, 9 × 9 on top, and no more than 3-1/2 feet high. Again, more water might be added. Ripening would take about one month. Howard's measurements showed that after a month's maturation the finished compost should be used without delay or precious nitrogen would be lost. However, keep in mind when considering this brief ripening period that the heap was already as potent as it could become. Howard's problem was not further improving the C/N, it was conservation of nitrogen.

The Superior Value of Indore Compost

Howard said that finished Indore compost was twice as rich in nitrogen as ordinary farmyard manure and that his target was compost with a C/N of 10:1. Since, it was long manure he was referring to, let's assume that the C/N of a new heap started at 25:1.

The C/N of vegetation collected during the year is highly variable. Young grasses and legumes are very high in nitrogen, while dried straw from mature plants has a very high C/N. If compost is made catch-as-catch-can by using materials as they come available, then results will be highly erratic. Howard had attempted to make composts of single vegetable materials like cotton residues, cane trash, weeds, fresh green sweet clover, or the waste of field peas. These experiments were always unsatisfactory.

So Howard wisely mixed his vegetation, first withering and drying green materials by spreading them thinly in the sun to prevent their premature decomposition, and then taking great care to preserve a uniform mixture of vegetation types when charging his compost pits. This strategy can be duplicated by the home gardener. Howard was surprised to discover that he could compost all the crop waste he had available with only half the urine earth and about one-quarter of the oxen manure he had available. But fresh manure and urine earth were essential.

During the 1920s a patented process for making compost with a chemical fertilizer called Adco was in vogue and Howard tried it. Of using chemicals he said:

"The weak point of Adco is that it does nothing to overcome one of the great difficulties in composting, namely the absorption of moisture in the early stages. In hot weather in India, the Adco pits lose moisture so rapidly that the fermentation stops, the temperature becomes uneven and then falls. When, however, urine earth and cow-dung are used, the residues become covered with a thin colloidal film, which not only retains moisture but contains combined nitrogen and minerals required by the fungi. This film enables the moisture to penetrate the mass and helps the fungi to establish themselves. Another disadvantage of Adco is that when this material is used according to the directions, the carbon-nitrogen ratio of the final product is narrower than the ideal 10:1. Nitrogen is almost certain to be lost before the crop can make use of it"

Fresh cow manure contains digestive enzymes and living bacteria that specialize in cellulose decomposition. Having a regular supply of this material helped initiate decomposition without delay. Contributing large quantities of actively growing microorganisms through mass inoculation with material from a two-week-old pile also helped. The second mass inoculation at two weeks, with material from a month-old heap provided a large supply of the type of organisms required when the heap began cooling. City gardeners without access to fresh manure may compensate for this lack by imitating Howard's mass inoculation technique, starting smaller amounts of compost in a series of bins and mixing into each bin a bit of material from the one further along at each turning.

The passive backyard composting container automatically duplicates this advantage. It simultaneously contains all decomposition stages and inoculates the material above by contact with more decomposed material below. Using prepared inoculants in a continuous composting bin is unnecessary. City gardeners cannot readily obtain urine earth. Nor are American country gardeners with livestock likely to be willing to do so much work. Remember that Howard used urine earth for three reasons. One, it contained a great deal of nitrogen and improved the starting C/N of the heap. Second, it is thrifty. Over half the nutrient content of the food passing through cattle is discharged in the urine. But, equally important, soil itself was beneficial to the process.

Of this Howard said, "[where] there may be insufficient dung and urine earth for converting large quantities of vegetable wastes which are available, the shortage may be made up by the use of nitrate of soda... If such artificials are employed, it will be a great advantage to make use of soil." I am sure he would have made very similar comments about adding soil when using chicken manure, or organic concentrates like seed meals, as cattle manure substitutes.

Control of the air supply is the most difficult part of composting. First, the process must stay aerobic. That is one reason that single-material heaps fail because they tend to pack too tightly. To facilitate air exchange, the pits or heaps were never more than two feet deep. Where air was insufficient (though still aerobic) decay is retarded but worse, a process called denitrification occurs in which nitrates and ammonia are biologically broken down into gasses and permanently lost.

Too much manure and urine-earth can also interfere with aeration by making the heap too heavy, establishing anaerobic conditions. The chart illustrates denitrification caused by insufficient aeration compared to turning the composting process into a biological nitrate factory with optimum aeration.

Table 9.16 Making Indore Compost in Deep and Shallow Pits.

	Pit 4 Feet Deep	Pit 2 Feet Deep
Amount of material (lb. wet) in pit at start	4,500	4,514
Total nitrogen (lb) at start	31.25	29.12
Total nitrogen at end	29.49	32.36
Loss or gain of nitrogen (lb)	-1.76	+3.24
Per centage loss or gain of nitrogen	-6.1%	+11.1%

Finally, modern gardeners might reconsider limiting temperature during composting. India is a very warm climate with balmy nights most of the year. Heaps two or three feet high will achieve an initial temperature of about 145°. The purchase of a thermometer with a long probe and a little experimentation will show you the dimensions that will more-or-less duplicate Howard's temperature regimes in your climate with your materials.

WEEDS

COMPOST farming is a type of soil fertilization that dates back to the first recorded agricultural history. One modern dictionary defines compost as "a fertilizing mixture." Which really doesn't define a great deal, for there are many fertilizing mixtures that fall far short of properly built compost. In ordinary language, compost is what results when vegetable materials are thrown into a hole or stacked up on the level in some out-of-the-way place and permitted to rot as they will.

Scientific compost making, however, follows a more exacting formula. A true compost is a mixture of plant ingredients, all right, but there is more to the processing than is generally believed. Actually, almost anything organic short of saw logs can be turned into good fertilizer if the right procedure is followed.

Probably the first compost formula was the one introduced and developed by Marcus Cato, a Roman scientist, statesman, and general all-round farmer who lived and lectured on agriculture some two hundred years before the Christian era. At least, I think Cato's compost formula is the first that history records. Until the fall of Rome, the teachings of Cato were the last word in farm management. There is little doubt that this old Roman was one of the world's greatest agriculturists. Many of our modern agricultural discoveries were advocated by him.

Cato was a strong believer in compost as *the* soil builder. Indeed, one gets the idea from his writings that he considered compost making and compost fertilization indispensable if one expected to hold one's land to a high production level. Farm animals were kept as much for what they could supply to the compost pits in the way of manure as for any other purpose.

Cato's method of compost making required two deep, covered pits, one to hold the finished fertilizer, the other to take the stuff as it came from the barnlot or field. On the larger estates the pits were in charge of men who were thoroughly versed in the science of compost making.

As a first step in getting the materials ready for the pit, Cato directed that everything should first be scattered in the corrals or used as bedding in the animal stalls, to be trampled under the feet of the livestock. Treating the vegetable materials in this way did two very important things: the trampling broke up the roughage and insured quicker disintegration in the pits; also the spongy material collected the liquid manure which otherwise would go to waste.

After this initial treatment, the ingredients went into the pit, where they remained a year. During this period the stuff was turned periodically to bring about uniform disintegration and assure against loss from firefanging.

One of Cato's most interesting — and certainly progressive — agricultural principles was that the raw materials must always be composted before being inculcated into the soil. This, he claimed, saved the plant roots from having to do a lot of extra work that was not directly connected with the production of crops. He wanted plant food materials served ready for immediate consumption. No raw manures or other undecayed ingredients should ever be applied directly to the soil.

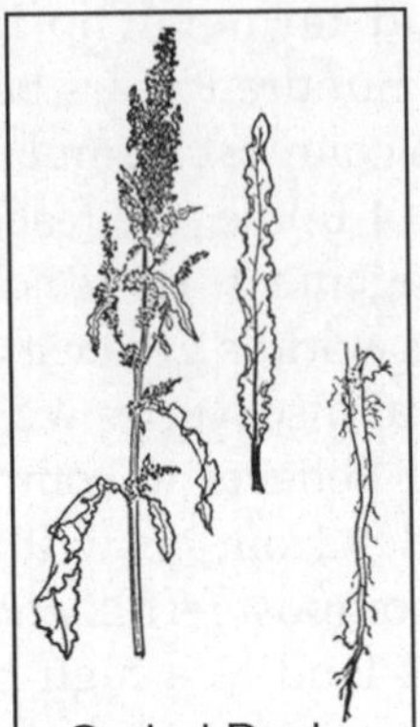

Curled Dock

Some suggest that the Romans may have learned compost making from the Chinese. I doubt this, for the Romans seem to have employed only dry materials for making their compost, whereas the Chinese always have preferred green vegetation. It is true that dry rubbish is never wasted in China; but during my explorings over there I never met a farmer who did not rank the green vegetation above straw and other dry refuse.

The only reason I could discover why the Chinese were partial to the green material was because the processing was quicker. A few farmers I talked to also considered the 'green compost' more quickly available when applied to the soil. I found only occasionally a Chinese farmer who was building or had built what he considered a complete compost, though any of them could tell you all about Chinese composts.

Green weeds would be the best possible materials for making composts, they say, but these are no longer to be found in sufficient abundance on the hills. As a general rule, like the old Chinese woman already described, they chop up the small amount of green stuff they are able to gather and apply it directly to the soil.

The people in several countries of Europe prior to the outbreak of the last war were far more compost conscious than American farmers and gardeners have ever been. Farmers in

America seem to think of compost making as kid work; not a man-size job of farming. Compost for a small house garden is all right, some will tell you; but for a cornfield — well, men have enough to do without wasting time hauling and tossing rubbish into a hole in order to get a hatful of fertilizer after waiting several months. To compost organic materials into the superb fertilizer that is possible is a man's job from start to finish. Yet the composting of plants or plant refuse is simple in comparison with the results obtained. Nature's constructive laws are usually like that. They are exacting but easy to follow, and the returns are great.

An English agricultural scientist, the late Sir Albert Howard, was beyond doubt the outstanding compost authority of modern times. Making use of the best compost knowledge to be found in the Orient and elsewhere, he added to this the results of his own extensive experience and experiments in several parts of the world, until he came up with a formula which, if followed, results in a fertilizer that ranks with Nature's best.

Fertilizer made according to the Howard formula will re-establish balance in weak soils in a much shorter time than will any of the fertilizers with which most of us are familiar; and it reveals its richness in the harvested produce in a way that is almost unbelievable. Both quality and quantity are enhanced. In some respects, soil built up by means of the Howard compost surpasses virgin land in that it can be held to a more uniform balance because the farmer has the soil-improving operations completely under his control.

For full information about the Howard compost, its method of processing and so on, the reader is referred to *The Soil and Health*, by Sir Albert Howard, the great scientist's own record of his life work.

What I wish particularly to bring out here is the place of weeds as compost material; weeds in the light of the Howard compost. Just as the Chinese have proved through long experience that weeds, when used green, differ in their fertilizing ability, so should we expect to find that different kinds of weeds in our own country will differ in their ability to enrich the soil, both while they are growing and foraging for food materials and when they are employed for making compost.

Unfortunately, our knowledge of this difference between our valuable weeds is at present very limited. What we do know is that several familiar weeds are excellent soil improvers and that all weeds rank high as compost material. Consequently, the farmer or gardener should employ in his compost as many kinds of weeds as he can get hold of, from sunflowers to carpet weeds, with all the in-betweens, and at every stage of growth.

Most farms have an abundance of compost material. Here is one worthy use for the weeds along the road or highway. Those weed areas should not be denuded. Ample weeds should always be left to hold the soil and to provide seed for the next crop. And rare is the farm that does not have some vigourous weed patches temptingly available other than the weeds along the highway: next to fence lines and in fence corners; around out-buildings and here and there in the barnlot. Also, there are those weed strips along the forest edge, or weed coves that have grown undisturbed for a long period of time. On depleted land and on eroded farms, weeds are likely to be scarce. At least, the most desirable weeds. In such cases the roadside weeds may prove to be a valuable asset capable of lending aid well worth considering in soil conservauon.

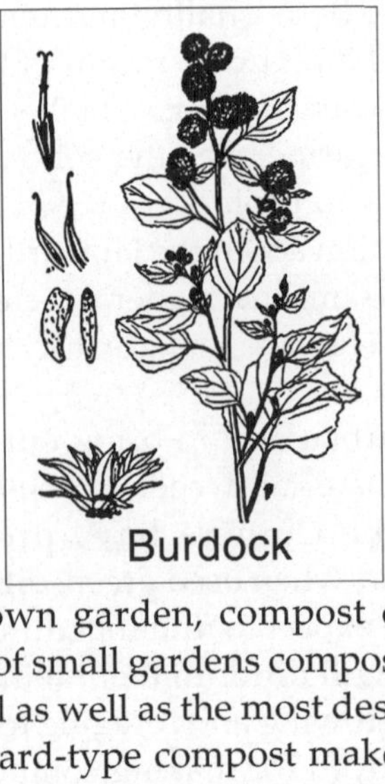
Burdock

In the small town garden, compost can really prove its worth. For all types of small gardens compost is beyond question the most economical as well as the most desirable fertilizer. This is because the Howard-type compost makes it possible for the gardener to get an amasingly high production of quality vegetables from a small plot. For vegetable plots, shrubbery, or flowerbeds, compost made from weeds combined with barnyard manure, the mixture correctly processed, will satisfy every plant-food demand. The town gardener, though his plot may not be larger than a four-by-ten table, should learn how to build compost the Howard way, and then use it for all it is worth along with green weeds turned under occasionally, and with mother weeds in his plots wherever the latter is practicable.

As a compost gardener, the town gardener will then never burn the leaves from his street trees. Fallen leaves are tops as compost material. Aside from containing excellent fibre, which all soils need, tree leaves are rich in minerals. Do not forget that tree roots delve deeply into the soil for food and moisture. They bring up enormous quantities of these food substances, a goodly portion of which go back to the soil when the leaves fall, after having completed their work as the food-processing laboratories of the plant.

In case a gardener does not feel he can spare the time and effort to build a Howard compost pile, he can still make use of his fallen leaves in a manner that will give him a lot of feeding material for his garden, his flowers in the yard, his lawn, or his shrubbery.

A simple compost stack—or pit—can be built to meet restricted conditions in town. And here is a word of caution about the composting of leaves: weeds should always be mixed with the leaves when building the compost, whether a shallow pit is used or the stack is built on level ground, since, the leaves, when piled up alone, have a tendency to compact together. This compacting of the leaves prevents suitable aeration while the stack is processing. By alternating a layer of weeds with a thin layer of leaves, this can be eliminated. And in order to have a more nearly balanced fertilizer, there should also be a layer, some two or three inches thick, of reasonably fertile soil, this also alternated regularly with the leaf-weed layers.

The soil, wherever possible, should be mixed with poultry or other animal manure, as well as a bit of slaked lime or ground limestone. If dry materials are employed for making the compost, all of the stuff should be thoroughly soaked with water as the different layers are put in.

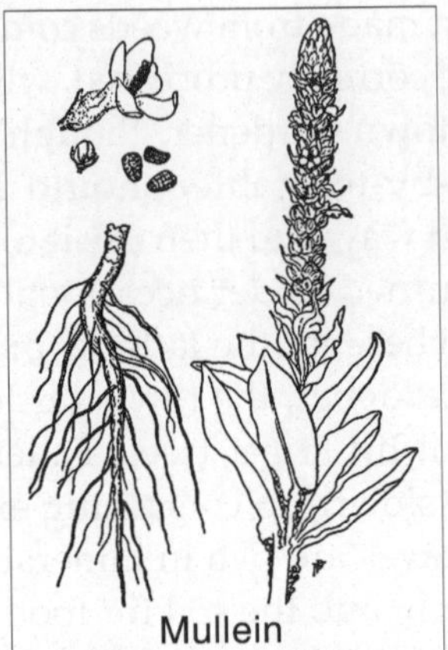
Mullein

Being unable to meet all the requirements for an ideal compost mixture should not deter one from doing the best one can. Weeds and leaves alone will give back a very desirable fertilizer. If you have some reasonably good dirt handy, just build a three-layer stack as follows: weeds, leaves, soil; weeds, leaves, soil, etc. Or, weeds and soil; weeds and soil. Where manure is used, weeds, manure, leaves; weeds, manure, leaves, work out well. The point is, make use of those lawn mowings, fallen leaves —all stuff that will decay in a reasonable time—for making a better fertilizer than you can possibly buy.

No farmer or gardener has a valid excuse for not getting some value out of his weeds. If he is unwilling to welcome weeds as a green manure in his rotation, or as mother weeds in his cultivated crop, he can still compost his weeds into a fertilizer that will live up to every claim made for it. And once tried, those thistles and pigweeds and sunflowers—all kinds of weeds will be seen as possessing some worth, though many may rightly be pests in some situations. Some of the very worst weed villains make the very best of compost.

In a town where there are gardening enthusiasts, there should be compost clubs in which the Howard system of compost making should be studied as a science and through actual demonstrations. This can be done, and is practical. After a gardener learns through his own efforts what quality of flowers or vegetables he can harvest from a few square yards of land, that gardener will be a compost booster wherever he goes. He may even reach the point where, like many gardeners in Europe at the present time, he will plant weeds in a special plot so as to make sure of an ample supply of this best of compost material. He will discover also that practically all vegetable refuse and discards from the kitchen, lawn mowings, prunings, garden leftovers, fallen leaves—all can be turned into rich plant food—a far better fertilizer than he can purchase on the market.

WEEDS AS FOOD

A VERY largre per centage of our soil-building weeds are in one form or another edible. Most of them are very nourishing. And my Nature-loving mother did know her potherbs. She searched the forest and meadows for her weed greens, often the very same weeds she fought so relentlessly in her garden. Mother considered the wild, eating weeds far superior to any greens that even she could grow. She planted mustard to give a bit of tang to the more delicate wild plants, or to assure our daily minerals if something prevented her gathering the wild greens. Turnip greens she grew in the fall when edible weeds were not plentiful. But the domestic greens were only for emergencies. Wild plants when available were the favourites.

In the spring, from the time of the first chirp of the little bird she always called the pewee, we were constantly cautioned to be on the lookout for the old standbys in the coves or in the protected forest spots. As soon as we reported that the young weeds were two inches tall, every morning soon after breakfast mother was off for the fields, her 'yarb' kettle on her arm. Neither rain nor mud stopped her. Those weeds that she hated in her garden were now a special gift to her from Nature; weeds were now food, not pests. Mother's weed collection was not large.

The poke weed, known for its poisonous roots, was particularly prized because it was the one weed that mother liked to cook with her meat. And because of the danger of harvesting a bit of the poison-filled root, she wouldn't trust anybody but herself to gather those 'asparagus' shoots of the poke. She served up to us the sow thistle, the smooth-leaf pigweed—but never the coarse-leaf villain. Stinging nettles occasionally came onto the table when the plants were young and tender. Dandelion and wild lettuce were sometimes combined, but as a rule they were served alone like other weeds. These two weeds were looked upon as a sort of 'Sunday greens,' because they were rarely abundant on or near our farm, and Mother was especially fond of their flavour.

As I recall, our weeds were always cooked much the same way: boiled in a large kettle and seasoned sometimes with a bit of bacon or ham grease, or more often served without any seasoning at all. Each of us seasoned to suit his taste. And it was a long time after my mother's day that I learned why those wild plants were so much more savory than the majority of cultivated vegetables: even young weeds, by the time they are big enough to start going into the 'greens kettle,' are foraging extensively; their husky roots are already near, or in, the lower soils, feeding in that rich store-house down there.

Pokeweed

The Pawnee Indians almost invariably cooked their weeds with meat of all kinds, preferably after the meat had become stale. Before edible weeds appeared abundantly in their cultivated fields, the squaws were weed gathering daily in the forest and gulches. The Indian women harvested all the weeds that were my mother's favourites, plus many others. They prized the rough pigweed, and purslane they also valued highly, often drying the stems and succulent leaves of the latter for winter food. The Pawnees—the very old members of the tribe—ate weed roots of several kinds. The wild morning-glory and the wild turnip I remember particularly. Weed seeds were eaten, but probably not so extensively as with Indians of some other tribes. The seeds of both pigweed and lamb's quarter were harvested by some of the squaws and ground or pounded into a sort of flour to be mixed with meal in making bread or porridge.

Professor Edward F. Costetter of the University of New Mexico, in his studies of the food habits among some of the Indian tribes of the Southwest, has brought to light interesting information on the use of many common weeds as human food. The Indians of Arizona and New Mexico still employ weeds much as did the Pawnees formerly. Some weeds, however, are put to more extensive use. Pigweeds, for instance, after being first boiled, are then fried in lard. These weeds are also canned for winter food. The Southwest tribes commonly grind the seed of both pigweeds and lamb's quarter for bread and porridge.

Several years ago, while exploring in Arizona and old Mexico, I now and then ran onto small plots of wild lamb's quarter that was being grown for the seed. Professor Costetter reports that the common milkweed is especially prized in some places, the young stems and leaves being cooked with meat. The roots and young pods of this plant are eaten both raw and cooked.

The late war in Europe, despite the suffering and destruction it brought about, gave birth to a new weed knowledge that should play an important role in rebuilding some of those ravaged countries. Necessity forced the investigation of the food value of many weeds that until then had been given little attention. Some weeds that had long been looked upon as worthless were found to be highly nutritious fodder for livestock. Once these weeds were correctly processed, that is, cut and cured into hay or made into ensilage, livestock not only devoured the hay and silage, but gave back gratifying returns. American farmers will probably be more than a little surprised to learn, for instance, that the detested bindweed, when cured into hay, gave returns from dairy cows considerably above either alfalfa or clover. Many weed experiments were carried on at one of England's leading experiment stations, where the weeds, of course, were under control.

Thistles of several kinds, when treated correctly, were also found to rank high as stockfeed. Thistle ensilage is not entirely unknown in the United States. Stinging nettles, a European weed that is now established in many parts of our own country, the English investigators found to be excellent feeding, when cured, for both dairy cattle and poultry. These nettles are rich in protein, and laying hens, fed the cured leaves and stems as a major part of their ration, showed a marked increase in egg production. With dairy cows, nettle hay produced a very noticeable increase in milk and butterfat.

How well I recall those dense patches of stinging nettles that we had to wade through bare-legged to reach the best fishing places! We could have made an abundance of chicken feed and cow feed from those nettles had we only known. Mother knew the nettles made good greens, but never dreamed of drying them and feeding them to her hens. Acres of those weeds, growing along the creek and in uncultivated bottoms, went to waste every year — and are probably still going to waste. The searching English scientists also discovered that many other weeds needed only a bit of special treatment to bring out their value as food for livestock. The rough-leaf pigweed was found to make excellent hay. Pigweed hay and thistle hay brought returns only slightly below those received from bindweed hay.

Any weed that gave the least promise as human food was tested thoroughly with the aim of helping out the limited ration of a hungry people. Rural America today is more or less familiar with the common yellow dock, one of the most famous greens of the South. Many southern housewives will tell you that no potherb can excel the dock in richness. And they are right. The yellow dock stands near the top of all potherbs in food value. Every garden should have a patch of this dock, especially since, it requires no care once it has become established in a fairly damp spot. During spring and carly summer a few square feet of these weeds will give an abundance of solid nourishment.

Dandelion

As a general thing, American farmers have given little thought to the curing of weeds for hay. It has long been known that sunflowers make excellent ensilage. And I have seen several other weeds used in the same manner. Giant ragweeds for one. One farmer told me he obtained his best ensilage when he mixed weeds with his cultivated legumes in the silage trenches. The stock seemed to prefer this ensilage to all others. Wild hay always contains a per centage of weeds. As a rule these weeds have passed beyond their valuable food stage before the grass is ready for cutting, but stock will go for many of them after the weeds have passed through the sweat in a stack.

But not all Americans are unaware of the value of weed hay as a forage for livestock. Lately I have had some very interesting reports on ragweed hay, and from widely different sections of the country. In every case the farmer was enthusiastic about the results he had obtained from this much-maligned weed: "Cattle preferred it to alfalfa and did well on it," one said. Another wrote me, "This hay is not bitter when cured and stacked right, like green ragweeds are. My cattle seem to like ragweed hay better than any other forage."

These farmers indicated that they were using identical methods for making the hay: the weeds are cut when lush and green, but before they become too woody. The hay is left in the swath or shock for a short period, the same as alfalfa, but when stacked it is given a bit of salt now and then as the stack goes up. These farmers seem to think that the salt in some way improves the value of the hay other than to perk up its flavour.

It goes without saying that the seed problem will enter in until somebody comes along with a satisfactory solution to it. The annual ragweeds must of course be planted each year save where a crop is permitted to go to seed on the land. Since, no farmer has written me about planting ragweeds, I take it that all depended on natural seeding, or they were making hay from the common perennial which is found in many sections. However, annual ragweeds are heavy seed producers, and gathering and threshing the seed should not be difficult. A few years hence, ragweed hay may well be filling an important forage niche on many American farms.

If a weed makes better hay than alfalfa or clover, then that weed *must* be good. Now, we have proof that many weeds will come close to doing that if they are cut at the right time and cured correctly. But any farmer who does not wish to make weed hay can turn his weeds into high-class ensilage. For making silage, weeds can be cut almost any time so long as they are not completely dry.

Why so many wild plants are repulsive to white people is difficult to understand, especially since, many of these same plants have been ranked as nourishing food by our Indians as well as other primitive people since, the beginning of time. One such plant is the common milkweed, a native perennial found generally throughout the United States. When the tender stems are boiled in two or three waters so as to remove the milky sap, the resulting product is a fair substitute for the best spinach. The small pods when cooked resemble okra — some who have tried it consider the milkweed pod more savory than okra, though the milkweed is not so easily cooked. And the milkweed roots are not bad "potatoes" — once you remove the original bitter taste.

Then there is the wonderful ground cherry. The ground cherry, a valuable weed in any field, has been ignored too long. Its fruit, produced in a husk, is most delicious whether eaten raw or made into preserves or pies. This weed should be a companion in every garden where it can be made to grow. One member of the goldenrod tribe has long been known among the Indians as a favourite tea plant. This variety, often listed as the "sweet goldenrod," can be distinguished from the other strains by crushing and smelling the leaves, which have a delightful aroma, resembling anise. It is a tall, slender plant and grows along the edges of fields or near the forest where the soil is a bit sandy. The beverage made from the cured leaves is very pleasing.

Now *my* favourite beverage: sumacade. Gather the common sumac panicles in late summer when the berries are brilliant red and sour. Then squeeze out the juice in any manner you like, strain, add water, a bit of lemon, sugar to taste—and drink ice-cold.

A research botanist remarked to me not long ago: "Rare is the weed that is not edible. I have eaten almost everything in the weed line in every community where I have lived, and have seldom found one that was not pleasing to the taste; most were delicious." As Indian John used to say: "All wild plants good. Indian eat 'em and live long time!' It used to seem to me, when I was a lad in the Indian country, that Indians did outlive white folks. I don't know how much weeds had to do with it. Old John may have been speaking with more wisdom than I at the time suspected.

I remember how as a boy I enjoyed digging and eating raw the roots of the evening primrose, but I did not know that those roots were cooked and served as a root vegetable until I had traveled in Europe. Though the primrose is native to America, it was the Europeans who first discovered that the roots were highly nutritious. This weed is commonly grown as a choice vegetable in both England and Holland. It should also be given a place in American gardens along with other favourite root vegetables. And finally, I would put in a word for the lowly sheep sorrel, a weed found throughout most of our country in cultivated as well as neglected fields, or along the edges of woods.

This sorrel has pink flowers and thick juicy leaves, all of which are pleasingly acid. While most folks know that sheep sorrel is edible, few know that it is delicious when served in a salad, or when used as pie filling. Those sorrel pies my mother used to make! No, I don't know how she made them, but she probably applied her good cook's ingenuity to a rhubarb recipe.

WEEDS AND WILDLIFE

IGNORANCE of wildlife values on the farm is no more excusable than are our prevalent weed superstitions. Even the songbirds are resented by many, although the birds are among our best friends. Were it not for the helpful birds, insects would soon drive us poor humans off the earth completely, despite our sprays and other bug killers. Then there are the nonvenomous snakes. The childish fear perpetually manifested for these harmless creatures is hard to understand. One garter snake or one whip snake or one gopher snake will catch more mice and rats than sixteen cats. Even a small house snake will put to rout a giant rattler or copperhead—and get a kick out of doing it. Venomous snakes are cowards and usually have a strange terror of their nonvenomous cousins. As long as there are a few non-poisonous snakes around the house or barnlot, rattlesnakes are likely to make themselves scarce.

Even skunks are generally looked upon as odorous enemies of respectable folk. More need of understanding. Did you ever watch a skunk digging for insects in a pasture or meadow or orchard? The number of grubs and adult insects that skunks destroy each year is enormous. In the orchard the skunk is especially valuable, since, the larvae of many injurious insects are commonly found around the base of fruit trees. Skunks, if not disturbed too often, will frequent orchards continuously and thus do a lot of good by digging up and destroying these fruit pests. And there is no more ideal sanctuary for all such wild friends than rich coves of annual weeds growing in sheltered spots not too far from the house or barnlot. As I found in that weed cove of my boyhood, our friendly varmints prefer a weed patch to any other kind of cover, especially during the summer and autumn months.

There is an old story of a miserly farmer who possessed extensive orchards and gardens, the only orchards and vegetable gardens for miles in any direction. It was natural for the birds to move into those orchards in droves every spring—valuable birds and orchards were made for each other. At first the miser only grumbled as the birds went about their business of nest building.

But as he grew older, his grumblings became more threatening. He didn't like the noisy chatter of those birds. Still, so long as the birds didn't disturb his fruit, he'd tolerate them —and birds were not very troublesome in apple and pear orchards.

To add to his income, the miser planted a cherry orchard. The cherry trees at last came into bearing. The miser was counting a lot on the dollars he would get from those cherries. He visited his cherry orchard daily. The trees blossomed, put on the young fruit—and the fine cherries began to ripen.

Then the miser received his terrible shock. He went out one morning to find that the birds were pecking his cherries. They had eaten only a few of them, but the miser raged at what he saw. He swore then and there to drive every bird from his orchard. He'd destroy every nest and break every egg. And he did. It took his laborers several days to destroy all of the birds' nests, for there were many of them. Then the miser kept one man busy for several more weeks, keeping the birds from rebuilding their nests. Finally the birds gave up; went in search of new nesting grounds.

A grim silence settled down upon the orchards and garden then. The miser gloated over his victory—and the extra dollars he had gained by driving the birds away. He gloated over that grisly silence too. He liked the stillness. He gloated until...

Until one day he was startled by new and different sounds coming from his orchards and gardens; sickening noises they were—noises that kept up right through the darkness of the night. Now he was hearing the sounds of gnawing insects! The rasping, crackling sounds caused by insect mandibles! The insects stripped the miser's garden and orchards; then they began on the miser himself. The worms gnawed him; the bugs stabbed him and chewed him. They drove him mad. The miser went out screaming.

There are plenty of adults who need this lesson. Especially those adults who destroy or permit the destruction of valuable birds and their nests, who kill every harmless snake they see simply because it wriggles; or those who think that all the good that skunks do is to stir up a stink. Yes, and those folks who insist on destroying all weeds just because—they don't happen to understand and appreciate weed values.

Once a very admirable man moved into our Kansas neighbourhood. This man bought a sort of run-down farm and then proceeded to improve it not only agriculturally, but also by turning it into a haven for wildlife. And what a contrast was Uncle Les Mason, as we called him, to that miserly farmer! Uncle Les was kind to everybody and everything. He went out of his way to prove to us that wild things did appreciate human friendship.

He often told us that the wild things always reciprocated human friendship by helping them at every turn. Why, Uncle Les knew a whole brigade of toads as individuals and called each toad by its name. I remember one jolly-looking toad that Uncle Les called Charley. I was certain that Charley always blinked more excitedly whenever he heard his name. Uncle Les used to say it was a lot better to have a bevy of toads around to catch the flies than to be bothered with sticky flypaper.

It was Uncle Les's flock of birds that no boy could forget. Uncle Les surely knew his birds and their value as insect catchers in his orchards and fields. But it was the homey things that he made so interesting to us when he was talking; the idiosyncrasies of birds—or toads or harmless snakes or skunks—as they went about their daily businesses.

It seems but yesterday when I was trotting at the side of Uncle Les Mason, listening with open ears and open mouth as he pointed out to us the thickets and weed patches that were inhabited by his happy birds; his birds, which he considered as necessary in his very successful farming as were his fat team, his farm implements, and his dog, Rover. It must have been that I was always too interested in the antics of the birds themselves. Weeds were ordinary, whereas Uncle Les's birds were not. "Fish anywhere you want to along my creek, boys, except at the bends where the weeds are thick," he would tell us. "Don't go into those patches for your grasshoppers—those yellowlegs are for my birds. They need them to go along with the bugs and worms they harvest in my orchard and garden."

A fair-size creek angled across Uncle Les's farm, and the bends were numerous. In all of those bends were briar and weed patches that during the summer were alive with noisy birds. If Uncle Les ever planted weeds, I didn't know it; but I do know that he guarded his weed patches as carefully as he protected his small patches of grain planted especially for the birds.

Uncle Les Mason is an example of the value of a too-often-neglected side of most theories advanced relative to wildlife preservation: love and understanding for all wild things. The miserly farmer illustrates the value, too, in contrast. It goes without saying that there must be scientific planning and well-directed procedure, else accomplishments may result in little more than the sentimental hysteria which a bit of superficial knowledge about Nature seems to arouse in so many people. Folks gush over the sublime beauty of redbuds, for instance, then proceed to mutilate the shrubs while gathering the blossoms. Such people haven't the least comprehension of Nature. But stern science, without a measure of sentiment—true Nature-sentiment—swings the pendulum too far in the opposite direction. Such naturalists know toads scientifically; they never see the jolly Charleys. They possess the letter of Nature, but too much of the soul is lacking. Anyone who thinks that he must kill a bird in order to study it thoroughly is not a naturalist. He is an anatomist who should work in a museum.

With the present interest in wildlife preservation, we need practical biologists in our schools who can interpret the biology of field and stream and forest—who are able to read Nature's books. We need a few textbooks or guidebooks that tell the full story about wildlife habits and habitats. While I have not scrutinized all books written on wildlife preservation, I have yet to discover a book or bulletin or pamphlet that gives weeds the place they merit as wildlife feeding grounds and covers. Rabbits or quail or other birds of many kinds—a weed jungle is an ideal hideout for them.

It provides them with protection and food and, in winter, warmth. Of the covers usually found on any farm where there are timber and brushy draws, shrubbery and vine thickets rank first and heavy weed growth second. Grass makes a good cover, but more wild things prefer weed coves or weedy fields than open prairie lands, however dense the grass. These quail are not often disturbed and have easy access to a dense grass area, a field of either oats or wheat, a spread of fairly thick timber, and a patch of vigourous annual ragweeds.

The quail seem to know they are as safe in one place as another, but during the many months I have been watching this flock, rarely have I routed the birds out of the grass. In the hot part of the day in June, July, and August, the birds usually spend several hours in the woody thickets. They also feed part of the day in the grainfields after the grain has begun to ripen, but considerably more than half of the time is spent in the ragweed patch. This, too, when there are no ripe seeds on the weeds. I attribute this conduct of the quail to something more than a partiality for ragweed feeding.

10

Manure Biomass

GENERAL

Several research groups have introduced systems for converting animal wastes by biotechnological processes into products having a greater nutritive and thus commercial value. The magnitude and complexity of this problem from the scientific and technological points of view are enormous, because animal wastes are high in complex populations of wild micro-organisms concerned with eating each other more than the biological waste itself.

According to Brown, anaerobic processes are generally easier and cheaper, but yield less profit and are hampered by the discharge of effluent, or even solid waste, which is incapable of anaerobic conversion. On the other hand, aerobic processes are necessary when manures (cattle manure for example) are rich in ligno-cellulosic constituents digestible only by aerobic action.

Based on mesophilic fermentation, bacteria offer a wider range of micro-organisms and require less controlled conditions. Thermophilic fermentation, however, offers a higher degree of safety through prolonged exposure of the biomass to higher temperatures, eliminating pathogens and pasteurising the product. In addition, the thermophilic process yields more biomass, as it also utilizes the ligno-cellulosic constituents. For this reason, most scientists turn to thermophilic organisms that offer high protein substrate (50 to 60 per cent) and are rich in nutritionally important amino acids (lysine, methionine, cystine and tryptophane), usually limiting in livestock rations. The degradation of organic matter can be accomplished by psychrophilic, mesophilic and thermophilic micro-organisms. Coulthard and Townsley prefer the following temperatures:

Type of Bacteria	Temperature°C		Greatest Activity °C
	Min.	Max.	
Psychrophilic	-4	25–30	15–20
Mesophilic	+10	40–45	30–37
Thermophilic	+45	75	55–65

AEROBIC FERMENTATION PROCESSES

Several aerobic processes have been developed for converting animal wastes into single-cell protein (SCP), yeasts or other types of protein biomass. Aerobic processes produce, from 1 tonne of manure (DM), about 500 kg of dry product (SCP and yeast) containing 50 per cent crude protein, with amino acid patterns similar to those of soya. The value of such a protein concentrate would be in the range of $180–$220 per tonne. Lower protein yields (35–50 per cent crude protein) have been obtained from materials such as feedlot waste.

Item	Unit	Quantity
Major chemicals		
Caustic soda	tonnes	714
Ammonia	tonnes	736
Sulphuric acid	tonnes	736
Labour		
Direct	man/hours	29,000
Indirect	man/hours	25,000
Utilities		
Electricity	10^6kW	14.9
Fuel oil	joules	2.7×10^{12}
Water	hl	242,000

Based on the processing of 18,000 tonnes of feedlot waste from 25,000 head of cattle, the cost of plant was estimated in 1973 at $5,5 million, producing 3,600 t/year of 100 per cent protein, or

8,182 tons of protein concentrate similar to soybean meal (44 per cent). Operating costs per year can be established for specific conditions from the following data:

This plant represents a minimum economic scale for production of feed supplement. A commercial system for manure (and other organic, agriculturally related waste) conversion into protein feed supplement has been developed by Parsons Brinckerhoff Quade and Douglas, Inc.

The process involves size reduction of waste by grinding, hydrolysis of the volatile organic fraction, separation of the ligno-cellulosic fraction, submerged fermentation of the cellular biomass, and dehydration. The process yields SCP biomass containing 45–50 per cent crude protein and discards the lignocellulosic fraction after separation in a primary, mechanical separator. Data from commercial applications are not available.

ANAEROBIC FERMENTATION PROCESSES

A batch process for fermentative conversion of feedlot manure filtrate into protein feed supplement for ruminants has been developed by Erdman and Reddy. The process involves dilution of feedlot wastes with water (1:1), agitation and filtration through a No. 8 sieve. The filtrate is fortified with a carbohydrate source (in this case, cheese whey) and fermented under anaerobic conditions. The indigenous microflora inherited from the filtrate and whey is used as a productive micro-organism. A constant pH is maintained by continuous addition of ammonia as a buffer to neutralize volatile fatty acids generated during the anaerobiosis. The best yields were obtained at pH 7 and 43°C, at a concentration of fermentable carbohydrates of 3.5 to 10.0 per cent. The process yielded biomass rich in CP, of which however 60–70 per cent was in the NPN form (ammonium salts or organic acids), while the residue consisted of microbial cells. In view of the simplicity of the process, the authors claim it can be easily adapted to the farm level.

More and Anthony, fermenting cattle manure under anaerobic conditions for 3 days, found a significant increase of protein, from an original 16.99 per cent in fresh manure to 43.26 per cent in fermented manure with a net increase of amino acids more than 20 per cent. The level of volatile fatty acids indicates that during the anaerobic process a very intense synthesis of organic acids occurred, and the authors reported that in 16½ hours of incubation at 37°C, the pH of the fresh manure dropped from 6.25 to 4.00.

Yeast has been produced from separated solubles (from fibres) of cattle manure. The recoverable, soluble portion of cattle manure represented 69 per cent of the DM. The process elded 40.9 per cent CP (on DM) in the final product.

Table 10.1 Manure: Composition Change By Fermentation.

Item	Fresh Manure (%)	Fermented Manure (%)
Organic acids		
Acetic	—	7.20
Propionic	—	1.27
Butyric	—	1.34
Valeric	—	0.11
Lactric	—	16.83
CP	16.99	43.26
Amino acids	16.98	40.74

THERMOPHILIC PROCESS

Recent Nebraska researchers have reported the development of a successful process for converting animal wastes into methane and protein concentrate by thermophilic anaerobic fermentation and centrifugation. Protein yields were as follows:

Products Recovered	Crude Protein (% DM)	Organic Protein (% DM)
From fermenter effluent	31.5	26.7
From centrifuge cake	18.5	14.8

The protein biomass of fermenter effluent contained a very high level of nutritionally important amino acids: lysine, threonine and methionine. The level of these amino acids in centrifuge cake was also relatively high as compared with soybean meal or lucerne hay.

Feeding trials showed that the fermenter effluent can be favourably compared with soybean meal. The economics of the process have been evaluated for a feedlot of 10,000 head. In summary, the following parameters were obtained:

	US$ Per Head
Capital investment cost	85.00 to 131.00
Methane value	7.65
Protein value of the fermenter effluent	82.90
centrifuge cake value	14.50 to 41.50

Table 10.2 Dried Fermenter Effluent, Dried Centrifuge Cake, Lucerne Hay And Soybean Meal: Essential Amino Acid Composition (g AA Per 16 g Organic N Except as other Wise Noted)

Item	Fermenter Effluent	Centrifuge Cake	Lucerne Hay[a]	Soybean Meal[a]
Phenylalanine	4.78	3.95	3.54	5.30
Threonine	4.60	4.74	4.11	3.94
Methionine	2.30	1.44	0.57	1.14
Valine	6.20	5.12	4.11	5.20
Leucine	6.44	8.37	5.87	8.08
Isoleucine	5.58	4.29	4.70	5.23
Lysine	5.36	4.74	3.54	6.58
Histidine	1.44	1.43	1.76	2.74
Arginine	3.93	4.88	4.11	7.06
Total essential AA	**40.63**	**38.96**	**32.32**	**45.25**
Total essential AA, % DM	**10.84**	**5.75**	**5.49**	**23.67**

The centrifuge cake value depends upon the capture efficiency of the centrifuge. The thermophilic anaerobic system appears to be an economically feasible process for a larger operation.

Thermophilic processing of pig waste conducted by Canadian researchers involved batch processing of pig sludge. A stabilized, odourless sludge, when dried, was considered by the authors as suitable for feeding.

DEVELOPMENT STATUS

All fermentation processes are still in the stage of pilot plants or small commercial operations. Thermophilic types appear to be most promising.

HEALTH HAZARDS

All fermentation processes are completely safe.

FUNGI AND MOULDS

The use of fungi and moulds as potential production micro-organisms has recently been reviewed by Calvert. Current studies indicated that some types of fungi grow satisfactorily on animal wastes, but the problem of toxicity affects the otherwise promising results.

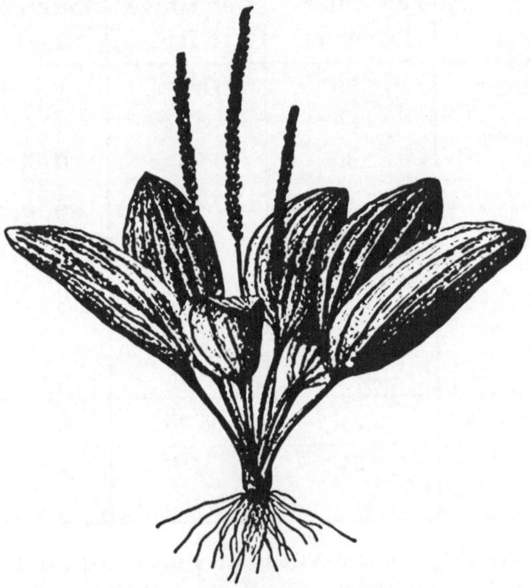

Rugel's Plantain

Quail are partial to ragweed cover because of some benefit they get from the soil where ragweeds grow. Ragweeds do enliven the soil. The soil where thick prairie grass grows is also richer than that found in most cultivated fields, but in sod it is not so easy for the birds to get close to mother earth.

Which brings us to one of the most tragic causes of wildlife depletion in many parts of our country: soil sterility. The garden toad, once so familiar around the doorsteps almost everywhere, or in the kitchen garden, or milk house near a cool spring, is now rare.

Then I went to call on a friend of those yesteryears, a friend whom I had not seen since, those days of my early youth; those years when we both cut weeds for Sol Benson and others. And I mentioned not finding any toads in the spots where they had once been so numerous.

A reminiscent shadow slid across my friend's face. "Toads! I recollect how thick they used to be when we were kids. Fly-catchers, we used to call 'em! I don't remember seein' hardly any toads for thirty years or more — "The everyday life of the humble toad is tied in with soil fertility. The toad is more dependent on fertile soil than many other wild things familiar to us: rabbits, gophers, skunks, and snakes. Toads haven't a great many enemies among other wildlife. Even snakes don't care much for toads. But toads soon disappear from land that is weak in organic substances, though the insects on which they feed may be plentiful. Earthworms and toads — their absence spells weak or depleted land.

Throughout the United States some species of birds have become rare for the same reason: our eroded or exhausted soils are not providing birds the nourishing foods which for many of them are essential. On eroded land even weeds do not produce high-quality seed for the seed eaters. Granted that many other factors share responsibility for the depletion of our valuable birds, low-quality grains and the persistent destruction of weeds have, either directly or indirectly, taken a heavier toll than is usually recognized.

Whenever I visit a weed cove, which is one of my chief outdoor sports, I inevitably compare it with that one particular cove of my youthful years. That cove was wildlife at its best. In summer or winter the cove was activity plus. In it, many wild things found food, either insects or seed, and protection and warmth, preferring it to the surrounding rich fields and meadows and forest in which food was abundant.

Such weed coves are not often found now. Where there is continuous erosion the water often sweeps through the coves and disturbs the soil-mellowing work of the weeds. Either poor soil is washed into the coves, or the dead plant bodies are carried away. The weeds may struggle along and make a fair growth, but they are not able most of the time to build up a rich, mellow earth.

Dense shrub thickets provide a bit better cover than weeds, since, these thickets are more permanent and enemies cannot penetrate them so easily. A wise farmer, instead of destroying his thickets, will encourage them to grow in all places where land can possibly be spared. And not all of the thickets should be located in pastures.

The best wildlife thickets are those completely isolated from all farm activities, located where domestic animals cannot browse in or near them. Permanent weed coves should be left as undisturbed jungles.

An ideal setup for many species of wildlife is a dense, well-shielded thicket that stands near a small field that has been released to weeds. I know an almost impenetrable plum thicket situated near such a weed patch. The weeds in the small field have been permanent fixtures for only a few years, but even when that field was under cultivation there usually was a good growth of weeds in it late in the summer after crops had been laid by.

This plum thicket and field have long been a favoured spot for migratory birds. Many species have for many years spent a part of each year here, some for only a few days, while others have come down from the north to remain for the winter.

During late years, though, the bird population of this thicket has shrunk to a mere fraction of what it formerly was. I am quite certain that the birds haven't shifted their course. The birdlife has vanished in direct proportion to the depletion of the farmlands.

Just lately I watched from a concealed spot the activities in and around this thicket. I had seen some migratory birds near the house, which immediately brought the thicket to mind. I found a few migrants in the thicket in addition to the two or three species of small birds that make the thicket their permanent homes. But the migratory birds were few. In an hour I saw only two species, and I could have counted all of those on the fingers of my two hands and had a finger or two left. I decided to go out into the weed patch, hoping I could in that way add more visitors to my count. But at that same moment I caught sight of something that caused me to change my mind: a wild house cat. The cat was easing its way towards the thicket, bird hunting, of course.

The prowling beast soon disappeared into the brush. Immediately birds came fluttering out. I ran to the thicket and routed the cat, after which I said a few uncomplimentary things about people who cast off their cats to hustle for themselves. One can't blame the starving cats. But why can't people put the cats out of their misery and thus save a very large number of valuable birds? Cats may be questionable pets; they don't help to produce and conserve food—save for an occasional worthy mouse catcher.

Birds do. One spring I kept a record on a pair of friendly wrens that had built their nest in an old bucket near my garage, which stood near the garden fence. For four uninterrupted hours I checked the number of worms the birds brought from the garden to their five young: every forty-five seconds one of the birds returned from the garden with a worm! I know, because I timed them carefully with my watch. I was a wreck when I finally gave up.

And that wasn't all: those faithful little labourers had been at it since, daylight. I have no doubt they continued their work until dark. Where those tiny nestlings put all those worms is still a mystery to me. But I am very certain those two wrens were largely responsible for some excellent cabbage in our garden that summer.

While wrens as a rule do not frequent weed patches, many other valuable birds do: for seed or for insects — or just for cover when they are not busy elsewhere. If two wrens in a few hours could do so much valuable work, think of the good all birds taken together must do. Then add to this the joy they bring us in friendship and song.

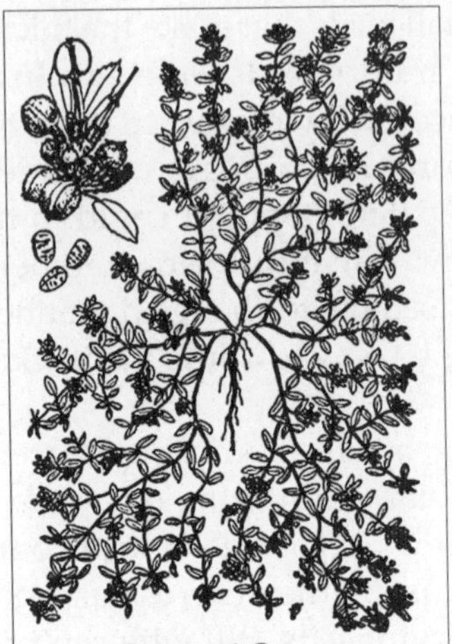

Spotted Spurge

The 4-H club work, dealing with wildlife preservation, is a grand movement and should receive hearty support from everyone. However, there is danger of this work's becoming too mechanical. Boys and girls should be taught in school and in club meetings that the first step in learning how to preserve the wildlife is to learn to love the outdoors—and to understand the outdoors. They should be taught how to study the wild things in the fields and forests—and weed patches. In this way they can best learn the relationship that exists between the birds, for example, and man's well-being. In this way it will be possible to present to the boys and girls the sentiment factor more realistically, for to see wildlife in action in the field will teach more than whole libraries of books.

As the young naturalist systematically studies his wild friends—and they should be looked upon as friends even though they do scamper away when he approaches them—he will often find his path leading straight towards a weed patch. And he may be a bit surprised to discover that so many of the inhabitants of the big outdoors depend upon weeds for food and shelter. From then on, as a true naturalist, he will see weed coves in a new light. Weed patches, with their seeds for his valuable bird friends; weed patches for cover for other wild things—they all belong together. And all are man's trustworthy friends.

FARMS UTILISING ANIMAL WASTES

INTRODUCTION

The conflict for land and other natural resources increases sharply as populations and living standards grow. Integrated farming, which maximizes food production, optimizes land use and minimizes environmental pollution, is a concept which has become an imperative for developing countries with limited natural resources but unlimited demands.

There are many methods of farm integration, but a suitable model can be established only when all the segments of the ecosystem are carefully considered. The examples set out here are therefore only indicative, and their economics are inevitably outlined very roughly. Nevertheless, most of these integrations exist as realities in various forms in Asia and elsewhere.

A typical example is Kamchai's farm (10,000 pigs) in Thailand. This integration involves a layer-pig-fish recycling principle; it is therefore applicable to a landless farmer, but it requires a fish pond. This type of livestock integration is usually applied on swampy or other lowland areas near urban centres, where cropping is less profitable while demand and animal product prices are high. Another Thai farm applies successfully an integration involving starch waste from a rice-flour mill and bakery by-products which are fed to pigs (4,000 head/day), while all pig wastes are discarded to ponds as the sole feed for fish. One pig produces about 35 kg of fish biomass annually.

Another agro-industrial integration approach, using all possible segments of modern recycling technology, is applied at Maya Farms (23 hectares), in the Philippines.

The individual components of this complex are:

- Pig farm (about 4,000 pigs at any time);
- Biogas plant (24 digesters of different types—Germany, China, India);
- Flour and feed mill;
- Abattoir;
- Rendering plant;
- Cannery;

- Crops (rice, beans, vegetables, fruits and others);
- Mushroom production;
- Algae/fish ponds.

The pig farm produces annually about 10,000 pigs, which are slaughtered and processed at the abattoir and meat processing plant. Several other farms, integrated with Maya farms, also supply the abattoir and meat processing plant with pigs, buffaloes and cattle. Processed meat is partly marketed, partly canned in the cannery. Abattoir waste and by-products (including blood), processed in the rendering plant (run on methane gas) generate feed which is recycled via the feedmill to pigs.

Manure from the pigs is washed with water into the biogas plant, which provides most of the electrical power required for lights, engines, deep-well pumps, dryers, smoke generators, burners, cooking and scalding tanks, refrigerators, etc. Digested liquor from the biogas plant is funnelled to the lagoon, where it yields algae, kang kong and fish. Sludge from the settling tanks is partially dried (using biogas and rice hulls). Most of it is utilized, via the feedmill, for pigs and other livestock, and the remainder as organic fertilizer. The paddy fields are fertilized by nutrient-rich liquid effluent. Rice straw as a by-product is used as a medium for mushroom production.

The main income from the recycling of wastes derives from feeding sludge to pigs, which provides more than five times the income derived from methane. Some of the practically applicable, simple models involving recycling of animal wastes among livestock species are as follows:

These integrations are quite common in Thailand, the Philippines and several other countries in Asia. They are operating on both small and large (commercial) scales and there is naturally no limit to the number of possible modifications of the integrations designed above. All these systems are in reality a substitute for the common soil-plant-animal cycle, because they convert all waste resources into animal products more effectively than traditional disposal methods. In addition, they ensure a clean environment with a minimum labour requirement.

Layer	Pig	Fish		
Broiler	Dairy Cow	Fish		
Layer	Dairy Cow	Fish		
Layer	Pig	Dairy Cow	Fish	and/or Cropping
Broilers	Dairy	Biogas	Fish	and/or Cropping
Pig	Biogas	Fish	and/or Cropping	
Pig	Dairy	Biogas	Fish	and/or Cropping
Layer Broiler	Pig Dairy	Biogas	Fish	and/or Cropping
Layer Broiler	Dairy	Sheep	Vegetable (for arid areas)	

Such operations would require about 4,000 m^2 (0.4 ha) of land if fish pond and cropping area are to be included, but they can also be modified for landless farmers or for farmers with very small plots. Under such conditions, fish and cropping would be excluded, and discarded animal wastes would be converted into biogas.

Most of the systems outlined above are suitable for lowland humid areas, and fish-ponds can be partially used for alternate cropping, rice in particular. For these smallholding models, the following standard units would constitute the circular integration.

LAYERS

The flock would consist of 100 layers fed on a conventional layer mash with an annual production of 165 eggs per bird; approximately 80 per cent of the birds would be sold ($1.50/each) at the end of the laying cycle.

In the case of layer-pig integration, layer cages would be fixed above the pig pen, and all falling layer manure would be consumed instantly by pigs. The layer manure contribution as a direct benefit on feed saving per pig/year is estimated to be $6.00 to $14.00.

Where layer-dairy cow integration is foreseen, layer waste would serve as a protein feed for the dairy herd; it would be collected daily, chemically treated and substitute for most of the protein requirement (60 to 90 per cent) of the herd. Another option would be to ensile wet, freshly collected, layer waste with forages, feeds or other wastes (grass, tubers, leaves, fruit waste and other resources), giving enough soluble carbohydrates to ensure proper fermentation and to maintain the moisture content of the silage in the range of 40–65 per cent. Ensiling would require 10–21 days and could be carried out in re-usable plastic bags. The farmer would prepare and use (10–21 days later) one bag (about 35–50 kg) of the silage daily.

Broilers

Broiler-dairy cattle integration would require about 500 broilers kept on wood shavings or any other ligno-cellulosic bedding material. Broilers would supply about 25 to 30 per cent of the total DM requirement and most of the protein requirement (70 to 90 per cent) of the cow. Broiler litter would be either chemically treated or ensiled together with forages, feed or wastes as indicated above.

Pigs

A simple wooden slatted house divided into 2 or 4 pens, for housing 20 pigs, would be constructed by the farmer at a cost of $300. The estimates assume the purchase of 20 piglets at 15 kg liveweight; they reach 100 kg (85 kg weight gain) within 170 to 180 days (feed efficiency 3.5); with a mortality allowance of 5 per cent, 19 porkers will be sold.

In pig-fish integration, all faecal waste generated by pigs will be directly discharged through slats into the fish-pond. In pig-dairy integration, the pig pens would require a concrete flooring which would facilitate the collection of waste for further handling. In this case, freshly collected pig waste will be ensiled for 14–21 days with suitable forages, feeds or wastes.

Dairy Herd

The herd would comprise 2 milking cows of a value of US$500 each, with a 520-day calving interval. The herd would generate 10 litres of milk daily (5 litres per cow/day). Milk is to be sold at an estimated $0.22 per litre. The feed input would consist of broiler litter or layer manure (20 to 35 per cent of DM requirement of dairy rations), 1 kg of feed concentrate per cow/ day during 300 days only, forage (leaves, fruit and vegetables) or its substitutes (grass growing within the premises of the farm and higher aquatic plants recoverable from the pond).

Sheep

The sheep herd would consist of 20 head of sheep yielding wool and meat. Dairy cattle-sheep integration would be applicable in arid areas where all cattle waste would be recycled to sheep. It is estimated that about 35 per cent of the DM feed requirement of sheep would be met by cattle waste in the form of silage with other available forages, feeds or wastes.

Fish

There are several suitable species of tropical fish, of which the best appear to be *Tilapia* (particularly Tilapia mossambica) and catfish. A small multiplication pond for sexing of fingerlings is necessary to control the number of fish in the pond because *Tilapia* and some other tropical species have an enormous reproductuve capacity which could cause overcrowding of the pond.

Although most of these species can survive under a low oxygen supply and poor water management, the yields of fish biomass can be significantly increased with good water management on one hand and control of the waste flow on the other.

Water hyacinth and other higher plants usually growing in the pond can cover about 10–15 per cent of the DM forage requirement of dairy cows, and in pig-fish integraton about 5–10 per cent of the DM requirement of the pigs. In addition, higher aquatic plants, where available in excess, can be chopped finely and returned to the pond as a feed for fish.

BIOGAS

The biogas installation would consist of one or two underground digesters with tanks, resettling ponds and the necessary infrastructure including feed funnels and piping for gas distribution.

CROPPING

In lowland areas rice (2 crops/year) will be the main crop, with some intercropping of forage for cattle and vegetable/fruit for family use; the required area would be about 4,000 m^2 = 0.4 ha. The smaller the land area the more intensive cropping programme could be applicable. In all these recycling systems the first limiting dietary factor in ruminant feeding would be feed energy. Therefore the choice of ingredients in humid tropics would be centred on root crops, cassava in particular; in arid areas the feed energy requirement could be balanced by dates and their waste products. Approximate financial estimates of some of these integrations at the small-farm level are given in Tables.

Table 10.3 Layer-Pig-Fish Integration: Economic Characteristics*

Item	Unit	Layers	Pigs	Fish	Total
1	2	3	4	5	6
Investment					
Assets	US$	150.00	300.00	50.00	500.00
Working capital	US$	216.00	2,437.00	10.00	2,663.00
Total investment	US$	366.00	2,737.00	60.00	3,163.00
Income	US$	1,192.00	3,800.00	570.00	5,562.00
Expenses					
Production costs					
Feed	US$	675.00	1,624.00	0.00	2,299.00
Drugs, medicines, etc.	US$	11.00	49.00	12.00	72.00
Labour	US$	91.00	274.00	91.00	456.00
Fixed costs					
Depreciation	US$	30.00	60.00	0.00	90.00
Interest (farm loan 10%)	US$	36.60	273.70	6.00	316.30
Total expenses	US$	843.60	2,280.70	109.00	3,233.30
Net Return	US$	348.40	1,519.30	461.00	2,328.70
Net Return	%	29	40	81	4
Return On Investment					
Average investment	%	190	111	1,537	147
Initial investment	%	95	56	768	74

1	2	3	4	5	6
Annual cash inflow	US$	378.40	1,579.30	461.00	2,418.70
Payback period	years	0.96	1.73	0.13	1.30

Table 10.4 Broiler-Dairy Cow-Fish Integration: Economic Characteristics

Item	Unit	Broilers	Dairy Herd	Fish	Total
Investment					
Assets	US$	650.00	150.00	50.00	850.00
Working capital	US$	1,180.00	1,000.00	10.00	2,190.00
Total investment	US$	1,830.00	1,150.00	60.00	3,040.00
Income	US$	3,600.00	943.00	570.00	5,113.00
Expenses					
Production costs					
Feed	US$	2,250.00	84.00	0.00	2,334.00
Dssssrugs, medicines, etc.	US$	100.00	10.00	12.00	122.00
Labour	US$	366.00	274.00	91.00	731.00
Fixed costs					
Depreciation	US$	130.00	30.00	0.00	160.00
Interest	US$	183.00	115.00	6.00	304.00
Total expenses	US$	3,029.00	513.00	109.00	3,651.00
Net Profit	US$	571.00	430.00	461.00	1,462.00
Net Profit	%	16.00	46.00	81.00	29.00
Return on Investment					
Average investment	%	62.00	75.00	1,537.00	96.00
Initial investment	%	31.00	37.00	768.00	48.00
Annual cash inflow	US$	701.00	460.00	461.00	1,622.00
Payback period	years	2.61	2.50	0.13	1.87

Table 10.5 Layer-Dairy-Fish Integration: Economic Characteristics

Item	Unit	Layer	Dairy	Fish	Total
1	2	3	4	5	6
Investment					
Assets	US$	150.00	150.00	50.00	350.00
Working capital	US$	212.00	1,000.00	10.00	1,222.00
Total investment	US$	362.00	1,150.00	60.00	1,572.00
Income	US$	1,192.00	943.00	570.00	2,705.00
Expenses					

1	2	3	4	5	6
Production Costs					
Feed	US$	675.00	84.00	0.00	759.00
Drugs, medicines, etc.	US$	11.00	10.00	12.00	33.00
Labour	US$	91.00	274.00	91.00	456.00
Fixed Costs					
Depreciation	US$	30.00	30.00	0.00	60.00
Interest	US$	36.20	115.00	6.00	157.20
Total expenses	US$	843.20	513.00	109.00	1,465.20
Net Return	US$	348.80	430.00	461.00	1,239.80
Net Return	%	29	46	81	46
Return on Investment					
Average investment	%	193	75	1,537	158
Initial investment	%	96	37	768	79
Annual cash inflow	US$	378.80	460.00	461.00	1,299.80
Payback period	years	0.95	2.50	0.13	1.20

Table 10.6 Layer-Pig-Dairy-Fish-Crop Integration: Economic Characteristics

Item	Unit	Layers	Pigs	Dairy	Fish	Crop	Total
Investment							
Assets	US$	150.00	300.00	150.00	50.00	0.00	650.00
Working capital	US$	212.00	2,437.00	1,000.00	10.00	42.00	3,701.00
Total investment	US$	362.00	2,737.00	1,150.00	60.00	42.00	4,351.00
Income	US$	1,192.00	3,800.00	943.00	570.00	620.00	7,125.00
Expenses							
Production costs							
Feed	US$	675.00	1,624.00	84.00	0.00	0.00	2,383.00
Drugs, medicines, etc.	US$	11.00	49.00	10.00	12.00	0.00	82.00
Labour	US$	91.00	274.00	274.00	91.00	280.00	1,010.00
Fixed costs							
Depreciation	US$	30.00	60.00	30.00	0.00	0.00	120.00
Interest	US$	36.20	273.70	115.00	6.00	4.20	435.10
Total expenses	US$	843.20	2,280.70	513.00	109.00	284.20	4,030.10
Net return	US$	348.80	1,519.30	430.00	461.00	335.80	3,094.90
Net return	%	29	40	46	81	54	43

(Contd...)

Return on investment							
Average investment	%	193	111	75	1,537	1,599	142
Initial investment	%	96	56	37	768	800	71
Annual cash inflow	US$	378.80	1,579.30	460.00	461.00	335.80	3,214.90
Payback period	years	0.95	1.73	2.50	0.13	0.12	1.35

Table 10.7 Broiler-Dairy-Biogas-Fish-Crop Integration: Economic Characteristics

Item	Unit	Broilers	Dairy	Biogas	Fish	Crop	Total
Investment							
Assets	US$	650.00	250.00	125.00	50.00	0.00	975.00
Working capital	US$	1,188.00	1,000.00	0.00	10.00	42.00	2,240.00
Total investment	US$	1,838.00	1,150.00	125.00	60.00	42.00	3,215.00
Income	US$	3,600.00	943.00	50.00	570.00	620.00	5,783.00
Expenses							
Production costs							
Feed	US$	2,250.00	84.00	0.00	0.00	0.00	2,334.00
Drugs, medicines, etc.	US$	100.00	10.00	0.00	12.00	0.00	122.00
Labour	US$	366.00	274.00	24.00	91.00	280.00	1,035.00
Fixed costs							
Depreciation	US$	130.00	30.00	6.25	0.00	0.00	166.25
Interest	US$	183.80	115.00	12.50	6.00	4.20	321.50
Total expenses	US$	3,029.80	513.00	42.75	109.00	284.20	3,978.75
Net return	US$	570.20	430.00	7.25	461.00	335.80	1,804.25
Net return	%	16	46	15	81	54	31
Return on investment							
Average investment	%	62	75	12	1,537	1,599	122
Initial investment	%	31	37	6	768	800	56
Annual cash inflow	US$	700.20	460.00	13.50	461.00	335.80	1,970.50
Payback period	years	2.62	2.50	9.25	0.13	0.12	1.63

Table 10.8 Pig-Biogas-Fish-Crop Integration: Economic Characteristics

Item	Unit	Pigs	Biogas	Fish	Crop	Total
Investment						
Assets	US$	300.00	125.00	50.00	0.00	475.00
Working capital	US$	2,437.00	0.00	10.00	42.00	2,489.00
Total investment	US$	2,737.00	125.00	60.00	42.00	2,964.00
Income	US$	3,800.00	50.00	570.00	620.00	5,040.00
Expenses						
Production costs						
Feed	US$	1,624.00	0.00	0.00	0.00	1,624.00
Drugs, medicines, etc.	US$	49.00	0.00	12.00	0.00	61.00
Labour	US$	274.00	24.00	91.00	280.00	669.00
Fixed costs						
Depreciation	US$	60.00	6.25	0.00	0.00	66.25
Interest	US$	273.70	12.50	6.00	4.20	296.40
Total expenses	US$	2,280.70	42.75	109.00	284.20	2,716.65
Net return	US$	1,519.30	7.25	461.00	335.80	2,323.35
Net return	%	40	15	81	54	46
Return on investment						
Average investment	%	111	12	1,537	1,599	157
Initial investment	%	56	6	768	800	78
Annual cash inflow	US$	1,579.30	13.50	461.00	335.80	2,389.60
Payback period	years	1.73	9.25	0.13	0.12	1.24

Table 10.9 Pig-Dairy-Biogas-Fish-Crop Integration: Economic Characteristics

Item	Unit	Pigs	Dairy	Biogas	Fish	Crop	Total
Investment							
Assets	US$	300.00	150.00	125.00	50.00	0.00	625.00
Working capital	US$	2,437.00	1,000.00	0.00	10.00	42.00	3,489.00
Total investment	US$	2,737.00	1,150.00	125.00	60.00	42.00	4,114.00
Income	US$	3,800.00	943.00	75.00	570.00	620.00	6,008.00
Expenses							
Production costs							
Feed	US$	1,624.00	168.00	0.00	0.00	0.00	1,792.00
Drugs, medicines, etc.	US$	49.00	10.00	0.00	12.00	0.00	71.00
Labour	US$	274.00	274.00	40.00	91.00	280.00	959.00
Fixed costs							
Depreciation	US$	60.00	30.00	6.25	0.00	0.00	96.25
Interest	US$	273.70	115.00	12.50	6.00	4.20	411.40
Total expenses	US$	2,280.70	597.00	58.75	109.00	284.20	3,329.65
Net return	US$	1,519.30	346.00	16.25	461.00	335.80	2,678.35
Net return	%	40	37	22	81	54	45
Return on investment							
Average investment	%	111	60	26	1,537	1,599	130
Initial investment	%	56	30	13	768	800	65
Annual cash inflow	US$	1,579.30	376.00	22.50	461.00	335.80	2,774.60
Payback period	years	1.73	3.05	5.55	0.13	0.12	1.48

Table 10.10 Layer-Pig, Broiler-Dairy, Biogas-Fish-Crop Integration: Economic Characteristics

Item	Unit	Layers	Pigs	Broilers	Dairy	Biogas	Fish	Crop	Total
Investment									
Assets	US$	150.00	300.00	650.00	150.00	250.00	50.00	0.00	1,550.00
Working capital	US$	216.00	2,437.00	1,188.00	1,000.00	-	10.00	42.00	4,893.00
Total investment	US$	366.00	2,737.00	1,838.00	1,150.00	250.00	60.00	42.00	6,443.00
Income	US$	1,192.00	3,800.00	3,600.00	943.00	100.00	570.00	620.00	10,825.00
Expenses									
Production costs									
Feed	US$	675.00	1,624.00	2,250.00	84.00	0.00	0.00	0.00	4,633.00
Drugs, medicines, etc.	US$	11.00	49.00	100.00	10.00	0.00	12.00	0.00	182.00
Labour	US$	91.00	274.00	366.00	274.00	48.00	91.00	280.00	1,424.00
Fixed costs									
Depreciation	US$	30.00	60.00	130.00	30.00	12.50	0.00	0.00	262.50
Interest	US$	36.60	273.70	183.80	115.00	25.00	6.00	4.20	644.30
Total expenses	US$	843.60	2,280.70	3,029.80	513.00	85.50	109.00	284.20	7,145.80
Net Return	US$	348.40	1,519.30	570.20	430.00	14.50	461.00	335.80	3,679.20
Net return	%	29.23	39.98	15.84	45.60	14.50	80.88	54.16	33.99

(Cont...)

Return on investment									
Average investment	%	190	111	62	75	12	1,537	1,599	114
Initial investment	%	95	56	31	37	6	768	800	57
Annual cash Inflow	US$	378.40	1,579.30	700.20	460.00	27.00	461.00	335.00	3,941.70
Payback period	years	0.96	1.73	2.62	2.50	9.25	0.13	0.12	1.63

Bibliography

Bailey, D. and B.W. Brorsen.: *Dynamics of Regional Fed Cattle Prices*, Madison: American Press, 2001.

Bayri, T., K.A. Rosaasen and W.H. Furtan.: *Limit Pricing in the Nitrogen Fertilizer Market: An Application to the Saskatchewan Market*, Madison: American Press, 1998.

Boyle, G.E.: *Modeling Fertilizer Demand in the Republic of Ireland: A Cost Function Approach*, Journal of Agricultural Economics: Ireland University, 1998

Burrell, A.: *The Demand for Fertilizer in the United Kingdom*, Journal of Agricultural Economics: United Kingdom Press, 2004.

Carman, H.F.: *The Demand for Nitrogen, Phosphorus and Potash Fertilizer Nutrients in the Western United States*, Western Journal of Agricultural Economics: Oxford, 1998.

Denbaly, M. and H. Vroomen.: *Dynamic Fertilizer Nutrient Demands for Corn: A Cointegrated and Error-Correcting System*. American Journal of Agricultural Economics: American Press, 2004.

Griliches, Z.: *The Demand for Fertilizer: An Economic Interpretation of a Technical Change*, Journal of Farm Economics: Harvard University, 1999.

Griliches, Z.: *Distributed Lags, Desegregation, and Regional Demand Functions for Fertilizer*, Journal of Farm Economics: Harvard University, 2001 .

Gunjal, K.R., R.K. Roberts and E.O. Heady.: *Fertilizer Demand Function for Five Crops in the United States*. Southern Journal of Agricultural Economics: United States, 1996.

Heady, E.O. and Martin H. Yeh.: *National and Regional Demand Functions for Fertilizer,* Journal of Farm Economics: Harvard University, 1997.

Lingard, J.: *Aggregate Demand for Nitrogenous Fertilizer in the United Kingdom: Another Look,* Journal of Agricultural Economics: American Press, 2000.

Payne, G.D.: *Spatial Fertilizer Pricing in Western Canada,* Ms.c Thesis, Department of Agricultural Economics: University of Saskatchewan, 2001.

Pidgeon E. and L. Kiwanuka.: *Regional Fertilizer Demand Analysis,* Agriculture and Agri-food Canada: Cambridge University Press, 2004 .

Roberts, R.K. and E.O. Heady.: *Fertilizer Demand Functions for Specific Nutrients Applied to Three Major U.S. Crops,* Western Journal of Agricultural Economics: Taxes, 2004.

Acharya, C. N.: *Organic Manures,* Indian Council Agriculture Research: New Delhi, Scientific Publishers, 1997.

Law, James P.: *Agricultural Utilization of Sewage Effluent and Sludge,* U.S., Taxes, 2001.

Jeris, J. & P. McCarty.: *The Biochemistry of Methane Fermentation,* U.S.A., American Press, 2000.

Gotaas, H.: *Composting: Sanitary Disposal and Reclamation of Organic Wastes,* U.S.A, Oxford Press, 1998.

Dugan, Gordon L.: *Photosynthetic Reclamation of Agricultural Solid and Liquid Wastes,* U.S.A., University of California, 2002.

Hart, Samuel.: *Sludge Digestion Tests of Livestock Manures.* U.S.A, University of Califronia, 2001.

Index

L

M

O

P

R

S

T

V

W

X

Z